FIRST THINGS FIRST

The first thing you have to do when you begin a business at home is to realize that it is not a hobby. It is a money-making operation with all the risks and rewards of one.

The second thing you should do is carefully read this book. It will give you the guidance you need for every problem you encounter and every decision you have to make as you work to make your business work for you.

Whether you are selling a product in person, at markets and trade fairs, through the mail, to retail distributors, or exporting it abroad, you will find invaluable aid in every line of this guide, which puts the bottom line on top.

VALERIE BOHIGIAN is the owner of her own home-based business. Her articles on business and marketing have appeared in national magazines such as *Woman's Day*, *Redbook* and *Self-Reliant*. She is the author of *Successful Flea Market Selling* and <u>*Real Money From Home: How to Start, Manage and Profit from a Home-Based Service Business*</u> (available in a Plume edition).

ⓂMENTOR

ALL ABOUT BUSINESS

(0451)

☐ **DOING BUSINESS WITH THE JAPANESE by Mitchell F. Deutsch.** There is a logic behind Japanese business practices—and this book will show you how to recognize and use it to your own advantage. Designed to help American executives bridge the East-West "knowledge gap," this step-by-step guide to negotiation offers a wealth of invaluable advice.
(623495—$4.50)

☐ **HOW TO START AND MANAGE YOUR OWN BUSINESS by Gardiner G. Greene. Revised and Updated.** Step-by-Step instructions for a successful small business operation: how to choose an ad agency, how to obtain government aid, how to incorporate and form partnerships, plus much more. (624017—$4.50)

☐ **HOW TO KEEP SCORE IN BUSINESS: Accounting and Financial Analysis for the Non-Accountant by Robert Follett.** A practical and realistic look at the financial workings of the business world designed to give nonfinancial managers the knowledge necessary to succeed on the job. Presents the primary financial reports and statements, main analysis tools, key vocabulary terms, significant trend indicators, useful ratios, and financial danger signals that all managers should be familiar with. Charts, glossary, and index included. (622596—$2.95)

☐ **HOW TO TURN YOUR IDEA INTO A MILLION DOLLARS by Don Kracke with Roger Honkanen.** A step-by-step guide to researching, patenting, financing, manufacturing, marketing and distributing new products. Appendices (Inventor's Checklist, Sources, Typical Marketing Plan) and Index included.
(624513—$3.95)

Prices slightly higher in Canada

Buy them at your local bookstore or use this convenient coupon for ordering.
NEW AMERICAN LIBRARY,
P.O. Box 999, Bergenfield, New Jersey 07621

Please send me the books I have checked above. I am enclosing $_____
(please add $1.00 to this order to cover postage and handling). Send check or money order—no cash or C.O.D.'s. Prices and numbers are subject to change without notice.

Name_____

Address_____

City_____ State_____ Zip Code_____

Allow 4-6 weeks for delivery.
This offer is subject to withdrawal without notice.

HOW TO MAKE YOUR HOME-BASED BUSINESS GROW

Getting Bigger Profits From Your Products

by
Valerie Bohigian

A SIGNET BOOK

NEW AMERICAN LIBRARY

PUBLISHER'S NOTE

This publication is designed to provide accurate and authoritative information in regard to the subject matter covered. It is sold with the understanding that the publisher is not engaged in rendering legal, accounting, or other professional service. If legal advice or other expert assistance is required, the service of a competent professional person should be sought.

NAL BOOKS ARE AVAILABLE AT QUANTITY DISCOUNTS WHEN USED TO PROMOTE PRODUCTS OR SERVICES. FOR INFORMATION PLEASE WRITE TO PREMIUM MARKETING DIVISION, NEW AMERICAN LIBRARY, 1633 BROADWAY, NEW YORK, NEW YORK 10019.

Copyright © 1984 by Valerie Bohigian

All rights reserved

SIGNET TRADEMARK REG. U.S. PAT. OFF. AND FOREIGN COUNTRIES
REGISTERED TRADEMARK—MARCA REGISTRADA
HECHO EN CHICAGO, U.S.A.

SIGNET, SIGNET CLASSIC, MENTOR, PLUME, MERIDIAN AND NAL BOOKS are published by New American Library,
1633 Broadway, New York, New York 10019

First Signet Printing, March, 1986

1 2 3 4 5 6 7 8 9

PRINTED IN THE UNITED STATES OF AMERICA

To my mother and father—whom I cherish

ACKNOWLEDGMENTS

I am grateful to the people in my business life, my professional life, and my personal life who contributed greatly to this book.

Many home-based entrepreneurial friends and acquaintances shared the details of their successes and their disappointments with me. They confirmed my belief that home-based businesses can be extremely profitable and pleasurable operations. They inspired me to tell their stories in the hope that others would be inspired to follow their examples. I am indebted to these entrepreneurs for showing me what the winners do right that the wishers can learn.

My very special thanks to Dominick Abel, a first-rate agent, for his honest evaluations, consistent encouragement, kind words, and professional guidance. Many, many thanks to Cindy Kane, a talented, meticulous editor whose enthusiasm for this project was strong and delightful from start to finish.

My deep appreciation to Robert Levine for his tireless proofreading of each new draft; to Renee Handler who generously supplied me with helpful information and material; and to Haig, Melanie, and Kara for providing me the joyful serenity of soul so important to a writer.

Contents

Introduction   1

1. CHECKING OUT HOME BASE
   Key points to remember in setting up
   your home base   6

2. WHEN THE "RIGHT" PRODUCT IS WRONG
   Getting rid of the enemy within
   the otherwise perfect product   23

3. TESTING YOUR PRODUCT (AND YOURSELF)
   IN SHALLOW WATERS
   Propelling your business beyond
   infancy and childhood   40

4. WADING INTO DEEPER WATERS
   Steering your company into a
   promising adulthood   60

5. BETTER BUSINESS THROUGH BARTER
   How and when to use barter to boost
   your business   81

6. ADVERTISING, PUBLICITY, AND
   PUBLIC RELATIONS
   Getting maximum public exposure
   on a minimal budget   95

7. DIRECT AND INDIRECT SELLING
   How to sell jointly into the best retail
   and wholesale markets   128

Contents

8. **GETTING EXPERT HELP**
   How to get the most out of
   the best specialists ... 152

9. **EXPORTING MADE EASY**
   How to painlessly and profitably sell
   to overseas markets ... 176

10. **AVOIDING COMMON HOME-BASED BUSINESS MISTAKES**
    How to avoid the subtle and simple mistakes
    that cost dearly ... 193

11. **CURING FIGUREPHOBIA**
    Acknowledging and treating the
    major home-based business sinker ... 212

    Conclusion ... 226

    Appendix ... 227

    Index ... 236

Introduction

Home base. In baseball it's a place where you're "safe." In business it's not too different. The home-based entrepreneur is safe from many of the problems of the marketplace worker. No layoffs, no commuting, no boss, no wardrobe worries, no childcare problems, no nine-to-five hours, no slaving for the greater glory of a faceless factory or corporation. There's only one problem—no money to enjoy your freedom from all the other no's!

If you're a home-based worker, it's quite likely that the idea of running your own business pleases you. You like the challenge, independence, and freedom of home-basing. You're well aware of the advantages of working for yourself. Your personality is right for home-based self-employment. You like having the comforts of home available to you at all times. The lifestyle is right for you. What's not right for you is that this lifestyle isn't bringing in enough money.

Two thousand, three thousand, four thousand a year; it was fine in the beginning, but now you feel ready to see your business really take off, become something more than a piddling spare-time venture. You've learned the basics; you understand what home-basing is about. Now you want to turn your cottage industry into a castle industry. And that's what this book is about—taking this economic lifestyle that you like and making it really pay off. You're ready to develop a credible, profitable enterprise. You're willing to invest a few more hours, and a little more effort, into the business you already have going in order to see your earnings rise to twenty, thirty, forty thousand a year and more.

The media have let you know that today there is a major trend away from the external marketplace, away from office- and factory-based employment to home-based employment. You don't need the media to tell you this. It's people like you who've been alerting them to the trend. You know lots of people who "make and take": the quiche lady who makes her gourmet specialties by the dozen and takes them to the local deli for consignment selling; the quilt lady who makes her colorful coverlets and takes them to juried craft fairs; the word-processing whiz who makes miracles out of messes and takes his finished products to the many local businessmen who avail themselves of his services. What you do want the media to tell you they haven't been telling you. Not yet.

The reporters, economic prophets, and sociologists who are applauding the maverick migration from marketplace to home-based employment as an heroic move toward financial self-reliance don't examine the little how to's which make the difference between self-reliance and self-defeat. What does the quilt lady do when she's rained out of her three most profitable juried craft fairs? Why aren't her quilts selling in Bloomingdale's when inferior work is? Why isn't she getting orders for her work from specialty shops around the country? What should she be doing that she's not doing?

These questions are too specific to be answered by those who are observing and evaluating the cottage-industry phenomenon. They are looking at this movement mainly as the completion of an historic cycle in American economic history, as a back-to-basics trend. But this orientation doesn't do much for the quilt lady, who'd like to, but can't, put her daughter through medical school on her earnings. And the basics aren't as basic as they used to be in the early days of America, when we, for the most part, had an agricultural and artisanal economy. Wants are bigger. Competition is greater. Break-even points are higher. Though there is a desire to return completely to the seeming success and simplicity of yesterday's cottage industry, that desire is generally unaccompanied by the necessary imagination and know-how.

Today's cottage-industry trend is largely, but not entirely, rooted in marketplace disenchantment, employee dissatisfaction, job insecurity and inflation. Many of today's home-based enterprises are the result of attempts to deal positively and courageously with firings, layoffs, and interviews that never materialize; many are attempts to supplement an inflation-worn outside income; and some are praiseworthy efforts to ensure a self-sufficient and busy retirement. But there is another impulse operating here. The home-basing trend is also an exciting phenomenon tied in with a current urge to be commercially creative—to create a company of one's own for the sheer thrill of doing so.

If the possibility of making big bucks today in your own home-based business sounds too good to be true, it's because usually it is—not because it's impossible, but because the process is naively approached. The word-processing whiz is probably a whiz at his machine, but not at marketing his know-how or output. Not yet. Within the next few years the hi-tech, computer, and information-processing crazes of today will be increasingly targeted toward making tomorrow's home-based business a financial triumph. Export options and media opportunities will be used regularly to increase sales dramatically. Home-basers will have greater access to such market expanders as barter exchanges and trade shows, which will permit them equal billing with top firms. These and many other trends are covered in this book now so that you can get a head start on making your home-based business soar.

One major reason why today's home-based businesses are seldom financial triumphs is that they're seldom taken seriously. Though they often supply a supplementary income or a needed margin of comfort, they're basically viewed as relatively insignificant by both business owner and customer: "Mary's quilts are nice; but if she really wants to make money she's going to have to get a 'real' job." Mary's customers see it that way, and so does Mary. Once Mary gets a few department stores as customers and a few publications to do feature articles about her and her quilts, things change tremendously. Mary is now viewed as a professional, an artist, a supplier, an inspiration. One success and mention leads to another. Now she's taken quite seriously, but she's considered the exception to the rule that real money cannot be made from a small home-based business. What's often ignored is the fact that if

Mary weren't home-based, she wouldn't be netting any real money because her overhead would disallow it.

Everyone has heard about a Mary, a mail-order maven who makes a million dollars a year from a desk in the corner of her bedroom, or an inventor who sells his garage-invented widgets to Fortune 500 companies. But there is still an air of unreality about it. Yes, home-basing lowers overhead—but real money? The average home-baser is not a big believer and does not have enough of the "I can do it" spirit. Impressive earnings can be made from home, but first a strong commitment must be made to treat your goal not as a semi-hope, but as something which you intend to realize within a very few years.

Over two million Americans now sell products from their homes. Ninety-five percent of them earn less than $5,000 a year. Why? Ask yourself. It isn't because you wouldn't love to earn a lot more. Nor is it because you're selling a poor product, or because you're a disreputable person. But you, like most home-based entrepreneurs, really don't know all the nuts and bolts of turning a sideline income into a profitable enterprise. You're not sure how to make it happen, or if it can happen. You know your product well, but you don't know how to market it to make real money. You're probably well aware of others who seem to be doing everything right, but you can't see what you're doing wrong, or not doing at all. Should you hit it hot for a spell, chances are you won't be able to keep the fire glowing. This book will change all that, and a lot of other things. It will help you to think, act, and earn differently.

All of the operating methods and strategies for success discussed in this book relate to the home-based *product* business; the focus is on selling products, not services—on marketing tangibles. Frequently, however, a clear distinction cannot be made between the home-based product and the home-based service businesses—a home-based manufacturer of floral centerpieces may also be a home-based wedding consultant, for example. Such overlapping will be discussed.

This book is the result of several years of formal and informal research which I undertook both as a home-based businessperson and as a professional writer. I began home-basing by selling decorator items at upscale flea markets and fell in love with the entrepreneurial spirit that pervades these events. Eventually I became a savvy "fleaer" and was offered a contract to write a book called *Successful Flea Market Selling* (Tab Books; Blue Ridge Summit, Pa., 1981). In the process of writing it I interviewed over a hundred successful home-basers who sold at flea markets, and more than two hundred avid flea-market shoppers. As I became more interested in home-basing, I investigated and experimented with new products and new marketing methods (such as mail order, consignment, barter, wholesaling, and multilevel marketing), all aimed at increasing my profits while still permitting me the luxury of working out of my home. I quadrupled my income within two years, yet had ample time to pursue my writing career and other professional and personal interests. While engaging in my business-building activities I wrote many how-to articles, and a monthly business column, for national magazines and trade publications. In these articles I described what I, and other home-basers I knew, were doing. I analyzed and evaluated my successes and failures and those of the home-basers whom I observed and interviewed, in addition to analyzing and evaluting the reader mail I began receiving. What were we all doing right? What mistakes were we making along the way? What was it that we wanted to get a handle on but couldn't? As both an entrepreneur and a writer I grasped every opportunity that arose to talk to home-based winners and "wishers," always with the intention of trying to find out what the winners were doing right that the wishers weren't. I have also been on the receiving end of questions from entrepreneurs and newspaper and television reporters, which has forced me into still more entrepreneurial probing.

At this point I know most of the questions, many of the mistakes, and a lot of the answers. I am passing along to you what I, and other successful home-basers, have learned through trial and error and endless questioning and evaluating. When you're finished reading this book, you'll be ready to transform the business you have into what you'd like it to be. Keep this book handy. Refer to it along the way. You won't be a "wisher" for long. The next few years will be your soaring years. Home base will become, as in baseball, a place where you're "safe" and where you're also a winner.

1

CHECKING OUT HOME BASE

For a business to soar, it must be credible. You must apply the same financial, organizational, and attitudinal standards to a home base that you would to any other business base. Johnny's gloves are not to be taken off in your office and dropped on your desk. Katy can't use your business phone to call a friend. Your office and work area must be used exclusively for business-related items. Any piece of paper you put down should be in exactly the same spot when you go to retrieve it. This all seems obvious, yet the foundation for success is often poorly laid because of a disregard for the obvious. Here are the nine key points to remember in evaluating your home base:

1. Think with your head, not your heart. Because home is a place where you rest your head, where you ease your survival instincts, where you reduce your self-discipline, it is a place where you're vulnerable. For this reason there's a tendency to think poor rather than rich when your business is homebased. Here's an example.

Nancy handcrafts wooden decorator items: wall plaques, jewelry boxes, stools, picture frames. She makes her goods in the basement of her home and four times a year she puts on shows in her living room. Her shows are well attended. People purchase her creations for themselves and for gift giving. She has a lot of repeat business. Her customers like her work. From her four annual shows she gets enough orders to keep her busy all year. She's doing a lot right: her work is excellent; she displays her products at festive, refreshment-rich shows; she personalizes her goods to meet her customers' tastes; and she maintains pleasant relations with her buyers. She even has an attractive, hand-drawn brochure which she distributes wisely and well. Yet she's doing one major thing wrong; she keeps her income under $5,000 a year.

Nancy thinks poor; and because she does she's earning peanuts for all her efforts. Not a year passes when she doesn't talk about "giving it all up and getting a real job." She doesn't see that she has a real job, a real business, and one that she loves. Her problem is that she's not using her business head the way she would were she working in a corporate office. Her guiding pricing policy is unbusinesslike and self-defeating. It keeps her poor. It is based on assumptions that profit-minded corporate America would never tolerate. If a great number of people seem to be ordering one of Nancy's offerings to the exclusion of some of her other products, she assumes that she has priced the seller too cheaply and at the next show raises its price tag "to even demand." Yes, she evens demand, and in doing so turns a winning product into a loser.

Why does Nancy do this? Because, like many home-basers, she sometimes thinks with her heart rather than her head. She loves working from home and, like most craftspeople, considers her output labors of love, more than products of keen business scrutiny. To meet the high demand for one particular product, and begin to boost her business, Nancy would have to hire help and delegate some parts of her work. Taking on help and delegating work are acts which make many home-basers clutch up and which Nancy consistently claims she's "not ready for." The thought of relinquishing any control upsets her. Until she is ready to think with her head instead of her heart, the way non-home-basers are forced to think in order to survive, home base is not a place from which Nancy will ever make big bucks. Even though certain decisions seem painful, a home-baser must make them and must make them correctly—based on financial, not emotional, sense.

2. Budget your time with military-style discipline. For a home-based business to soar, time must be tightly budgeted—yearly, monthly, weekly, and daily. Time must be thought of as money, just as it is in the commercial marketplace. This means having overall general tasks and specific daily ones, having a game plan, and committng it to paper. The best way to do this, and to keep home base from becoming time-sloppy, is to be a serious listmaker.

Formulate a list of all your business tasks for each time unit (year, month, week, day)—matters to be researched, publicity to be sought, products to be made or bought or inventoried, phone calls to be made, invoices to send, mail to be answered—and work from this list. When you were just starting your business you couldn't do this well because everything was new. It was difficuft to determine priorities. But now that you're no longer a novice, you must start to list your tasks in order of descending importance. These lists will enable you to establish moneymaking daily routines—and permit you to realize your overall goal of skyrocketing your business.

Take a look at the following lists. You will constantly be adding new activities to yours, and dropping completed ones. At the end of each day, make a new daily list for the following day by consulting the week, month, and year column. Carry over unfinished daily tasks to the next day's list. At the end of each week, month, and year, make new lists using this same carryover method. If you have any free time-slots on a given day, you can pull an appropriate activity from the weekly, monthly, or yearly columns to work on.

3. Use a flow chart. A flow chart is a diagram that illustrates the sequence of operations for a program of action. The formal operating logic provided by a flow chart goes a long way toward preventing a home-based business from becoming a high-stress, low-income operation. This logic is displayed by a series of boxes and arrows which help you to make necessary business decisions quickly (see page 11).

A flow chart for a home-based business (computer flow charts for programming into machine language are different and more difficult to create) is created by:

1. making a list of the five to ten major questions that keep recurring.

2. answering these questions with other questions that must be considered, or with solutions which have proven to be effective.

Checking Out Home Base 9

A flow chart imposes a sense of order on a home-based business by imposing a disciplinary routine on its owner. Consulting it weekly enables you to create your worklists and to view your enterprise with a detachment that would not be possible if you were simply trying to keep all the

Anderson Awards and Trophies Co.			
Year (1984)	**Month** (Sept.)	**Week** (2nd)	**Day** (Wed.)
1. Find & train 3 regional reps.	1. Design & print up new catalog.	1. Attend awards close-out auction.	1. Package & UPS Turner order.
2. Find new medals suppliers.	2. Send out invoices & pay suppliers.	2. Call *Journal* re editorial mention re contest contribution.	2. Send sample medals, flyers to YMCA
3. Attend awards conventions & trade shows.	3. Visit D & L Plaque Co.	3. Plan mechanical for newsletter ad.	3. Deliver trophies to Police Dept.
4. Visit athletic meets & talk to directors.	4. Get cable publicity.	4. Buy ribbons.	4. Assemble Tim's trophies.
		5. Answer letters requesting specific information.	5. Send out price-sheet requests.
			6. Call Bill re non-payment by City College.
			7. Draw mold sketch for J.C. Sports Assoc.

flow-chart information in your head. A flow chart should be updated periodically as new situations and choices warrant.

When you're home-based it's easy to become disorganized in your thinking. There are distractions that you don't have in a non-home-based office. Also, you probably don't have a lot of co-workers who'll bounce questions around and give you immediate help. Flow-chart logic (if *this*, then *this*) forces you to think and act quickly and correctly.

4. Attitude determines aptitude. How do you feel about working from your home? Does it delight you? Do you feel a pleasant sense of superiority over those poor souls who have to commute daily to a job that thrusts them into constant contact with people they would avoid were they given a choice? Or do you feel forced, for financial reasons, to home-base when you'd really feel happier, more important, and more professional working in an office building or outside shop? Do you feel defensive about telling people that your business address is your home address? Or are you proud of this fact?

The way you feel about working from home is strongly related to the degree of success you'll experience. The more the concept of home-basing pleases you, the better you'll do at it. You'll approach it as an exciting challenge, as a long-range endeavor to be taken seriously. You will be receptive to the tips and techniques which increase sales and profits. You will absorb the bits and pieces of information that are not picked up by the home-baser who apologizes for, or resents, his lifestyle. You may think, Look, I have no other choices; I'm stuck working at home; but I'm still interested in doing well. No doubt you are; but until your attitude changes, you'll be working at a strong disadvantage. Your aptitude, your ability to expand your business, will be impaired. If you have a negative attitude about homebasing, you must change it before going any further. Here's a case in point.

When Ralph was laid off from an assembly-line job that paid well and provided camaraderie, a friend convinced him to try multilevel sales. He began selling a muscle-building diet supplement for a multilevel marketing com-

Flow chart for Anderson Awards and Trophies Company

- **Low on necessary inventory?**
  - Y → **Can you order or make?**
    - Y → Begin today.
    - N → Find help.
  - N ↓
- **Dissatisfied with suppliers?** → Attend trade shows and visit new companies.
  - N ↓
- **Low cash flow?**
  - **Money owed you?** Y → Send polite second invoice.
    - N ↓
  - **Money you owe?** Y → Send please-be-patient note.
  - ↓
- **Outdated catalogs, price lists, etc.?** Y → Start creating new printed literature.
  - N ↓
- **Need ads, P.R., etc.?** Y → **Can you create?**
  - Y → Begin.
  - N → Find help or read up on subject.
  - N ↓
- **Customer waiting for order?**
  - Y → **Can you get it out?** Y → Package & ship.
    - N → **Insufficient supply?** Y → Visit new suppliers.
      - N → **Insufficient time?** Y → Get immediate help.
        - Call to explain delay.
  - N ↓
- **Recheck this chart weekly.**

Y = Yes
N = No

pany (where commissions are earned on many sales levels—on your sales, on the sales of people you recruit, on the sales of your recruits' recruits, etc.). As he was a serious body-builder and worked out in a gym, he had many contacts. He liked what he was selling and used it himself with impressive results. It was not hard for him to make sales, and he was surprised and pleased by his success. He enjoyed telling friends about how well he was surviving financially while he was "waiting to be rehired." Then something happened: he found out that due to financial cutbacks and his limited seniority, he wasn't going to be rehired. Suddenly his sales of the diet supplement began to decrease. Now, when he most needed to be able to survive financially, he was least able to. Why?

As long as Ralph considered his entrepreneurial endeavor to be temporary, he regarded it as an interesting diversion and challenge. And he was great at it. The moment he learned that he wouldn't be rehired, that his diversion was now all he had going for him financially, his attitude changed. He had never been a man wo secretly longed to be in business for himself, and now he felt cornered. Should he look for another assembly-line job? Should he try another kind of job? Should he get into an educational trainng program?

For a long time he did nothing. His diet-supplement sales plummeted along with his spirits. Then through his interest in cars, he met a man who ran a lucrative car-parts business from his home. Something clicked. One of the reasons the car-parts supplier was doing so well was that he was home-based with low overhead. The sociological climate was right for home-basing. People respected this man. Slowly Ralph's hostility toward home-basing began to evaporate. In its place came a determination to never worry about being laid off again. He looked at the multilevel marketing organization with different eyes. Now he was interested in selling the supplement, finding recruits, becoming a group counselor. . . . Ralph is now earning four times his assembly-line income. He has an office and storage area in his home, and doesn't know why he "didn't get into all this sooner."

Was Ralph lucky that it all worked out for him? No. Luck has little to do with success at home-basing. Ralph always had the personality for sales, and a product that he believed in. Things worked out for him because his attitude turned around 180°. He began to view home-basing as a positive lifestyle, and because he did, success followed.

5. Form follows function. The look of a home is determined by how it is used. This is important for a homebaser to understand. Certainly your home should serve your personal and family needs, but it must do more than this lest you give out mixed messages to yourself, your family, and your customers. *A portion of your home must seriously reflect the business use to which you are putting it.* This means thinking in terms of:

Credibility. A home-baser who gives conflicting messages loses credibility regardless of how fine his product is. When people come to your home on business, they are there to relate to you solely as a businessperson. The personal portions of your home—the places where you are a mother or husband, for example, more than a businessperson—should be off limits to customers. If Mrs. Cooper is purchasing some of your photographs, she shouldn't be doing so, or discussing the purchase with you, in your kitchen while you are preparing a snack for your child. The part of your home which demonstrates your function as a photographer is the only part that should be open to Mrs. Cooper.

Space. What if you don't have a specific portion of your home which demonstrates your function as a self-employed home-baser? Once you buy your next home, you'll have an office and a studio, but what about now? Your work is good. People are buying it. But let's face it, you're spread out all over the place. There is no one spot that you call your own. Basically you have a kitchen-table operation. What can you do? It may be only a little, but you must do something. One way to proceed is to *"divide and conquer"* — section off a part of a room, or an area, to be used exclusively for your business. This can be done vertically simply by using folding panels to screen off an area. Today many big businesses are doing just that—breaking down large spaces into modules that provide privacy. If you have high ceilings you may want to section off a work area horizontally, with a loft.

Another way to centralize your base of operations is with a *portable office*. This is popular because of the close quarters in which many of us are forced to live. The portable office is a multipart unit on wheels that may be custom-built or bought. Generally it includes space for a typewriter table, file drawers, a worktable, and shelves. It folds up into a small hideaway package and opens up into a remarkably roomy and functional mini-office.

Still another way to create a work area within a living area is to *move furniture around*— to make space by moving a few pieces into another room, by selling an unnecessary piece, or by reorganizing the way your room is laid out. Often the "push and shove and think" method produces very acceptable results. For extra ideas thumb through the many decorator magazines on the market. They devote a lot of attention to utilizing space effectively. Or you may wish to consult an interior designer. Often a professional can come up with a solution that just isn't hitting you. How you decide to carve out a work area will depend on your particular needs and what you have to work with. But don't put this off; it is crucial if your business is to truly soar. Your solution need not be ideal at the present time, but it must be a solid step above "kitchen-tabling it." You need this leap in order to make greater ones.

Color. Color may seem a trivial consideration for a work area, but it's not. Color influences mood and mood influences actions. If your work requires that you feel serene during the creation process, it's unlikely that the color red will make you feel this way. On the other hand, if you need excitement in order to create, red might be a perfect predominant color for your work space. Color, and color combinations, used in your work area need not be similar to colors used in other parts of your home. The function of your work area is different from that of your bedroom, living room, or kitchen area.

6. Equipment is everything. Today a prospective buyer wants a well-equipped house. He is usually not eager to consider a home without certain appliances, a garage, or a fireplace, unless he's willing to add these features himself.

Just as a house for living in must be properly equipped, so too must a house for working in. If your home is improperly equipped for the work you're doing, you're working at a severe disadvantage. Having the right tools for a job is essential, lest your work hours be needlessly prolonged, your output be needlessly inferior, and your business be needlessly curtailed. Don't skimp on the tools of your trade. Skimpers seldom soar.

Let's look at Kurt, a home-based manufacturer of wooden rocking horses, for a typical example of home-based, "penny-wise, pound-foolish" thinking. Kurt's highly polished and sturdy wooden horses are majestic creations. Because he lives in a status-conscious town, word-of-mouth alone was bringing him in an impressive number of customers. People were ordering his horses not just as toys, but as decorator items. He promised himself a much-needed new power saw as soon as it went on sale. Months passed without the saw going on sale. Because the old saw wasn't doing the job well enough for an expanding number of orders, there were long delays in customer deliveries. Eventually cancellations resulted, word-of-mouth lessened, and business slackened. Kurt didn't see what was happening. Because he kept thinking the saw would go on sale "in a week or two," and because he wasn't willing to invest $30 or $40 over sale price for the new saw he needed, he lost what ultimately could have amounted to thousands of dollars in new sales.

Kurt's "penny-wise, pound-foolish" thinking is not unusual for a home-baser. Most home-basers are not rich and do not think like experienced entrepreneurs. However, "tomorrow" thinking about needed equipment is the kind of thinking that will cause a home-based business to sink. Any equipment which helps you to make a better product faster, more economically, and with greater ease is a must and should be purchased promptly even if the equipment might be cheaper at another time. Don't be afraid to incur a small amount of debt for this purpose. *Business-investment debt is a world apart from ordinary consumer debt, and should be considered a positive course of action for increasing or maintaining sales.*

If a large amount of debt is necessary for the equipment you need, and you don't feel your business can presently justify it, or you only need the equipment for short periods, investigate equipment time-sharing. Here, instead of incurring heavy debt, or doing without, you pay a manageable fee. If, for example, it would help you greatly to have the use of a computer, kiln, duplicating machine, or a heavy-duty sewing machine, for a few hours a week, search out those people or companies who have this equipment and are not using it continuously. Many individuals and companies are well aware that frequently unused equipment is a nonproductive asset that can be turned into a productive one through the equipment time-sharing principle.

Sometimes it isn't "tomorrow" thinking that keeps your business from growing more quickly than it might; rather, it's the failure to recognize the need for supplemental equipment. Even a person smart enough to own all the obvious equipment needed to do a job well will often overlook the importance of good supplemental equipment. Lighting usually falls into this category. A home-baser will find that after two or three hours of work his eyes are bothering him. He'll stop for a while even though he's not at a point where he wants to break. Common sense should tell him that maybe if he changed his lighting his eyes wouldn't tire so easily. But it doesn't. Further, because supplemental equipment such as lighting is not directly related to getting a job done, it is often a low priority to be addressed. Beware of this. Lack of supplemental equipment can cost you dearly, just as lack of regular job-related equipment can. In addition to lighting, items such as heating and air-conditioning fall into this category. Even a radio or stereo does if you find music soothing to work by. Anything that increases your work comfort may fall into this category. Be alert to these indirect work aids, and invest in them.

7. The phone doesn't stop ringing just because you're out. The telephone is a critical instrument for the home-baser. You don't have a storefront, a mall spot, or an outside office. Customers aren't going to stumble upon you by accident unless your home is uniquely situated. Generally they're not going to stop by unannounced. And, in many cases, they won't bother ordering from you if they have to do so by mail. *The telephone is your business* *lifeline.* If you use it properly, it will serve you well. If you don't, not only won't your business soar, it might die! The following advice should be strictly adhered to.

During nine-to-five business hours someone must always be available to answer your phone. Customers and potential customers will stop calling and take their business elsewhere if they find you difficult to reach. Long-distance callers who might have considered you a large firm with commercial headquarters and placed large orders will quickly write you off as a small-time novice.

Messages should not be taken by just anyone. Under no circumstances should your business phone be answered by a child, by someone who speaks poor English or doesn't understand English well, or by someone untrained to take good messages. Your business phone should be answered with your company name ("Frank's Flowers, may I help you?"). Messages should be written down in an organized manner—caller's name, phone number, purpose of call, best time to return call.

Answering services should be used under certain circumstances. If your business is such that you must be away from home a lot, and you do not have daily help available to take phone messages, use an answering service. One home-baser built up a large and lucrative mail-order business though he was seldom home to receive calls. He found an excellent, small-business-oriented, computerized answering service that took messages and orders quickly and correctly. Customers who did not wish to write in their orders with enclosed checks were able to give the answering service creditcard numbers and receive prompt service. They didn't know whether they were dealing with a home-based business or a huge factory-based firm. And they didn't care. They received good products and good service, and that's what mattered. From the home-baser's point of view the answering service not only enabled his business to soar, it permitted him freedom of movement. Rather than staying home to take calls, he was able to be out finding rare offerings for his next mail-order catalog.

It is not only important that an answering service be used under certain circumstances, it is imperative that you seek out the right service for your particular needs. The mail-order man needed a service that could deal in high volume if need be, a service that could write up data-filled orders, mail printouts of a day's messages, and take short messages. To make sure all his needs were met, he was willing to pay about $2 per call-in order. If you don't need this much service—if, for example, you're a home-based graphic illustrator, you don't receive many calls daily, and you just need to be able to call in somewhere and receive names and numbers of people who called while you were out—you don't need the service just described. All you need is a reliable flat-fee service.

Don't use a call-interrupt phone system. Have you ever been deep into a phone call with someone when you heard a beep on his phone and he said apologetically, "Can you hold on a minute, I have another call?" It's upsetting. And it can be insulting if he returns to you and informs you that he'll have to get back to you. Aren't you as important as the interrupting caller? If you are important, and the man ignores the beep, okay. But what if there are several interrupting beeps? It's annoying to talk to someone under these circumstances.

As a businessperson, particularly one who may be getting a lot of calls, this is not a desirable telephone system to have. Even if you can turn off the interrupting beeper at will, you're not accomplishing your goal—to be aware of all incoming calls. There are better phone systems for the home-baser.

Investigate the various kinds of phone systems available. Today there are several phone-package options available and new ones are constantly being offered. Rather than the call-interrupt system, for example, you might have a system where, if you're on a call, a *recording device* would inform the interrupting caller of this. The message might be, "Our lines are busy at present; please leave your name and number and your call will be returned promptly," or anything else you might wish to tell the new caller. If this doesn't suit you, you might like a *call-forwarding* service, where all incoming calls to your home number are automatically forwarded to the number where you're going to be. Or perhaps your work is such that you don't want to be bothered walking back and forth to a phone location. How about a *portable phone* attached to your belt? Perhaps your business is such that it is frequently crucial for you to be able to talk simultaneously to two or more people in different locations. Have you heard of *teleconferencing?* This is expensive, but it might be a good option to look into.

Don't settle on a phone system that works against your success. Call your telephone-company business office and investigate all the options open to you, what they cost, and what modifications are possible.

8. *Imitation is the most sincere form of flattery*. Have you ever bought a piece of furniture, organized your furniture in a unique way, or made some home renovations, and been surprised to discover that your neighbor has copied you? (Or have you done this to your neighbor?) It happens a lot. It can be both offending and flattering depending upon how you view it. It's offending because you want your house to be unique; it's flattering because your neighbor is making it clear that your idea is better than what she was living with. Like it or not, it is a sincere form of flattery. The imitator has recognized your superior plan. Just as imitating a neighbor's home-decorating setup is a form of flattery, so too is imitating a home-baser's work setup. And it can be financially profitable as well as flattering. Do imitate a superior home-based setup; but:

Make your intentions clear to the home-baser whose setup you'd like to use as a prototype. If the superstar home-baser whose modus operandi you'd like to imitate is not local, chances are he'll be flattered without being offended, and willing to share with you some of his hard-learned lessons. You may be able to copy a home-baser's setup, or use him as a role model, without his being aware of what you're doing. But if he is aware of what you're doing, and willing to help you, you'll feel better, do better, and learn more if you talk to him about it. You'll feel free to ask pointed questions, seek specific advice, and take notes.

Don't imitate blindly. Not everything that works for your role model will work for you. Follow general guidelines, but beware of slavishly following specific ones. If your role model boosts his sales by giving how-to classes or seminars that tie in to what he's selling (for example, products such as diet supplements, cosmetics, and flower arrangements), consider strongly whether or not such a self-marketing technique will work well for you. Do you like teaching? Do you like speaking in front of large groups? Learn all you can about the specifics of such tie-ins, then try them yourself, if they're suited to your product and your personality. This is wise imitation. But where you might be wise to imitate a general business setup you'd be foolish to use office color schemes that are incompatible with your temperament, simply because your role model favors them.

Grow and show. Take the best from your prototype. Selectively choose those techniques which will serve your purposes and use them as the basis for improving your business. Introduce your own innovations. Add your own creative ideas to those used by your role model. Then, when you feel you've developed something superior to your original setup, because of your role model's input, invite him to evaluate, and perhaps benefit from, your clever offshoot ideas. In this way you are getting and giving—a "win/win" situation, where both parties come out ahead.

Snoop and interview. In order to imitate productively, you need a setup worth imitating. Very few home-basers are making big bucks. You must ferret out those who are. Sometimes it takes a lot of snooping to come up with successful home-basers in your county or state. Ask questions here and there about a superstar home-baser whom you've heard or read about, and who is succeeding splendidly in a business similar to your own. Follow up, in person, by phone, or by mail, relevant statements made at social gatherings. If you overhear someone saying that enterprising Evelyn is going to be showing her jewelry made of silicon chips at the Fashion and Boutique Trade Show in Los Angeles, don't let the statement drop. Don't worry about appearing snoopy. Find out all you can. How did Evelyn manage this? Can anyone exhibit at this show? Is it expensive? (See Chapter 4 for information on trade shows.) Is Evelyn doing as well as everyone believes she is? Question your informant and question Evelyn. Chances are good that if she's as successful as everyone believes, she knows the value of sharing information, of networking, and will not be turned off by reasonable requests for how-to information from another serious home-baser.

The few home-basers who are making the big bucks are usually doing things, or are in situations, that the average home-baser is not. You want to discover what they're doing that you're not, what they may have going for them that you don't. You want to make sure that your role models are really worthy of your admiration. Often an entrepreneur is doing well only because he or she has the right spouse or parents working behind the scenes. It's one thing for a home-baser to develop an ingenious and wildly effective marketing system by her own efforts. It's another thing entirely when so-and-so's stuff is selling fantastically mainly because her spouse is a prominent businessperson with infinite social contacts. Make sure you differentiate. Locate those entrepreneurs who are genuinely self-made; then write up four or five questions you'd find it valuable to have a particular entrepreneur answer. One of the best ways to go from here is to put your questions in a letter requesting a short appointment (include a self-addressed stamped envelope). When it's mutually convenient, conduct an interview. Your role model will probably enjoy the experience and so will you. (If he is timeshort, he may choose simply to answer your questions by mail, which is still helpful.) Repeat this procedure with the next admiration-worthy entrepreneur you've located. Again, it's important that your role models be solely self-made if you're working under the assumption that they are. It's okay if they're not, but you should know this, as you may be expecting more of yourself than is realistic. It's hard to imitate an entrepreneur who has a powerful behind-the-scenes support system that you don't have.

9. "Home" is a flexible term. A home can be an apartment, private house, or a mansion. In a home-based business it can also refer to mobile units—trailers, trucks, tents, boats, and station wagons. Being home-based means not being based in a formal outside office or factory. You can sell your homemade offerings from a mobile home at a flea market, a catering truck outside a suburban office complex, a tent at a juried fair, a boat docked at a regatta, or a station wagon at a country auction. You are basically home-based. You are just taking your goods to a mobile extension of your home in order to bring them to where the buying crowds are. Often this puts you steps ahead of the home-baser whose business is not easily mobile, who cannot effortlessly "wheel and spiel" or go back and forth between his home base and a lucrative extension. If you are fortunate enough to be able to be "wheel-based" at will, then your mobile home base must be set up for soaring just like your immobile home base.

2

WHEN THE "RIGHT" PRODUCT IS WRONG

Major manufacturers and corporations are well aware that sometimes a "right" product can be wrong—a product that could be selling briskly isn't. They invest fortunes in market research when they find that a basically fine product is not selling nearly as well as it should be. Usually their research tells them that if their product is to experience a turnaround in sales, certain steps must be taken. These steps are similar to the steps you must take if your "right" product isn't working, if sales and buyer response aren't what they could be. Let's look at why a "right" product can be wrong and see what can be done to change this.

IS YOUR PRODUCT REALLY "RIGHT"?

The assumption is made in this chapter that you have a product that is essentially "right": you're selling a well-made product with high sales potential which is not being realized. Your product probably does fall into this category or you would have given up by now. However, *sometimes a person becomes glued to a hopeless loser*. He refuses to see that regardless of any steps undertaken, sales will never substantially improve. An example of a hopeless loser is a product whose pulling power is dead or drying up; as eight-track tapes would be today, a product that is overly ordinary, such as a stuffed toy that's like dozens of others and not even attractively priced, or a product that is poorly made, such as a digital watch that runs slow or a chocolate-chip cookie that tastes doughy. Before going on, be certain that your product is "right"—that sales really can be better. *If your product is such that all markets for it have dried up, or it is excruciatingly ordinary or poorly made, face this fact. Come up with a product that won't doom you.*

DOES YOUR PRODUCT HAVE A SALES-SPURRING NAME AND LOGO?

If a product is good, it doesn't really matter what you call it, right? Wrong! Whenever possible, a product should have a name, and the name should:

Be easy to pronounce. People don't like to sound foolish when they talk. A cutesy, multisyllabic name is a turn-off to the average, hurried businessperson. If he has to ask for twenty Weenie Write-It-Right Pads, he may decide not to place his order with you.

Tell you something about the product. A Write-It-Right pad (without the "Weenie") is a good name, if you're selling a pad—as is one home-baser specializing in educational aids—which has a border composed of writing tips. A successful seller of home-baked, golden-colored brownies marketed them as Tannies. One man changed the name of his custom-designed children's saddles from Tot Trots, which is cute, but makes no specific sense, to Stay in the Saddles, which hints of safety. His sales have picked up considerably and he feels the name change is largely responsible.

Differ from the name of your company. A home-based manufacturer of hand-dipped chocolates was about to officially name her business The Chocolate Connection when her granddaughter said, "What if one day you decide to make gumdrops or taffy too?" The Chocolate Connection became The Candy Connection and for many years this home-baser sold several aptly named candy treats, in addition to her Hazel's Hand-dipped Chocolates, under the umbrella name prompted by her granddaughter.

Even though you currently may be specializing in one product, you may eventually decide to take on other products or drop that product entirely. If you don't yet have an official company name, choose a nonrestrictive one which will embrace new and related product offerings.

Be simple, but catchy, if possible. Write-It-Right for the pad described above, is a relatively simple, yet catchy, title. Most people remember catchy names. Children, in particular, do. Ask a child if he knows what a Shrinky Dink or Hula Hoop or Etch-A-Sketch is. If you're selling in the children's market, take great care to give your product an appropriate, yet appealing, name.

Be enticing. Not every product needs an alluring name; but if your product lends itself well to having a name that seduces the senses, why not go with it? Remember the perfume Evening in Paris? Do you think it would have sold so well had it been called Evening in Brooklyn?

Be changed if you think a change might help. Like the designer of children's saddles who was wise to change his product's name from Tot Trots to Stay in the Saddles, you should upgrade, or update, your product's name if you think doing so will increase sales. Also, if your product is already doing quite well, but you think it can do better with a name change that will alert customers to the fact that it's even better than ever, you can try what many major manufacturers do. Promote your product as "New, improved———."

Most people spend a great deal of time choosing names for their children and for their pets, boats, homes, and other prized possessions. Yet many entrepreneurs who would never carelessly grab from the air a name for their children will do just that for their products. Don't do this. Your products are also precious to you.

As important as a sales-spurring name is a sales-spurring logo. People like logos. And they recognize them, sometimes more than they do the actual name of a product. Which do you think is more familiar to most people, the name Izod Lacoste or the "alligator" shirt? If possible, your product should have a logo—one which is appropriate to all the products you may be handling and helps to increase consumer recognition. Consumer recognition increases consumer confidence (for some reason people associate a logo with a commitment to quality and longevity), and consumer confidence increases sales.

If you don't yet have a company logo, experiment with several. Seek other people's opinions and advice. Aim for a logo that is both clever and descriptive of your operation. A paintbrush and palette, knitting needles and wool, some cookies in an oven, a hammer and wood, flowers in a basket—all have been used as effective company logos by entrepreneurs whose operations were related to these items. Once you think you know what you'd like in your logo, put it together in a unique way. You want your logo to rouse people, not leave them cold. Cookies in an oven is fine—but what kind of oven (old-fashioned, ultra-modern?) and what kind of cookies (pure chocolate? big chocolate chips and nuts?)? Should someone (grandma? child?) be happily testing the product? *Remember, this is the trademark that will be on your product labels, on your company stationery, on T-shirts which you might one day distribute for promotional purposes, on everything that relates to your enterprise.* A "right" product should be linked to several supports (packaging, display, pricing) which jointly create customer recognition and a sales-spurring image. Name and logo are among the supports that will create the image you need.

DOES YOUR PRODUCT HAVE A SALES-SPURRING PACKAGE DESIGN?

Another thing that goes a long way toward creating a "right" product image is the packaging of your product. If your product is incorrectly packaged, it won't sell nearly as well as it could or should. Maybe you "can't judge a book by its cover," but, like most people, you probably do. And if you don't like a book's cover, you may not bother opening the book to see if it's worth purchasing. Right or wrong, that's the way it is. *There are lots of sellers competing for the same consumer dollar; and all*

When The "Right" Product is Wrong 27

other things being equal, the one whose product is in the most attractive and attention-getting package stands the best chance of getting that consumer dollar.

Sometimes packaging is so unusual that people buy a product they might ordinarily not buy just to get the package it's in. One home-based manufacturer of flavored popcorn was surprised to learn that people liked her popcorn, but more than that, they loved the colorful metal canisters she was selling it in. Long after the popcorn was finished, the canisters were still being used for storage and decoration. Not every product lends itself to such packaging; but if yours does, you may want to consider going all out with packaging—provided, of course, you're selling into a market where you can comfortably write into your selling price the cost of pizzazz packaging.

Just as people will sometimes buy a product to get the container it's in, they'll buy a product because it has some other type of "freebie appeal" related to its packaging. One man who sells thousands of holiday fruit baskets annually says that people buy his product only partly because his fruit is delicious and beautifully basketed. For years this man has been attaching magnificent flowers, made of wood shavings, to each basket. His customers have come to regard his wooden flowers as collectibles and display them proudly in little vases.

You may think, Baskets, wooden flowers; isn't this overpackaging? Not for this man, who buys in quantity thousands of wooden flowers from an importer he found at a trade show. The flowers cost him about fifty cents apiece, permit him to add at least a dollar to his selling price, are easy to attach to each basket, and have proven to be a definite buying incentive.

Certainly you don't want to overpackage. Time, money, and market should determine how far you go with packaging. Don't package your product so that the actual act of packaging is time-consuming. Don't get involved with fancy packaging or package design that causes your product to become overpriced. Packaging materials should not be so costly that you lose your competitive edge in the marketplace.

Don't engage in fancy packaging where it is totally uncalled for. Gifts, decorator and gourmet items, and crafts and goods that are prominently displayed in upscale outlets are among the products that lend themselves well to creative package design. Proper packaging of these items can make the difference between selling and not selling a good product. Here the right packaging can grab a customer and persuade him to buy. But avoid fancy packaging for a "no-frills" product in a "no-frills" market. If, for example, you sell kitchen utensils from a custom-designed catalog, you're dealing with an armchair consumer who just wants the basic item in the picture in front of him and expects it to come in plain wrapping. The same applies if you're selling socks at a flea market. Here customers are interested only in such things as size, color, style, price, and quality, and would just as soon not have to be bothered with packaging; they want to be able to touch their potential purchase. If your product lends itself at all to decorative packaging, don't put this sales-spurring step off. If your product is such that packaging it will in no way make it a more attractive buy, turn your attentions elsewhere.

IS YOUR PRODUCT DISPLAY RIGHT?

You can have the most perfect product, but if it's displayed poorly, it will sell poorly. Here we go from package design to product display. *A product can have the right name, the right logo, the right packaging, and still be a loser if it's not exhibited to maximize its selling potential.*

Merchandise should be displayed so that it is:

Easy to inspect all samples. One home-baser selling exquisite, well-priced, imported throw rugs displayed himself right out of an expensive trade show because he exhibited his wares foolishly. Instead of setting out his rug samples on racks so that buyers could easily inspect and compare different pieces, he heaped his rugs into piles thirty pieces deep. Most buyers were too busy, too weary, or too annoyed to be bothered lifting, pulling, and holding in order to examine his goods. If buyers have to work hard to see your line, they may just pass it by.

Easy to size. How large a package of cookies? What

size shirt? How long a gold chain? Many products are sized at point of sale. A customer comes to a flea market to buy an eighteen-inch gold chain. All other things being equal, will she buy from the vendor who has dozens of chains hanging together, intertwined, from nails on a wooden board? Or will she buy from the vendor standing behind five or six rolls of chain, each roll styled differently, all the chains easy to unwind, cut, and put a clasp on? If you're selling a product where size is a significant factor, set up your display so that sales proceed easily for seller and buyer. Don't throw different sizes and shapes together. Display neatly, putting likes with likes as much as possible. Spread out. If there's not enough horizontal space available to you, create vertical space through the use of racks, shelves, or screens.

Easy, or hard, for customers to handle. This means that if you want customers touching, trying, or tasting your product, your merchandise should be displayed in a manner that invites this response. One woman who runs a weekend fudge and jam shop from her home sets out an enticing array of samples beneath a sign that reads "Try Before You Buy." Customers who might ordinarily purchase just a single jar of jam or box of fudge frequently find themselves feeling that they must have two of this, one of that, three of these—precisely the response this entrepreneur is encouraging by making her product easily accessible to potential customers.

However, if you're selling a product which loses its attractiveness the more it's touched and picked over, display it in such a manner that customers can look but not handle anything, or touch only if you're monitoring their inspection.

Easy to find. When a consumer wants to purchase a particular item, his natural response is to go to that section of an outlet where it usually can be found. Make sure your item is placed with like items. However, if your product is such that it can logically be placed in one of two or three displays, try to have it placed in the display where it will most appear to be a unique and well-priced item. One woman who makes dramatic and amusing four-foot character dolls out of stuffed nylon stockings learned quickly that when her offerings were placed with other dolls, they appeared overpriced and did not appeal to most youngsters. She had her local department store move her dolls from the toy section, where sales were sluggish, to the decorator accessories section, where they became a brisk-selling novelty. Young married and gift givers took to them almost immediately.

IS YOUR PRODUCT PRICED TO SELL WELL?

Almost all people, even the rich, love a good buy and hate to feel they've overpaid for an item. A product can be "right" in every way, but if it has an inflated price tag on it, it won't sell well. People will look at it and admire it, but they'll be reluctant to pull out their wallets. A "right" product becomes wrong when it is overpriced.

A clear distinction must be made between "overpriced" and "priced too high." An overpriced product is one where seller greed is readily obvious to the savvy consumer —the vendor is aiming for a markup several times greater than comparable products get. A product priced too high is one that costs more than the average consumer will pay for it. If your product falls into the overpriced classification, you must modify your price immediately in order to boost sales and enable your business to soar. If your product is priced too high, you must ask yourself the following questions and act accordingly:

1. If I lower my price, will increased sales volume substantially increase my net profits? Or will my net profits remain the same, or shrink, because of the need for increased labor and supply costs?

2. Is there a modification, something that can be done to my product, to make it seem less expensive? Some sellers have found the answer to this in pretty packaging. Others have found it profitable to advertise "Buy four, get one free." (Of course, here you must have a product that lends itself to multiple buying.) Still others have thrown in an "incentive goody" which promotes impulse buying without substantially increasing marketing costs: "Take

home a cheesecake for dessert and enjoy a doughnut now!"

3. Am I selling to the wrong market? What one buying audience finds too high, another may find reasonable. If possible, try selling your product to a more upscale buying audience. If upgrading your product a bit will make this easier, you may want to try the "upgrade/upscale" approach: One photographer found that a more attractive frame around his pictures brought him the kind of customers who considered his product "a great buy." The cost difference between the frames he had been using and his new ones was minimal; and his increase in net profits was impressive.

4. Should I price my product even higher? Maybe what you think is "too high" can go even higher without being considered overpriced. This sounds absurd, yet sometimes the right product becomes wrong when it's underpriced in the eyes of the snobbish. Have you ever met someone who will ignore you when you say, "Why buy this in Bloomingdale's for $50 when Annie Sez is selling the exact thing for $35?" There are people who truly believe that, within limits, the more they pay for an item, the better it is, and reason won't reach these people. But you can reach them by accommodating them! Try, for example, placing your item on consignment in a snob outlet for three or four times your planned selling price. If it moves well, you'll be happy; your consignee will be happy; and your customers will be happy—a win/win/win situation.

IS YOUR PRODUCT PRESENTATION RIGHT?

Are you presenting your product to its (and your) maximum advantage? One home-baser was doing just okay selling imported shoes from a flea market when he came upon an idea that turned "just okay" into "sensationally well." This man frequently found customers complaining: "If only you had this shoe with that heel" or "What I would give to get that shoe in this color." He decided to give them exactly what they wanted. Next to his regular table he set up a Make-Your-Own Shoe table equipped with all the shoe parts, and tools, necessary to satisfy even the most outrageous tastes. His son manned the table, guiding the hammer-clumsy each step of the way. Overnight his booth became a teen-ager's delight—a shoe for every outfit, and a cute young boy to help put it all together! His sales quadrupled within a few months.

In many cases the make-your-own presentation can skyrocket a high-potential/low-sales item. Buyer labor meets buyer needs. The customer gets exactly what he wants without your having to increase your labor costs. It's amazing how many products lend themselves to this approach. One teenager paid her way through college with a Make-Your-Own Cupcake table which she set up at all sorts of weekend events patronized mostly by children. She baked a few hundred plain cupcakes and took them, along with a selection of icings, toppings, decorations, spreaders, and napkins, to each event. The children were delighted with the freedom she provided them; and she enjoyed watching them, and watching her savings account grow. This type of make-your-own presentation can be used with all sorts of things, from dolls to tacos, from jewelry to body or nail decorations.

Another way to successfully present a product is the *personalized presentation*. You've seen scarves, bags, wrapping paper, pads, barrettes, mugs, hundreds of objects sell just because the buyer is delighted to come upon his own name. Is your product such that you could possibly put someone's name on it? If so, try it. And don't think only in terms of names. Today color is almost as personal as a name. People think of themselves as pink people, yellow people, blue people. Think along with them. Present your product in the season's most popular colors and color combinations. Make it clear that color choices are readily available.

Still another successful presentation is the *multi-purpose product*. People are usually delighted to discover that an item which they thought had only one use can have two or three or four. One home-baser increased her sales many times by multiplying the purpose of the blankets she was selling. She went from selling blankets to selling The

Five-Way Blanket. She demonstrated to department-store and boutique buyers her product's versatility as a blanket, fireside robe, skirt, bedspread, and tablecloth. When her presentation became perfected, one department store made a videotape of her demonstrating the product's many uses and ran it continuously for their fascinated customers. (This clever entrepreneur, fast to follow a good idea, eventually made up her own videotapes for distribution to customers who could use them as selling aids.)

If you've created a product with only one intended use, don't close down your imagination. What else can your product do or be used for? A wall plaque can be used as a serving tray. A jam can be used as a cake filling or roast glaze. A fruit bowl can be used as a flowerpot. The more versatile a product, the more economical it becomes from a consumer's point of view—better to buy one wall plaque that can double as a serving tray than buy both a wall plaque and a serving tray. Often the multipurpose product is viewed as both a money and space saver.

No matter what your product, visual impact matters. Even if your offering is such that prettiness is unimportant, even if function is foremost, your product should still be as eye-pleasing as possible. There was a time when a teenager was thrilled just to have a working telephone in her room. No more. Now that phone has to be the right style and color. Present your product as thoroughly and imaginatively as possible and keep in mind that even when looks aren't supposed to matter, they do.

DO YOU UNDERSTAND THE DIFFERENCE BETWEEN THE PRODUCT AND MARKET APPROACH TO SELLING?

Many economists believe that one of the major reasons the Japanese have been more successful than we have in selling their manufactured goods is that they use the market approach and we use the product approach. Here's the difference, and here's how you can benefit from understanding it:

The market approach. You go into the commercial marketplace, analyze what is wanted and needed, make it, and sell it.

The product approach. You create a product for which you believe there is a market, then you go out, find that market, and sell them your product.

The market approach seems to make more sense—to be a more rational, safer approach. However, until recently, most American manufacturers operated under the belief that they could create a market for their products, or that they could introduce their products in small, test-size units, and manufacture based on initial marketplace response. This isn't a ridiculous belief. But for many reasons it has led to costly surplus inventories and forced writeoffs. You can benefit from understanding, and using, the market approach.

The average home-baser uses the product approach. He creates a product that he believes in and then seeks ways to market it. He hopes that others will agree that his item is wanted and needed. Basically he's banking on the idea that he is representative of the buying public to whom he hopes to sell. He can't afford extensive and expensive preliminary market research. Nor would he be certain exactly how to proceed if he could. Ultimately, how well he does depends on how truly in tune he is to what people want to buy. An ivory-tower type, who creates beauty for the sake of beauty, generally does not stand a great chance of making big bucks. A "people person," one who's constantly in touch with all kinds of people in all kinds of places, stands a much better chance.

Let's assume that you're a "people person" but that you don't want to rely exclusively on the product approach to selling. You want to use some sort of modified market approach to make sure your product is completely right:

1. Be a media-gulper. Read, watch television reports, listen to the radio, attend seminars. Take in all you can that pertains directly or peripherally to your product. While you can't conduct costly market surveys, you can benefit enormously from those that are conducted. But first you must learn of their existence. Once you become a "mediagulper," you'll take in all the information that is ignored, not only by the average person, but also by the average entrepreneur. In this way you can adapt your product, or your product line, to be totally in sync with the marketplace of the moment.

2. *Assume your product to be only partially "right."* Assume that your product is in the act of becoming a great seller, not in its final stage of development. Encourage and use feedback in order to perfect your product.

3. *Be a constant competition watcher.* Your product will definitely lose some strength if the marketplace becomes glutted with perfect imitations. You want to sell into a still-hungry market, and the best way to do this is to know who's feeding your market, how fast, and how well. Once you build a clientele you can keep it by maintaining quality control; but you must also be in the vanguard with innovations and adaptations. There's little doubt that if you're successful, you'll be copied. Your competitors will always try to capitalize on your good thing. But don't worry. It works both ways. They copy; you copy. They modify; you modify. The idea is to get in there early while there's still room for everybody.

Let's take a look at a home-baser who used a modified market approach, who pretty much followed the three steps just covered, and who, by doing so, turned a tiny enterprise into a solid moneymaker.

Carol started out as an overweight housewife in search of a part-time income. Someone put her onto popcorn as a friendly food for would-be skinnies. Popcorn, instead of more calorie-laden foods, became her quick hunger-fix. She became so high on popcorn as a weight-reduction aid that she started making it from her home and marketing it, in charming packages, to outlets which catered to the health- and diet-conscious. She wasn't making much money, but she was showing a small profit—mainly because her packaging was so appealing. Nevertheless, she felt encouraged and was eager to expand in some way.

Her opportunity came in the form of a television report (Carol was a mediagulper, step 1) on American's obsession with flavors. Carol soaked in every bit of it and came up with the decision to market flavored popcorn. She made up several distinctly flavored packets and placed them on a "let's see" consignment basis (step 2) in several different types of outlets. Within a month she learned what to make more of and what to drop (licorice-flavored popcorn did poorly, honey-flavored became a fast favorite among the health-conscious).

Predictably, Carol's idea was copied and one-upped. Someone not only came up with the same product, also cutely packaged, but introduced chocolate-coated popcorn as well. It was popular almost immediately. Carol, by now a businessperson, and on top of the situation (step 3), didn't despair. Instead she came right up with bittersweet, milk-chocolate, chocolate rum, and several other chocolate choices, all in her now recognizable wrap. Orders began to stream in and Carol's tiny business took off.

DOES YOUR PRODUCT HAVE LONG-TERM APPEAL?

For some products there always seems to be a market. For others the market is fleeting or whimsical. Unfortunately, it's difficult to forecast with certainty whether a product will have long- or short-term appeal. This is too bad because a "right" product can be wrong if it doesn't have a market of at least reasonable duration. However, there are certain things you can try to build into your product or associate with your product, which will help to ensure long-term appeal.

Reasonable obsolesence. Certainly your product shouldn't disintegrate the moment it gets into a customer's hands. However, if it is something which lends itself well to periodic updating, plan for this so that you don't have to depend only on new customers for cash flow. Fashion and decorator accessories fall firmly into this classification. If either is your field, by all means create "perennials," but think also in terms of "annuals." Give your customers some change each season, something new. Keep the best of the old, but add, modify, update.

Repeat need. Is your product such that when supply dwindles a customer's immediate response is to reorder?

This is an ideal situation and one that is particularly enjoyed by the producers of taste treats—the tastier a product, the faster it gets used and reordered. Repeat need also applies directly to cosmetics items and stationery supplies. If you have a repeat-need product, make sure to include a reorder slip in each order. If possible, have your reorder slip in the form of a self-addressed stamped post-card requiring the customer to do little more than check off boxes.

Collectible appeal. Can you build into your product a "one is not enough" customer response? Paul, a popular New England potter, has found that once people begin collecting his work, they return regularly to add a piece. He creates whimsical "people pieces" in mugs, lamps, teapots, plates, and intentionally makes pieces which go with other pieces. If your product has add-a-piece appeal, try to keep coming up with novel variations on your main theme. This gives your product long-term appeal and keeps you in the public eye in much the same manner as word-of-mouth advertising.

Gift-giving potential. Will your product make a great Christmas present or birthday gift? If so, promote it as such. Offer it in gift wrappings appropriate to different holidays. Have holiday sales and specials. This doesn't mean people shouldn't be encouraged to buy your product for personal use. It just means that they should also be induced to see its gift-giving potential. One home-baser, with a stocked greenhouse off her kitchen, has her greenhouse deliberately set up as a buy for yourself/buy for another operation. Not only is her pricing policy "Buy two, get one free," but she has plants in fancy containers, plants with baby, birthday, and holiday decorations in them, and plants with gift tags already attached to them, as well as plants for setting into her customers' own gardens or own containers.

HOW ENTHUSIASTIC ARE YOU ABOUT THE PRODUCT YOU'RE SELLING?

Certainly, if a product does not have long-term appeal it won't be a "right" product for very long. Nor will you be in business for very long. However, you can have a product rich in long-term appeal and spilling over with profit potential, and if you're not keen on it, this super product is wrong for you. If there's little chance of your coming to regard it more favorably, find a product which excites you more.

There are those who say, "Never mind the philosophizing; if my product's making money, I'm enthused about it!" This is like saying, "If my kid's doing great in school, I'm proud of him!" It's easy to respond passionately to a situation that's going the way you want it to. But if your child is not doing well in school, does this mean you're not to feel any positive emotions for him? Of course not; and the same thing applies to your product. *You must feel a sense of enthusiasm for the product you're selling, whether or not it's currently producing the way you would like it to be.* If you don't feel this way, being the owner of a home-based business will be a sour experience, and it's not likely that you'll be able to make your business soar.

One home-baser in Maine sells potatoes. How enthusiastic can you get about potatoes? Not very, if you're like most of the other potato vendors in that area, who sell potatoes (and some other produce) to eke out a meager living for their efforts. But if you're like this particular home-baser, who sees all sorts of exciting possibilities in potatoes—who displays them as potato people, gives out potato-pancake samples, has a special hot cheese dip for french fries, throws an annual potato-skin-eating contest, and sells, or does, other things related to potatoes—you can not only be a great potato enthusiast but quite an affluent one too.

WHERE, PRIMARILY, IS YOUR PRODUCT BEING SOLD?

A "right" product can be wrong if it's being sold in the wrong place. Where to market what you're selling will be discussed in detail. However, in closing this chapter it is important to note that a product must not be judged "wrong" or unsalable based on its performance in one or two locations. The story of Anna Moses illustrates how important it is to sell your product in the right place or the right market.

Anna Moses was eighty when she decided to try to sell a few of her paintings of the countryside and life she knew well. She took her art, along with some jams and jellies she frequently made, to a local fair. The jams and jellies sold. No one bought her artwork. She then placed her primitive scenes on consignment at a local drugstore. Lookers, but only one buyer—a New York art collector, Mr. Louis Caldor. Caldor was impressed enough with the inexpensive little scenes to show them in a museum exhibit along with the works of seventeen other American unknowns. Still, no acclaim or sales. But Caldor kept in touch with Anna and urged her to keep painting. Then, several months later, Caldor arranged for a one-woman show at the gallery of a man interested in American folk art. The show was called What a Farm Wife Painted. The gallery was the right place, the right market—acclaim, publicity, recognition, prizes, and sales followed. A reporter, and then everyone, dubbed Anna Moses . . . Grandma Moses. The rest is art history. Had Grandma Moses stopped marketing her art because it didn't sell at the fair, or had she not followed the lead of someone who knew the value of the right location for a "right" product, what a loss it would have been for her, and for America as well!

3

TESTING YOUR PRODUCT (AND YOURSELF) IN SHALLOW WATERS

Just as man can be said to pass through four stages—infancy, childhood, adulthood, and old age—so too can a business be described. Your business is now past its infancy. It's been born and nurtured. You've parented it as well as you've been able to; and you're going to do even better in the future. Now your business is in its childhood. You're going to have fun with it as you bring it to a strong, successful adulthood.

In Chapter 1 we checked out home base to make sure all is set for soaring into a strong, successful business. In Chapter 2 we made certain that your product is as perfected as it can be. Now your home-based business, like the solidly primed child, is ready to see what kind of impact it can make on the big world out there. Are you prepared to take a few small risks, make mistakes, get feedback? Are you ready to venture from the peace and solitude of home base and meet lots of different people? Are you ready to consider expanding your product line? Are you willing to undertake some business offshoots?

RISK-TAKING

There is a saying, "Don't hesitate to go out on a limb sometimes; after all, that's where the fruit is." The key word here, for the home-baser, is "sometimes." Risk-taking is a part of moneymaking and business boosting; but because it is also a part of money-losing and bankruptcy, it must be approached with great caution. When

Testing Your Product (And Yourself) In Shallow Waters 41

the consequences appear to be too painful, dangerous, or costly, it should not be approached at all. Let's start with the easiest types of risk-taking and work toward those that are a bit more demanding but still within shallow waters.

The best risks to begin with are those that don't cost you money if they don't work out. These are called *rejection risks*. You risk being turned down for something which could help boost your business. The local school is planning a fundraiser. You have five hundred four-inch Lucite picture frames. Would the school like to raise funds selling your product? If so, you will sell them the five hundred pieces at 50% beneath retail and they can mark up accordingly. If they like your idea, you make money and they make money. If they don't like your idea, you don't make any money and you don't lose any. All you've risked is being told, "No thank you, we don't want to buy your frames."

Because rejection risks are ego-linked, they are not undertaken enough by home-basers. No one likes to feel rejected; but home-basers are more sensitive to rejection than their more commercial counterparts. Often a home-baser doesn't feel like a real business person, or an important entrepreneur, until he starts making a lot of money. His business ego is not yet strong and he doesn't want to court rejection by picking up his phone and making a proposition to a school fundraising chairman. So he doesn't. And he doesn't make the sale. Meanwhile, his commercial counterpart in the little storefront off Main Street is working out delivery dates for five hundred Lucite bud vases with the grateful fundraising chairman, who was hoping a good idea would come along.

Don't wait to build your ego before taking rejection risks. One becomes confident by taking them. Sometimes these risks will work out; sometimes they won't. Eventually, if your product is right, it will be commercially received in several markets. But you must make this happen. Contacting fundraising chairpeople is just one kind of rejection risk you should attempt. What you must do is test your product in as many shallow waters as possible. You may get a bit wet, but you're not going to drown.

Another cost-free way to test your product is via party-plan selling. Here again you're risking being rejected, and you're investing some time; but you're not risking any money. Usually someone gets a group together in an informal home setting. In a low-pressure way you pitch your product to this group, demonstrate its value and virtues, and answer questions about it (see Chapter 7 for more on party-plan selling). If your audience likes you and your product, they may buy and rebuy and ultimately create a financially lucrative customer chain for you. However, if they don't like you or your product, or if they don't want to buy for one reason or another, they won't stone you.

You may feel a sense of rejection if party-plan selling doesn't pan out. But if you approach the experience professionally, it can ultimately prove useful. Ask yourself probing questions. Why are these people rejecting you or your product? Are you making any mistakes? Is something wrong with your product, your approach? Can you change your product, or your presentation, to change the situation? And should you make changes? Is this party typical of how you'd do at other, similar gatherings? Is party-plan selling the wrong marketing avenue for your product? Remember, you're testing your product, and yourself, in a nonthreatening environment. This is exactly what you must do with a business in its childhood stage of development. This is a muscle-flexing time for your enterprise.

This stage of business growth is the best time for seeking feedback, negative and positive; for finding out where you and your product do and don't belong. One home-based manufacturer of children's toys learned, to her surprise, that her offerings did not interest school fundraisers or suburban party-plan-goers, but that they greatly interested the grandparent market. She initially reached this market through a nursing-home fundraiser auction and later through special sales and direct mailings. Apparently, expensive handmade toys were not items quickly grabbed up by the average young mother trying to stretch her dollars; but they were products many gift-seeking grandparents, remembering the homemade quality of yesteryear's toys, were willing to spend on.

MULTIMARKETING

Multimarketing means marketing your product, and yourself, in multiple ways so as to maximize sales. (It is critical to sales program development for the home-baser—see Chapter 7). Approaching fundraising chairpeople and selling via the party plan are two free and easy ways to multimarket for valuable feedback. There are other product-testing ways which, though not necessarily cost-free, are inexpensive and very much worth trying. Into this category falls participation in such events as flea markets, fairs, mall shows, and auctions. Also there's participation in fundraisers where you act as a profit-sharing vendor, community demonstrations where you teach or inform, and seminars where you speak as part of a program on a certain subject.

The main thing to remember about multimarketing is that if you don't do it, chances are your business won't soar. You *must* multimarket! The more you and your business are in the public eye—the more people are seeing, hearing, and reading about you and what you're selling and doing—the better for your business. Those home-basers earning the really big bucks are those rich in entrepreneurial spirit, those who seem to be everywhere, doing everything, those who come across as authority figures, almost as public figures. Often the ability to multimarket oneself—to package for profit—makes the difference between affluence and poverty for the home-baser. Here's an example.

Linda is a talented artist specializing in watercolors. If she stopped at her present level of success, she would be like most artists—poor. But she doesn't stop there; and not only isn't she poor, but she earns more than most corporate executives, while thoroughly enjoying the lifestyle of a home-baser. In addition to selling her original watercolors to private buyers, Linda has her work reproduced and marketed in other media as well. Her reproductions are framed and sold in galleries. They are adapted to greeting-card format and sold as a quality stationery line. From a studio in her home, Linda also teaches art to children and adults. Based on her experience as an artist and an art teacher, she has written a book about art for children. She has made some videotapes on the subject and given seminar lectures. She judges community-art contests, acts as a consultant to local cultural clubs, and makes herself professionally accessible to organizations that wish to benefit from her status. With each activity Linda becomes more and more of an authority figure. Each multimarketing activity has led, or will lead, to still more opportunities. One activity feeds another as Linda gains more exposure and meets more people. A profitable spiral has taken shape, and a talented home-baser has become, in many ways, larger than her craft.

Can any home-baser do what Linda's doing? With appropriate modification, yes, but you must adhere to the following:

You must engage in "image making." Adapt yourself, and your product, to a few media. You don't magically become a "name." Package yourself into this profitable position by doing the kinds of things Linda does. Can you teach anything related to what you're selling? Can you speak publicly on a subject that ties into your product? Can the product you're selling be adapted to another medium or be used by a new kind of buying audience? Can you perform a public service that relates to your business? Extend your home-based status into the community, into the public arena. Tap your imagination for profitable possibilities.

One home-based manufacturer of Christmas-tree ornaments visited a local hospital and offered to decorate a tree with the help of patients in the children's ward. He would supply the decorations and guidance; the hospital would supply the tree. His idea turned into a local media event. The town newspaper did a feature on the tree-decorating ceremony, giving ample space to the ornament maker's role in the event and his place in the community as a manufacturer.

This manufacturer was now on his way to becoming a "name." A local cable-television station picked up the feature and interviewed the man. A department store in a neighboring town invited him to demonstrate his craft in their Trim-A-Tree department. Within one week, and while having a wonderful time, this man found that holiday orders had tripled those of the previous year, and there was strong interest in his work from local retailers.

You must be willing to expend some energy. Multimarketing need not be an exhausting experience; in fact, it shouldn't be. If anything, it should be exhilarating and stimulating. However, it does take a measure of energy. There must be a commitment to performing some activities only indirectly related to your businesss. Be eager to direct some of your energies into peripheral or satellite activities which might have a positive effect on your business. Initially some tasks you perform may seem nonproductive. Don't give up. It is the cumulative quality of multimarketing activities that makes a business soar. Try several possibilities and write off those that prove fruitless or that you dislike. One home-based photographer who wasn't doing well teaching photo development switched to teaching photo framing. This course proved popular and profitable. Many of the home-baser's students bought her works to put in their newly made frames.

You must be personable. This means easy to get along with and easy on the eyes. How are you at just being nice? Do you find it a great effort to smile? Do you like answering questions, showing people how to do things? Do you have a good sense of fun and humor? Is your dress flattering and nonoffensive? Do you appear clean and approachable? You needn't be a great wit or a raving beauty. But you can't come off as a slob either. If you are tense in social situations or stiff in your appearance, you can, and should, change these things. Practice a presentation. Try different outfits or makeup. Observe and take notes on social performances you admire. Work on your weak points. The more you practice and observe, the more you perfect. One of the great benefits of becoming a multimarketing pro is that you grow tremendously as an individual. In the process of doing things to boost your business, you're creating an improved self-image too.

You must work to avoid isolation. Not everyone regards home-basing as a desirable lifestyle. Many people enjoy being surrounded by co-workers. You may or may not feel this way. But even if you love everything about home-basing, you must not cherish your solitude so much that it becomes increasingly harder for you to get out with other people. You won't multimarket yourself if you become so intoxicated with a life of social isolation that the outside world looms as an obtrusive disturbance. The concept of multimarketing will become extremely disagreeable, and frightening, to you. And if you fervently don't want to multimarket yourself, and you fear it, you will avoid doing it even when excellent opportunities fall into your lap. Don't permit yourself to become a commercial agoraphobic. Impose a social schedule on yourself. Meet other home-basers for lunch. Attend conferences. Travel. Take courses. Network. Entertain customers. Do the kinds of things that force you away from the tendency to become too much of a loner.

You must welcome constructive criticism. You won't be able to multimarket yourself to entrepreneurial greatness if you hate to be criticized. Of course you don't want unjust, vicious, or jealousy-based criticism; but you must learn to accept, work on, and encourage constructive criticism. It is an excellent learning tool. If you send out the message to customers, contacts, relatives, and friends that all you're interested in is positive feedback, that's mainly what you'll get. And you'll be the loser. Compliments are wonderful, but if they're not combined with criticisms, you won't get a balanced progress report. Is your ego so weak that you have to believe you aren't doing anything wrong? If it is, do something about it, because it's hard to build a sturdy business on a fragile ego.

One home-baser, who was marketing a newsletter for singles, made a box at the end of one of his newsletters with a message inside that read, "Please drop me a line and tell me the one thing you dislike most about this newsletter." The man received several responses. One of the responses caused him to make a change which ultimately resulted in his publication gaining a substantial increase in income. The change provoking criticism read, "Your newsletter looks like something run off on a high-school mimeograph machine!" This home-baser was a sincere guy who believed that as long as he was presenting valuable information it wasn't terribly important that his publication looked beautiful. However, since enough people who responded to his request for criticism referred to his newsletter's appearance, he leased an electronic typewriter which produced attractive, margin-justified, printlike copy. Because he encouraged criticism, his newsletter not only ended up with increased subscriptions, but, for the first time, a few companies placed advertisements in it. Perhaps this publisher would have eventually gotten around to a more eye-pleasing format; maybe he never would have. But because he was ready to receive constructive criticism, and was prepared to act upon it, when there was something specific to focus on, he did make a valuable change. Customer criticisms, and compliments, must be built into the multimarketing process so that attempts can be made to reach, please, and keep those markets which sustain your business.

You must be genuinely interested in making your business soar. Are you ready to head a business that can make the transition from childhood to adulthood? Isn't this what a home-baser should want? Maybe not. One home-baser thought he was completely prepared for the big time until an excellent multimarketing opportunity came along and he found himself resisting it. Until then, he had been closing his eyes and ears to many multimarketing opportunities, though he wasn't aware of it. Now an opportunity was presented to him which demanded he respond. It was no longer a case of not seeking opportunity, or not being alert to possibilities. There it was right in front of him! He was an awards manufacturer and supplier, and a major school district was interested in buying thousands of pieces from him. This meant making up several new molds, buying special packaging equipment, taking on part-time help, and committing himself to a time expenditure which he was surprised to realize didn't excite him. This home-baser's business had been growing steadily and he was pleased. Occasionally he dabbled in business-related offshoots, or new products, and was satisfied with the results, but he had never really thought in terms of a quantum leap.

You don't *have* to turn your business into a major moneymaker. But you should decide whether you are really ready to make the transition from small time to big time. Some home-basers know, deep inside, that they're not ready for a quantum leap but superficially they're convinced they are, because they think an entrepreneur is supposed to be growth- and money-oriented. Do what's right for you at this time and don't give yourself conflicting messages.

PRODUCTIVE TESTING

This means testing a product to get information that ultimately will lead to increased sales. The following are outlets and/or methods for productive testing which a homebaser can (and should) try without having to worry about jeopardizing himself or his business in any way:

Flea-market testing. Flea markets can be excellent testing grounds; but before productive testing can begin you must be aware of several points.

You can make a killing at one flea market and not make a single sale at another. Flea markets differ and cater to different buying audiences. Some flea markets are mainly for basic bargains. Others are for interesting buys or goods finds. Still others are for tourists in search of local souvenirs. If there is to be productive testing, you must set up in the right flea market for your product.

The location of your booth or table is important at a flea market. There are usually prime locations and out-of-the way spots which are often never reached or are passed by. A prime location is one that is near a busy traffic area—the entrance/exit, a refreshment stand, the area where the busy, "regulars" set up.

When you set up at a flea market is important. Certain seasons are naturally busy; others are relatively slow. Christmas, for example, is usually a profitable season for fleamarket vendors. Midsummer, on the other hand, is generally a slow season except in tourist areas.

At all kinds of flea markets—anywhere, any time—the booths that draw customers are those which look promising at first glance—the display is neatly laid out, colorful, easy to examine, eye-catching, filled with enticing price signs.

Even if your booth is well located in the right flea market, during a busy season, and is such an eye-pleasing, browser-beckoning delight that people are approaching it—

Testing Your Product (And Yourself) In Shallow Waters

you can't just sit back and sell. This is unproductive testing because you're not coming up with enough useful information. What you must do is:

1. Take written notes. What colors, styles, sizes, and patterns are selling best? What age group is doing the most buying? What's not being examined at all? What's being looked at but not bought? Put on paper what you see, and hear, happening.

2. Experiment. Move items around on your table. Change prices. Offer gift wrapping. Throw in a freebie.

3. Eavesdrop. Act occupied, but listen carefully to what people are saying about your merchandise. Too expensive? Wrong color? Not as nice as similar ones seen? Nice but of no use? Beautifully made? Poorly made?

4. Question. Don't be shy. Whether or not someone's buying, extract all the information you can. Is she buying this for herself? Has she seen similar items? How does she feel these compare? Not everyone makes a good "interviewee." Question those who seem chatty and knowledgeable.

Keep in mind that your main purpose in "fleaing," at this point, is not to make sales but to gather information that will ultimately lead you to product improvement, profitable decisions, and increased sales.

Auction testing. Auctions, like flea markets, can be excellent product testing grounds if they are approached correctly.

There are several kinds of auctions—fundraiser auctions, trade auctions, estate auctions, country auctions, gallery auctions. Not every auctioneer will take your product; and not every auction is appropriate for your product. Many products don't have any auction potential at all. But you'd be surprised how many do, so check out this testing ground thoroughly. An offerng that a big-city gallery owner would sneer at might be a real moneymaker for the country auctioneer.

The advantage of testing your product at auction is that you can see how it fares in a fever-pitched setting. How much of an impulse buy is it? How much interest does it generate among bidders? What are the outer limts to which it can be bid? What is the auctioneer saying to keep the bidding going? Who's doing the bidding? One home-baser of custom-designed and -upholstered wicker furniture discovered to her surprise that her merchandise brought in twice as much money at many fundraiser auctions as it did at flea markets, retail shops, home shows, and crafts fairs.

Much of the same advice that applies at flea markets applies here too. Take written notes. Eavesdrop. Ask questions. These things can be done during the pre-auction viewing, the auction itself, and the post-auction period. Write down all that seems relevant. Don't be afraid to question bidders, or prospective bidders, who seem interested in your merchandise. Many auction goers get caught up in the excitement of the event and love to talk. The person to whom you're speaking need not know you're the consignor of the object under discussion if you feel it is to your advantage that this information not be revealed.

Community programs. Community programs are neighborhood or local events held primarily to inform, entertain, or help area residents. Here participation requires that you talk and that your talk adds something to the program. Now you're not just testing your product; you're also testing yourself. If appropriate, mention your product; but your presentation musn't seem self-serving. It must have a public-service quality about it.

The more you participate in these programs, the better you get at it. You may do poorly the first time you participate in a community program or address a group. You may not be able to sell yourself or your product to the audience. You may not sound like yourself. You'll sound nervous. You'll perspire. You'll sound insincere. You'll forget a lot of what you want to say. You'll answer questions foolishly. Don't worry. Regard the experience as a testing ground, not a final judgment. Any schoolteacher can tell you it takes practice, but once you master the methodology, it's fun, easy, and challenging.

Audiences can differ tremendously. Often there is chemistry, postive or negative, between speaker and audience. One audience may seem to embrace you, bring out the best in you, love what you're selling, order in great quantity. Another audience can make you feel uncomfortable, unliked, that you're selling junk. Once you build up a protective veneer, you'll find community programs an excellent way

Testing Your Product (And Yourself) In Shallow Waters 51

to test and expose yourself and your product, but it takes some getting used to.

When you appear in a spotlight setting, where you have to speak and all eyes are on you, be extremely self-critical when it's all over. Have a tape recording or a videotape made of your presentation. Ask audience members, relatives, and friends for an honest evaluation of your performance. Write down the good and the bad. Make lists of what to do and not to do next time around. This is a constructive procedure used by many successful business executives on the advice of business consultants who know that a product well plugged on a popular talk show can enjoy ten thousand extra sales.

To greatly boost your popularity as a community-program participant, present facts that most people want and can't easily get. One potter used facts and slides to mesmerize a community audience who had assembled for a talk on fire safety. The home-baser, familiar with the clay firing process, had made up slides which showed the damage done by fire of various intensities. The audience sat silently digesting what could happen in twenty seconds, three minutes, one hour. They remembered the facts presented. And they remembered the potter.

Customer testing. Multimarketing entails not just testing your product, or yourself, in a particular setting, but also testing your company's flexibility given a specific set of requests. Through their various requests, customers can provide you with the opportunity to expand your line, add to your production techniques, or adapt your product to a new medium. Remember, however, that a customer's goal is to get custom-tailored merchandise, not to provide you with a growth-producing testing ground. Don't let yourself get sucked into something counterproductive. For instance, don't agree to fill an enormous order in a small time span without first carefully investigating the financial and time commitments involved.

Try to engage in customer testing that appears to have widespread applicability to your particular business interests. The potter mentioned above was asked by a customer who had bought a few large vases for his personal use if she would be interested in "firing up a couple of hundred ashtrays" for his delivery company to use as premiums for new clients. The potter liked the idea. She could envision it as a possible beginning of an off shoot business—the manufacturing of small pieces of pottery for use as business premiums or buying incentives. She fired up two hundred ashtrays, the delivery service had its logo affixed to them, and she was on her way to becoming a "premium potter."

When testing your company's ability to meet unique customer requests, as with other kinds of product testing, evaluate your performance with an eye toward product perfection as well as business growth. The more perfectly produced or crafted your product, the more successfully it will compete with the products of other manufacturers. Quality is always in vogue.

With any kind of testing you should stay as much on the amateur level as possible. Keep testing and retesting your product, yourself, and your company. Be persistent. The more you can learn about the strengths and capabilities of your product and yourself, the more your business will grow in a healthy, long-term way.

TO WHOLESALE OR RETAIL YOUR PRODUCT?

As a home-baser you probably won't start making really big bucks until you set up your company either as a strictly wholesale operation or as a wholesale and retail operation. *It's unusual for a home-based business to make huge profits solely as a retail operation.* You can have great days at a flea market, enjoy sizable profits from a shop set up in your home, or make a respectable profit retailing in other ways, but real growth begins when someone other than yourself is marketing your product to the public. This is where the quantity orders start coming in. Chapter 4 will discuss how to reach for the large wholesale buyers and how to profitably process their orders. But first you need to practice wholesaling your product in a small way, getting a feeling for what wholesaling is all about and looking at your business as a supply company.

Testing Your Product (And Yourself) In Shallow Waters 53

You must develop a "middleman mentality." A middleman is someone who acts as a link between you and the buyer of your product. As a home-baser you may not have thought yet in terms of middlemen. You've always had face-to-face relations with your customers. This can be an appealing way to do business, especially if you're a craftsperson. However, though a middleman takes away from the personal part of customer relations, he can add a new and profitable dimension to your business. There are several ways to try middleman marketing.

Bring in some product samples to those community shops where you think they might sell. Visit stores that are currently carrying goods similar to yours and those that aren't but could conceivably do so. Most small storekeepers can't afford to stock large inventory. Chances are you'll only sell (or consign) a few pieces, which is just what you want for now. Should a shop owner order a large amount, more than you anticipated, give him a temporary exclusive and visit no further until you're able to comfortably mass-produce. Certainly he won't mind; and this keeps the pressure off you.

Arrange with a store owner or manager for you to install and stock a rack in a section of his store. Check the rack periodically, keep it stocked, and you and the store share the income. Here the rack, as well as the storekeeper, acts as a silent middleman. If it is too much for you at this point to maintain several racks, try just one or two.

You may not want to, or have the time to, present your product in a party-plan setup, but try having one or two neighborhood notables pitch your line to their friends (for an incentive, of course). This will enable you to see how you might do as a multilevel sales distributor. (See Chapter 7 for more information on multilevel selling.)

Approach community group leaders. Local clubs, church groups, nursery schools, and school organizations often buy in quantity for their members or for fundraising projects. Arrange to have a couple of group leaders examine your offerings for purchase by their organizations. If your product is acceptable, sell to the group leader, who'll take it from there.

In positioning yourself as a supplier, in talking to potential middlemen, readjust your general selling approach.

Remember, here you're not selling a customer on the merits of your product. Though you may or may not be dealing with a professional retailer, you are dealing with someone who is going to be thinking beyond his own pocketbook and beyond his own tastes. A middleman's main interest is not whether he wants your product, but whether those to whom he plans to sell will. You must sell him on the salability of your merchandise. This goes beyond pointing out the virtues of your product. You should make him aware of all your product's fine selling features so that he can pass this information along to his buyers. But, more important, present him with the kind of information which will make your line an attractive "take-on." Why will the people he deals with want your product? Why will your product be easy for this middleman to sell? Why is your product a better "take-on" than a similar one might be? Anticipate as many questions and objections as you can. One home-based supplier of sun catchers (colorful stick-ons for windows and doors) convinced a local parent-teacher organization to purchase three hundred of them for use in a fundraiser drive and as contest giveaways. She presented her product as something small and colorful that the children would enjoy hawking to friends and neighbors, as a safety item that parents would buy to keep youngsters from walking into a glass door, as a decorator item that could be affixed to many objects, and as a gift-boxed item that would make a nice prize in school contests. This home-baser, acting as a potential supplier, had formidable competition; but she beat them out because she took great care to present her sun catchers as an excellent "take-on" for the parent-teacher organization, rather than just as a good product.

TO MANUFACTURE, PARTIALLY MANUFACTURE, OR BUY FOR RESALE?

If you are making what you're selling, should you continue to do so? Or should you partially produce, or buy your product partially made and complete it? Or should you have someone make it up for you and just distribute it?

There are many ways to handle product production. Just because you have been using one procedure to obtain a finished product, there is no reason you must continue with this procedure. If another method might be easier, or more interesting to you, or would save you time, money, or both, why not consider it? Some home-basers, not wishing to relinquish all control of the manufacturing process, have found it profitable to partially manufacture and partially delegate. Following are two examples.

Bob and Diane turned their garage into a workshop from which they produced high-quality dollhouses, kiddie desks, high chairs, toy chests, and other kinds of furniture for children's rooms. All their pieces were unique and charming. Slowly but steadily, their business grew; they were getting a lot of orders but were working far too many hours for much too small a profit. They were already getting top dollar for their efforts and couldn't raise their prices. They didn't want to turn over their designs to someone else for mass production. They had all the part-time salaried labor they could afford. They were totally averse to buying what they considered to be inferior merchandise, touching it up a bit, and selling it as their own. Their solution? To partially manufacture—to sell a prefabricated line in addition to their regular line. They created high-grade do-it-yourself kits in different stages of completion. Some of these kits could be satisfactorily delegated to mass-production methods. A customer, depending upon his inclination and abilities, could buy an object in twenty, ten, or five parts, with nails, paints, decorations, and instructions included, or could buy the furniture already assembled but unpainted and unadorned. Because Bob and Diane could offer their kits at a price substantially lower than their finished products, and because their kits were designed for easy success, many customers turned in this direction. Bob and Diane no longer had to work to the last nail with each order. Though they still had major control over their operation, they found they were working fewer hours and yet were able to meet their customers' needs while realizing a much greater profit than before.

The decision to relinquish product completion in favor

of presenting a prefabricated do-it-yourself product is just one example of testing an alternative method of product production. Another home-baser decided to try "not going it from scratch any longer" and found that her decision also resulted in increased profits. In this case, Nicole, who had been designing and making hair decorations, decided that it was too much work for her to make the component parts, put them together, and do the decorative work. She found a bulk manufacturer who offered to make and assemble some of the parts, thus permitting her the luxury of concentrating on the painting and embroidering of her pieces (the two parts of her operation she most enjoyed). She explained to the manufacturer what she needed and was pleased to learn that for a modest sum she could have exactly what she wanted without sacrificing quality and without investing tedious hours. Ultimately she was able to take and process quantity orders in fast time, something she couldn't do before farming out a segment of her product production.

Like many home-basers, Nicole initially resisted the idea of not being totally in control of production. She was sure she'd never find anyone able to mass-produce to her specifications. But once she decided to become more commercial, she made the time to visit several manufacturers. Eventually she came up with someone who could handle the job. Now that her business is taking off she views herself as an executive as well as a designer and manufacturer, and wonders why it took her so long to test other methods of production.

Procrastination over trying alternate methods of product production is common with home-basers. Pride and fear combine to create what the novice perceives as a stalemate. The home-baser is certain that no matter how he proceeds, things won't work out, so he sticks with production methods that work against his business soaring. Don't do this. The idea of testing a product in shallow waters is to take the kinds of chances which, if they don't work wonders, don't create disasters either.

As your business begins to grow, it is quite possible that the production methods which worked fine when your company was in its infancy are no longer working well. Many major corporations have realized that if they are to enjoy substantial profits, they must change their production techniques. You've heard how many car manufacturers have had to resort to producing their cars in two or three different countries, using the best facilities of each. Many large clothing manufacturers, in order to keep labor costs affordable, have resorted to a corresponding solution.

Similarly, many forward-looking home-basers are beginning to understand that just having the low-overhead advantage of home-basing is not enough. Once a business starts to reach the point where a leap from childhood to adulthood is possible, various low-overhead methods of production must be considered. This means delegating the parts of production you least enjoy to those who can best handle them; or buying your product in a more finished stage. It means keeping the best of home base and modifying what is no longer in the best interests of your entrepreneurial advancement.

FINDING THE RIGHT SUPPLIERS

Whether you're buying component parts, a partially produced product, a finished product, or packaging materials, you have to deal with suppliers. They can vary tremendously. Often, when starting out, a home-baser will purchase supplies locally, if possible. It's convenient. The fact that a neighborhood supplier may charge more than a distant supplier doesn't seem too important at this stage. The amount of supplies being purchased is relatively minimal. As your business grows, however, you will need more supplies, and cost will become increasingly more important.

Never assume that suppliers, wholesale or retail, all charge roughly the same amount for their goods. Get out your Yellow Pages and call around. Visit trade shows. Send away for catalogs. You'll be amazed how prices vary. One home-baser was shocked to find that his local lumber yard was charging twice as much for lumber and skydomes as were lumber yards in two other towns. Another home-baser couldn't believe her luck when she discovered that she could buy from a fabric mill for two-thirds the price she was paying at a "trade-only" fabric showroom.

Not only do suppliers' prices vary widely, but often the lines between manufacturer, distributor, and retailer are fuzzy. You may think you're purchasing wholesale from a distributor or showroom, and you may be, compared with purchasing from a general retail outlet; but you may still be paying a lot more than you would were you buying directly from the manufacturing plant. Not every manufacturing plant will sell directly to you. Some will only deal with distributors. However, many will deal with you directly, particularly if they see you as a serious repeat customer. Don't be afraid to inquire.

As you grow and reach for more markets, it becomes extremely important that your product be both price-/and quantity-competitive with similar products. Using the right suppliers is a major way to keep your company profitably competitive. If you're paying more for supplies than a competing company, you'll reflect this overcharge in higher selling prices. This may well lose you customers. Don't feel bound to any supplier. Continually be on the lookout for new or adjunct suppliers who may be able to offer you better deals on some items than you're currently getting. You must do this in order to come up with a winning product—one that you can present to buyers as an attractive, well-priced find.

When you comparision-shop for new suppliers don't think only in terms of finding someone who will give you what you're already using at a better price. *Keep an eye out for alternative supplies—for supplies that are different from those you're currently using, but that can do a job as well or better.* One home-baser, who sells cosmetics by mail order, was upset to learn that her packaging supplier was raising the prices of the mailing boxes she used. She checked with other box manufacturers and found that, even with the price increase, she was not being overcharged. Nevertheless, she felt she would be paying more than she wanted to, that there might be a better way to ship. And there was.

One of the box suppliers suggested she try padded mailing bags. She tested some of her products in these bags and was pleased. Many of her cosmetics were easier to package this way, just as safe as in boxes, and cheaper to ship. Because the bags were less expensive than the boxes, her overall profit margin was larger. Eventually this home-baser found a wholesale stationer, directly affiliated with a paper mill, who offered to sell her even thicker bags for still less money. She approached her original bag supplier with a "meet-it-or-beat-it" proposition. He couldn't meet the competition. She switched suppliers and further increased her bottom-line figures.

In dealing with suppliers you like, you may find it useful to bear in mind the saying, "It's good to combine business with pleasure, but it's better to combine business with profit."

4

WADING INTO DEEPER WATERS

> Don't be afraid to take a big step if one is indicated;
> you can't cross a chasm in two small jumps.
> —Lloyd George

Lloyd George's advice is good so long as your "big step" is a precise one. In this chapter, you're going to learn how to sell your product in major wholesale and retail markets—how to supply the trade. Mistakes can be cosly here. Thorough figuring and planning is essential; and a detailed journal should be kept.

CAN YOU PRODUCE IN QUANTITY?

Chapter 3 discussed trying alternative methods of product production as your business expands. One of the main reasons for this is to come up with a plan that yields sufficient quality output to meet increasing customer orders.

Suppose that a major department-store chain places an opening order for a thousand of your widgets, to be delivered in three months. This order will net you $3,000. Can you produce it within the given time period? If you can't, you're not ready to wade into deeper waters. In order to make your business soar, you must be able to mass-produce.

In Chapter 1 we looked at Nancy, who handcrafts splendid wooden decorator items, puts on well-attended home shows, distributes an attractive, descriptive brochure, and is frustrated because she's earning peanuts. The reason for her low profits is that she does not mass-produce. When confronted with a large demand for one of her creations, rather than finding a way to meet that demand, she diminishes it by boosting the price of the item. She justifies her business-dooming act by claiming she is "evening demand," so that all her crafts will be purchased. She is not thinking like an ambitious entrepreneur.

In Chapter 3 we saw Linda, a watercolorist earning more than most corporate executives. Watercolors are not usually hot sellers; and Linda's work, though delightful, is not out of this world. But Linda is reaping huge financial rewards because she is willing to approach her business world head-on. One of the ways she is doing this is by mass-producing her originals into price-friendly media which make her work widely accessible and affordable—they are reproduced and marketed as posters and greeting cards. This means five or five thousand replicas of Linda's work can be sold with no additional labor necessary on her part.

Both artists are creative and talented. But only Linda is drawing the dollars—because her work is available, in some form, to as many people as want it. Once she set her mind to making her art business soar, Linda systematically investigated all possible ways to engage in quantity, or mass, production. She pursued two paths which seemed possible and profitable.

There is no one right way to mass-produce, to set up your business to handle a flood of orders. Depending upon your particular business and your personal preferences, you can do one or more of the following:

Hire in-house business help. Bring in workers whom you can train to do some of the time-consuming chores related to your business. These chores can range from product manufacture to product packaging or delivery.

Hire in-house domestic help. Bring in workers to relieve you of your nonbusiness chores. These workers can clean, garden, baby-sit, pet-sit. They can free you to devote more hours to your business.

Hire marketing help. It takes time to market a product —to find buyers, to set up displays, to seek out profitable P.R. situations, to demonstrate your product's capabilities, to do whatever has to be done away from home base to make people want to buy what you're selling. If this is not a favorite part of your operation, you may wish to delegate marketing responsibilities to others and oversee their efforts.

Hire outside help. Depending on what you're producing, you may find it cost-effective to have factory labor or machines manufacture a portion of your product. Nicole, in Chapter 3, did this with her hair decorations.

Modify your product to an alternative medium. Often a product that is salable in one medium is also salable in another, easier to produce, medium. Linda's watercolors being reproduced as posters and greeting cards are an example of this. Think of all the Smurf, Garfield, and Snoopy similar-scene products on the market. Thousands of Smurf stickers, for example, are being sold with scenes identical to those on Smurf posters, plates, and shirts.

Try the "pre" method. Pre-frozen, pre-cut, pre-fabricated—you may find it most profitable to sell your product in a stage of partial completion. Or you may find it advantageous to order your product in a stage of partial completion, finish it, and then sell it.

Bring machinery into your home. Having a duplicating machine, an industrial cake mixer, a dry-cleaning machine, or welding machinery on hand can make a big difference. However, sometimes legal authorization is necessary to bring major machinery into a residential dwelling. Check up front by contacting your local business-licensing office. Special permission is usually required to bring in equipment that may present a health or safety hazard (a kiln, for example) if certain set standards are not followed. Usually before being issued authorization, a business is inspected to see if it qualifies.

When you come up with a seemingly attractive method of mass production, make sure it is a financially and legally sound way to go. It's easy to say, "Yes, I'll bring in help to package and deliver my homemade bagels and croissants," but finding cheap, reliable labor is not always easy. Often an intense labor search is necessary. In all cases, local hiring laws must be investigated. Some successful home-basers have found hiring quality student labor to be an excellent answer. Students often need spending money, and in certain communities and depending on the kind of work they're doing, can work beneath the minimum wage. Their input into your business can be mutually rewarding. They learn as they get paid. They grow into responsible young adults; and their growth helps your company to grow without burdensome labor costs. Because students are often strong and fast, they can smile through tasks which older helpers might find oppressive.

Some home-basers have found contracting out-of-country labor to be financially sound. They have learned, as have many major corporations, that often "Made in U.S.A." means "no profit possible." (See Chapter 9 for information on overseas marketing.) You must carefully calculate and compare the financial costs of all possible methods of mass production to come up with the most cost-effective, and personally pleasing, solution.

Mass production for the home-based business does not mean competing with industrial America. No one suggests you personally manufacture millions of items, assembly-line-style, from the basement of your home. This is impossible and unnecessary. Rather, mass production means finding some way to profitably handle a fair-sized, and growing, number of orders. The methods just suggested are particularly applicable to the home-baser who finds that what worked when sales were in the dozens per month no longer works with sales in the hundreds per month.

Assuming that you can produce in fair or substantial quantity, you now need the opportunity to do so.

TRADE SHOWS

Trade-show presentations can be the easiest and most cost-effective way for a home-baser to collect rosters of new customers and solid leads. These commercial forums provide the power of numbers plus the appeal of one-on-one contacts. By adopting this marketing method you can shave other, more traditional, time-consuming, and expensive ones. The most successful home-basers have found trade shows to be a low-stress, profitable, approach to maximizing sales and minimizing marketing expenses. Many have found that these shows account for up to 50% of their sales volume, and they look forward to participating in several a year.

Trade shows are the main arena for the display, demonstration, and sale of an industry's goods and services. They are where manufacturers, middlemen, and retailers meet and touch base. You can get more orders at one of these events than from dozens of spread-out and costly sales calls or advertisements. Here you can show an entire line to hundreds of prospective buyers in a single shot. Rather than employing a standard traveling sales representative with many lines, should you be considering using one, *you* are meeting with prospective customers. This means potential buyers will be talking to the one person who is most committed to seeing your business grow, who can best answer all questions, who can pitch the line with genuine knowledge and enthusiasm, who knows exactly which details to point out and will take care to do so.

Although trade shows can substantially boost sales and give a small homebased business equal billing with major corporations and manufacturers, they can also be nothing more than financially and emotionally exhaustive fiascos if you approach them incorrectly. There's more to a tradeshow presentation than setting up a display and writing orders. Meticulous planning is essential. Following are some guidelines for productive trade-show tapping.

Be highly selective as to where you choose to exhibit. Booth rentals, though not prohibitively expensive, do not go at flea-market rates. Figure about $10 to $30 per square foot. Also, unless you happen to live near a major convention center, consider transportation costs.

Trade publications and groups can supply you with a list of shows potentially profitable to you. Show managers can provide profiles of previous years' events so you can determine which shows will provide the best sales prospects for your offerings. If possible, first visit a show you're considering exhibiting at. Be wary of renting a booth at a new, unestablished show, which has no performance history or records. The show may never take place. You may not get your booth deposit returned. Or the show may well fail to generate the kind of exhibitor and trade attendance which makes trade shows profitable events. (See appendix for representative list of trade shows.)

Consider booth-sharing. There are several advantages to booth-sharing for the home-baser. It can save you money;

it can allow you to display in a larger, more open, more inviting area (some trade-show buyers are reluctant to enter a tiny booth manned by a single exhibitor); you have someone in attendance if you want to, or must, temporarily leave your booth; and you can benefit from the drawing power of another vendor's line. If you decide to share an exhibit space, find someone whose line (and personality) complements, or is compatible with, yours. One homebaser who sells silkscreened T-shirt dresses always sets up with a small manufacturer of belts and sandals. Each tried exhibiting alone; both discovered they sell more, and have more fun, together.

Get a good location. Usually all floor locations cost the same per square foot. However, just as at flea markets, certain exhibit spots are better than others. Entrance/exit spots are good. Spots near eating areas, lounges, and washrooms are good. Spots that are located in out-of-the-way areas which many buyers don't get to, should be avoided. Negotiate for the best spot possible. Often the more you become a regular at a show, the more negotiation power you have. Many exhibitors choose to return to the same spot year after year. Their regular customers go to that spot looking for them and for a chance to see their current samples. Some home-basers have found they do best setting up in a floor section populated with "like-product" vendors. If you're selling leather bags, for example, busy buyers who won't tour the whole show will miss your table if it isn't set up in the leather-bag section.

Create a crowd-pleasing, easy-to-examine display. Whether you're exhibiting at a local flea market or a major industry trade show, you're in competition with a lot of other vendors (and at trade shows, some quite famous and experienced ones). Assess what your competition is doing to attract orders, and, when applicable, imitate and improve upon their performance. Why are their displays eye-catching? Are they giving samples? Attractive models walking about? Don't look to kill the competition. This ultimately injures an industry. Just look to improve yourself as a trade-show participant, to make your product as marketable and appealing a buy as it can be.

Make ordering easy. All items should be clearly priced. Have a chair available for an ordering customer to sit in.

Ordering forms should be at your fingertips. Have preset ordering specifications—minimum-order requirements ($100 minimum purchase, two dozen pieces, etc.), shipping terms (COD, net 15—fifteen days to pay—prepayment, etc.), delivery dates, and so forth. The customer should find it easy to order from you. All technicalities should be clearly spelled out to avoid any misunderstandings.

Let your regular trade customers know you'll be at the show. Send out mailers advising these customers when and where the show will be, what booth you'll be at, and what new items or updates they can expect to find. Though many may not come to the show, you're still keeping them aware of what your company's doing and of the commercial status of your operation; and this is sound business promotion. If you're selling to a seasonal market, make sure you're showing well in advance of the season—about six to eight months before.

Charge the trade correctly. Keep in mind that most trade buyers expect to purchase a product for half its retail asking price. Can your product take a 100% markup on your asking price and still be competitive in most retail outlets? Is there enough profit built in for you? If the answer to both these questions isn't yes, it's back to the drawing board for some serious modifications.

Be a buyer, a learner, and a networker. You may be at a trade show mainly as a seller, but go also as an explorer, a potential buyer. Several exhibitors may be selling products which your company can use or is presently purchasing from other suppiers. See if you're buying from the best possible sources. How do the ribbons (or pins, or paints, or baking supplies) that you're presently purchasing from Main Street Supply Co. compare to others at the show? Often an exhibitor can buy, off the floor, at show's end, from another exhibitor. This can be very beneficial.

In addition to selling and buying, a trade show affords the opportunity to learn what's going on in a trade, what companies similar to yours are doing, what the trade in general is recommending to its members. At the best shows a lot of information is available under one roof. Very often special speakers are on hand to present pertinent advice to show participants. Exhibitors and buyers are versed on topics ranging from low-cost shipment packaging materials to new industry tax write-offs. Pick up all the relevant information you can. Mingle with members of your trade. What's The Candy Connection doing to market its candy creatures as Christmas-tree ornaments? How is Wooden Wonders reaching for the teen market? Observe. Take notes. Listen to problems, and solutions, that come up. Try to talk to several other small business owners. See how their problems, products, prices, and profits compare with your own. Many home-basers have found trade shows can provide networking opportunities with their counterparts in other sections of the country and the world. Don't forget that part of the joy of being a business owner, home-based or otherwise, comes from being able to socialize within a trade that excites you.

VISITING BUYERS AND BUYING OFFICES

This is the part of product marketing that many home-basers like least—going to the pros. At a trade show the pros come to you. That can be fun; and, even if your line doesn't have them queuing up to order, no one's brushing you off either. This is not necessarily so when it comes to visiting the trade.

America is a product-glutted country. Usually many sellers are competing for the attention of a single buyer. And many buyers and shop owners don't wait for suppliers to approach them; they go on buying trips and to shows in search of what they believe will do well in their departments or shops. This situation is less than encouraging for the average home-baser. Many home-basers tell stories of being treated brusquely by buyers, or of buyers who set up appointments which they don't keep and don't take the time to cancel. One home-baser traveled fifty miles, through a storm, with her carefully packed samples, to keep an appointment with a department-store buyer she had been waiting months to see. The buyer was "suddenly called out of town—no time to cancel."

Add to this sort of shabby treatment the fact that department-store buyers are switched around a lot. Often the buyer you're planning to see, or have just managed to interest in your line, has been replaced. It's not hopeless, but you do need a systematic, hard-nosed, plan for dealing with buyers.

Research and prepare. Don't go near department-store buyers or buying offices until you're really smooth at presenting your line, negotiating, answering questions, and writing orders. Major buyers are almost always hurried and impatient. Study a store long before you set foot into it as a seller. What is its image? Why is your product in keeping with it? Which of your products will be most likely to sell well there? When you present your product to a buyer it should be clear that you're approaching the store as a carefully-thought-out market for your offering. You're familiar with the department, with its customers, and with the amount of money customers are prepared to spend for items such as yours.

Assuming you've presented your line properly, and the buyer is interested in placing an order, now the negotiating begins. How many? By when? At what price? On consignment? You're a professional. Be sure of what you want, but don't be inflexible, or unimaginative. One home-baser lost what could have turned into a valuable account because he couldn't be "pressured" into an early delivery. Had he explained to the buyer that he wanted his goods to be as perfect as his samples—that, because of the requested early delivery date, he could deliver only half the order on time—the buyer would have gone along with him. But because he felt he was being treated as a laborer, rather than a craftsman, it did not occur to him to present a compromise situation. Don't permit yourself to be taken because you're so eager for a major account. But don't be so unyielding, or proud, that you become unattractive to do business with regardless of how attractive your offering might be.

Try to anticipate any questions a buyer might ask you. Have good answers ready. Your answers should be what the buyer wants to hear, but they should also be honest. Don't promise a wide range of colors, sizes, or fabrics if you know you can't properly produce them. Don't promise anything you can't do or know you won't do. One homebaser, eager to establish an account with an upscale department store, assured the querying buyer that her store would have an "exclusive." The buyer ordered and was furious to learn that the home-baser was selling the line, on Sundays, at a flea market less than a mile from the store. When the buyer confronted the home-baser with the fact that she was not only retailing the "exclusive" but severely undercutting the store, the home-baser justified her actions by insisting that the store did have an exclusive since no other store was carrying the product. It doesn't matter here who's technically right or wrong. What matters is that the home-baser deliberately concealed important information. She never mentioned to the buyer that she might exhibit at flea markets. Had she done so the buyer might not have ordered, or might have insisted that the product not be sold at any flea markets within twenty miles of her store, or that the fleamarket price be competitive with the store's price. Be careful not to doubledeal with the retail community. It can kill your reputation and your business.

Finalizing a deal with a buyer is as important as initiating it. Be prepared here too. Have whatever you need on hand to write up an order quickly and efficiently. Make sure your invoice includes all the important specifics—colors, sizes, delivery date, payment terms. Give a copy of the invoice to the buyer along with your business card. One successful entrepreneur also gives out an attractive pen with her home-based company's name, address, and phone number imprinted on it.

Deal with the best buyers. "Best" here means best for your interests. A department or a shop can have more than one buyer. Try to find out which buyer will be most likely to like your merchandise, or will be most likely to like you and give you a good chance to pitch your product. Buyers are people with particular preferences. What appeals to one buyer doesn't necessarily appeal to another. What one buyer sees as perfect for the store, another won't. You want a buyer who'll respond with enthusiasm to your product, one who'll order it, then push it once it's in the store.

Certainly you can't run a preference and personality

check on every store buyer, but you can do some investigating. If, for example, you're planning to approach a department-store buyer, go to the store. Find a friendly salesgirl. Tell her, or show her, what you're selling. Ask her which buyer she recommends you speak to, and why. Rare is the employee who doesn't like to feel her opinion is sought.

Similarly, if you're planning to approach a neighborhood shop, ask any locals you know, or can strike up acquaintances with, for the names of people to talk to. Find out as much as you can about the buyer you're going to meet prior to the actual meeting.

One home-baser secured prime rack space for her homemade handbags in a chain of women's clothing stores by doing a bit of preliminary investigation. Ana queried a few longtime customers of one of the stores and learned that one buyer for the chain was from her native Hungary. On a hunch she made an appointment with that buyer. It turned out to be a wise and lucrative move. Certainly a common ancestry alone would not have put Ana's bags in prime locations in three different cities. However, Ana is sure that meeting with a buyer with whom she had something important in common was the "clincher." That, combined with the fact that her merchandise was extraordinary, tipped the scales in her favor.

Start small. Approach small, local shop owners with your wares before heading for the big department-store buyers. It's the least intimidating encounter of home-baser and buyer, and a good preparation for selling to more formidable markets. Small shop owners are often more sympathetic to homebasers than are department-store buyers. They identify with the entrepreneurial spirit and want to see it fostered. Often they feel it is commercially profitable to promote local talent. If they are community-minded, many will give your goods a chance they might not give to those of an out-of-towner.

Sometimes a local shop owner will offer to take your goods on consignment. Don't turn down this opportunity, feeling that because there's no payment up front your merchandise won't be promoted. Look at it this way. You're getting free display space—this alone is a vote of confidence in your goods. Also, if your merchandise moves, the shop owner will begin to talk it up, move it to a prominent place in the shop (assuming it's not already there), and perhaps offer to buy outright. For now, the shop owner gets a chance to see how your merchandise fares; so do you. Also, by consigning locally, you have the advantage of being able to get continuous feedback and act on it immediately—for example, you can drop in regularly to see which items, colors, or sizes are moving and which aren't, and restock accordingly.

Use truly representative samples. Do not show samples to any buyer that are of superior quality to those you can mass-produce. Several homebasers have had the disappointing experience of joyfully writing up a major order only to see their delivered goods turned away because they did not live up to the promise of the sample. Make sure you maintain quality control. Do not ship an order you have not inspected. Do not let inferior pieces slip in. A buyer has the right to expect an entire shipment to be like the samples; and you have a reputation to uphold.

It is better to show less-than-magnificent samples than to show magnificent samples that won't be duplicated. If a buyer orders from an honest sample, it is unlikely there will be disappointment or return upon delivery. Also, only present, or agree to produce, choices (colors, fabrics, sizes) which you know you can comfortably and properly provide at a given price. One home-baser agreed to produce two dozen pillow shams in satin without taking into account the fact that her pieceworkers seldom worked with satin. The buyer expected the satin shams to be similar in quality to the cotton samples which had impressed her. They weren't; and the order was rejected. Remember, if in doubt, only make a tentative promise and call to confirm when you're certain you can properly provide a specific request.

Be persistent. "Hello, Neiman Marcus? This is Jane Doe; I'd like to come in and show you some extraordinary widgets which I believe would sell well in your store." "Glad you called, Ms. Doe. When would it be convenient for you to come in?" This would be lovely; but it's not the way it goes. First of all, you must call a specific department, and, if possible, as explained before, the best buyer for your purposes within that department. Then you must be prepared to hear that the buyer is out, or "in a meeting." Keep trying. Send her a note with photos and sales literature enclosed. Call again. Leave a message. Drop in if you're nearby on a Tuesday, Wednesday, or Thursday (Monday and Friday are bad days to approach a buyer for the first time). Eventually you'll get to her; but you must be persistent. Don't be sensitive and don't let the procedure weary you. Buyers really are busy. They are the sought-after celebrities of their little worlds. Some are very hard to get to; but once you reach them with a product they judge to be perfect for their departments, you may well find yourself writing up many lucrative repeat orders.

USING AGENTS

Do you love having your own business but hate the selling aspects of it? You might want to consider using an agent. There are positives and negatives to using selling agents, or reps, as intermediaries between you and the buyers for retail stores. The positives are:

Your ego stays intact. Some people are more sensitive, less rebuff-proof, than others. If you find it hard to talk to strangers, hard to sell something regardless of how convinced you are of its worth, hard to shake off a rejection, you might be most comfortable having a good agent represent your business to the trade.

You have more time for other business tasks. Finding the most appropriate retail outlets, and buyers, for your product takes a certain amount of time. So does talking to prospective buyers, which is a necessary part of business boosting. An agent can free you from these tasks so you can concentrate on production, product improvement, order processing, advertising.

The industry regards agents as pros. To a busy buyer you may be an unknown he or she will put off seeing until you're just too worn down to keep trying. An agent, on the other hand, will get more respect. He'll be seen more quickly. He is known to buyers. He handles several lines. He deals with winning products. He socializes within the trade. He knows the industry gossip, the industry jargon, the industry's fears. He can get his foot into a door that might slam in your face. Often an agent can work wonders for you that you could not work for yourself.

The negatives to using agents are:

Top agents are not easily available to home-basers. Unless you have an unusual product with something of an impressive sales record, a top agent will not take you on. It's not in his best interests to do so. He wants to deal with a known, or an easy-sell, situation. He wants to write up volume sales, to make good commissions. You'll probably have little difficulty finding a poor, inexperienced agent; but is that what you want? If you can't get the best, you should find an enterprising beginner, like yourself, who one day will be among the top agents. Don't give up on getting a good agent, if you want one, but search carefully for one who will represent you well.

Rare is the agent who can talk up your product the way you can. You know your product inside out. You're genuinely enthused about it. You can demonstrate it perfectly. You can answer all sorts of questions about it, highlight its unique features. You can't expect an agent to be as intimately informed about your product or business as you are. No matter how much he may like your company or your product, you are still one of several accounts he must serve. And, if you're not one of his favorite accounts, your product may not get much talking up at all.

You don't make industry contacts. As a member of a particular trade it is helpful to know a lot of people within the trade. Information sharing and networking can help a home-based business to soar. If you are represented by an agent, you miss out on meeting a lot of buyers who can give you valuable advice—for example, information on co-op advertising, in which your advertisement is tied into that of another business person.

THE CORPORATE MARKET

Selling to the corporate market is different from selling to retail stores. When you sell to retail outlets you're selling for resale. The buyers are purchasing with the sole intention of selling your product to the public. This is usually not the case when you sell to corporations. Most often when a corporation buys a product from a small entrepreneur it is for one of two reasons:

They see the product as an ideal premium item. Periodically, enterprising home-basers come up with innovative items that strike the fancy of corporate marketing managers. These items are viewed as buying incentives or giveaways which are a departure from the usual premium fare—particularly if they are cleverly presented. A home-based maker of "splendid scents," for example, sold many hundreds of packets of her scents to a corporation that distributes plumbing supplies. She presented her samples, color-coordinated to blend with all plumbing fixtures, as intended for bathroom and kitchen use. A few of her samples were already imprinted with the corporation's name and logo, "just to give the corporation's marketing manager a look at the finished product." The corporation loved them and ordered and reordered—they were easy to distribute, inexpensive, attractive, and of long duration.

They have use for the product within the corporation. Frequently home-basers come up with products that are not produced by major suppliers, that are more attractive buys than those offered through standard supply channels, or that corporate buyers hadn't thought about needing until confronted with a good buying opportunity.

One home-baser, who imported colorful hand-painted vases from Mexico, found it fairly easy, and a learning experience, to sell her imports to corporations, institutions, restaurants, and clubs. A restaurateur, who didn't want to be bothered placing, and waiting for, an order told her, "If you want to sell me all your samples, I'll buy them now; otherwise I'm not interested." The home-baser sold all ten samples on the spot and approached future customers with the options of ordering, buying on the spot, or doing both. In this case, you have a home-baser who not only created a market for her product but who learned while selling it that it had value as an impulse item, something to be purchased immediately.

Don't be afraid to move in on the corporate market if you have a product that you believe they can use and that you can produce in sufficient quantity. Several enterprising home-basers, selling items ranging from miniature "executive trampolines" to awards and trophies, and vertical window blinds, have brought their net profits to over $40,000 a year simply by trying the big guys. They had enough confidence in their products, and themselves, to approach corporate buyers professionally with what they considered good deals or good buys. Some corporate buyers responded and some didn't. In many cases those who responded more than made up for those who weren't interested or who wouldn't give the home-baser a chance.

The most important thing here is to try, to be unintimidated by the fact that you're small and they're big. Your product is what matters. A corporate buyer who wants what you're selling doesn't care (or necessarily know) how small you are, so long as you can deliver the goods.

Assuming you're willing to try the corporate market, how do you begin? Whom do you call or go see? Begin by defining the "corporate" market for your use. Consider it to consist of not only corporations but all sorts of commercial institutions that are not retail stores—companies, schools, hospitals, clubs, organizations. By doing this you give yourself a lot of possibilities and starting points. Now, look locally and choose that corporation or commercial institution which you believe to be your best bet, the easiest place for you to begin moving in. Do you have contacts in the local hospital, children in the local school, friends in local clubs, companies, organizations, or corporations? Have you ever worked directly, or indirectly, with, or in, any one of these places? Basically what you're doing here is thinking, Do I have a good "in"? You're acknowledging the fact that while it's important to have a good product, contacts also count.

If you can come up with a good contact, that's a good place to start. Call or visit your contact, explain what you have in mind, and ask whom you should see; would your contact serve as an introduction to this person? Is there a particularly good way to approach this person? Of course, the more your contact can do for you, the better. However, in many cases it is helpful just to have someone who can direct you to the right person to talk to about your product.

In many corporations, or commercial institutions, there is a person, a variety of people, or a purchasing department, with the authority to order from selected vendors. It is important that you find out the names of the people with this authority, and, if possible, the name of the one person most liable to like what you're selling. If you have a contact, this may be easy. If you don't, you may have to make several phone calls before you come up with the name of anyone in a position to buy from you. Don't let this stop you. One home-baser was cut off twice and given the wrong information three times while attempting to find out whom to see about having his diagrammed exercise guides racked in a certain hotel chain's health clubs. No one seemed to know or want to take the trouble to help this author, until by mistake he reached a health-club maintenance man who gave him the exact name he needed. The "exact name" not only agreed to take and place several guides on consignment, but was impressed enough with the guide to recommend it to some professional friends in the fitness field who purchased a few hundred copies outright from the author. Reaching the correct person to talk to can often be infuriating; but it does pay to be persistent.

Once you find out whom to speak to about purchasing your product, make sure you have a well-prepared presentation, good samples, good sales literature, whatever will make it easiest for you to sell your product. Chapter 3 discussed honing your product, and your presentation, to perfection in the smaller markets. Now you're ready not only to reach for major markets, but to do so with some ease. However, no matter how experienced you are, you have greater hopes and fears invested in your presentation. Just remember, don't, for one minute, view yourself as a supplicant talking to a formidable giant. Before you shake hands with a potential corporate buyer, ask yourself, "What can I say to the 'giant' that will make him want to purchase my product?" If you can answer this question well, you may land yourself a major account.

One home-based woman wanted to sell floral centerpieces made of silk, cloth, and wood to the manager of a catering establishment that worked closely with a local florist. This home-baser knew the manager couldn't care less that she hoped to cut into the fresh-flower market. But he did care about increasing his business. When she showed him her samples, she saw he liked her work and was pleased when he asked for her business card and price list. Then, before leaving the card and price list, she turned one of her samples upside down, pointed to a pretty gold-foil label with her company's name, logo, and phone number on it, and said, "If you decide to purchase my centerpieces, I will have your company's name and information put on similar stickers. Since one person at every table usually gets to take the centerpiece home, that person will have a permanent reminder of the affair with your name on it." The manager hesitated—ten tables per affair, ten affairs per week, one hundred permanent reminders per week with his name on them. He invited the home-baser to sit down, checked in with a bride-to-be who had given him carte-blanche, and gave the home-baser an opening order for one hundred centerpieces.

PLATEAU PERIODS—A TIME TO LOOK INTO STILL DEEPER WATERS

Your business is going to go through stages where nothing particularly exciting is happening and where there's nothing simple you can do at the moment, which you haven't already done, to generate new business. Things are humming along, quietly, steadily. You're in a plateau period. This is a good time to enjoy and reflect. It is also a good time to explore new "deepwater" possibilities. Is your product such that it might be of interest to the government? If it is, you might want to learn how to approach the government as a buying market. Uncle Sam is the country's biggest purchaser of goods and services. Various government agencies solicit bids daily on items ranging from plaques to paper clips to print-out reports. A home-baser can often compete successfully with a major company for government contracts if his products qualify, if he can produce according to set specifications. If government contracts interest you, now is the time to look into them. The Small Business Association can supply you with the details of how to proceed. The process is not difficult. It takes a bit of time; but it can be time very well spent.

Local SBA offices can be found in counties all over the country.

If government contracts don't interest you, franchising might. Have you created the kind of business which, under your supervision, can be successfully duplicated in other cities and states? Would you like to develop and market a turnkey package, everything provided, that would enable would-be entrepreneurs to have a business such as yours, that would teach them how to run a similar moneymaking home base, stock them with the necessary supplies and equipment? Can you produce a program that will train your home-based franchisees to solicit business, produce a prime product, advertise effectively, package properly, ship economically, and cover all the do's and don'ts that pertain directly to your unique kind of enterprise? Will your program provide the often-needed emotional support system? Can you spot those who will succeed in a home-based business such as yours and those who won't? Can you sell your idea—make it sound intriguing enough for would-be entrepreneurs to invest their savings in it?

If you think you'd like to go from mass-producing your product to mass-producing your home-based business, there are authorities at the Small Business Administration who can advise you on how to proceed—and if you should proceed; on the legal and financial ramifications of franchising; and on alternatives to franchising. Fortunes have been made in franchising everything from chocolate-chip cookies to picture frames to rug-cleaning services. They have also been lost. If you're fascinated by the concept of becoming a franchiser, explore the subject thoroughly. In addition to consulting franchise authorities, read books that have been written for franchisers and franchisees. Seek advice from people who have successfully transformed small businesses into thriving franchises. Visit franchise operations similar to what you'd like to develop. Talk to the franchisees. It won't take you long to learn whether or not you can profitably bring off the idea. There is a certain amount of risk-taking involved; so proceed optimistically, but with caution.

Before exploring franchising you might want to look into a related possibility that could pave your way into franchising—mass-produced teaching aids. These include

Wading Into Deeper Waters 79

items such as manuals, videotapes, and cassettes. Here, rather than creating a total, turnkey package, you'd be creating instructional material which would enable a would-be entrepreneur to buy your knowledge and experience in some sort of home-study format. He wouldn't be embraced into success as he would be with a franchise, but he wouldn't be spending much money either. His ultimate success would be related to his determination and initiative and to the quality and comprehensiveness of your teaching aids.

Though producing a teaching aid is not as time-consuming or intricate a procedure as developing a franchise operation, it is not something that can be successfully brought off on a slow Wednesday. Here again a plateau period is needed. First you must investigate the technical, financial, and marketing how-to's of manual, videotape, or cassette making. Then a proposal or outline must be drafted. Next you must write, film, or record; and rewrite, refilm, and rerecord several times until you come up with a perfect product.

You have to take all your experience, know-how, successes, and failures, and devise a product which will, in a reasonably simple way, take the novice's hand and say, "This is the beginning. Follow me step-by-step and when we're finished you will be able to create and build a profitable home-based business such as mine." This is not hard, but it does demand attention to detail, making sure no steps are omitted, a willingness to revise and edit many times before seeing a finished, marketable product. If you're interested in producing teaching aids, examine those already on the market, read up on the subject, submit a proposal to publishers and agents who market these aids.

Plateau periods are times to investigate the various quantum leaps your business can take. Whether you're interested in trying a special or trendy method of mass production, becoming a franchiser, seeking government contracts, or exploring any large new endeavor which seems well suited to your particular home-based business, it is important that you press ahead with caution. The sweet smell of success has caused many ambitious entrepreneurs to spread themselves too thin.

One home-based baker who was featured in her local

newspaper, and who became a local celebrity, got so inebriated by the attention that engulfed her that she let herself be talked into writing a cookbook for bread and cake bakers. Her book might have done well and made her a tidy sum. There is a strong market for cookbooks. However, this woman did not approach writing in the same professional manner she approached the baking and marketing of her goods. She took valuable time away from her business, which caused her sales to drop; and then she produced a sloppy, poorly-organized and written work that no publisher wanted. Her big mistakes were allowing herself to take on a new offshoot without protecting her original endeavor and assuming that because she was a good baker and businesswoman she would automatically be good at writing what she knew about. This is an arrogant assumption made by many specialists. Beware of it.

Writing, like baking, woodworking, painting, designing, or sewing, is a craft unto itself. Take the time to learn the how-to's of the trade so you can write something that others will benefit from reading. All of the good plateau-period activities can have a positive impact on your business, but again, you shouldn't plunge too quickly into these particular "deep waters."

5

BETTER BUSINESS THROUGH BARTER

When you hear the word "barter," what comes to mind? Making a deal? Trading one item for another? Swapping baseball cards? As a home-baser, have you ever thought of barter as an important business booster? Do you know how it can be? Are you aware of the different kinds of barter that you can use to help your business soar? Do you know how to approach barter as a business aid and when to avoid it? Do you know what your business can get, and give, on a barter basis? Do you know what to look for and what to beware of?

WHAT IS BARTER?

Barter is a cashless exchange of goods, services, or both. It is a form of trade that can improve your home-based business and requires no cash outlay. Here's a simple example. You sell home-made, gift-boxed candies. There is a surplus on hand. You need some mailers made up for your next sale. The local printer wants to give some gifts to special customers. He prints the mailers you need in exchange for your candies, which he will distribute to his special customers. No cash exchanges hands.

Why is this exchange a business booster? First, you had candy that wasn't selling, which means it was a nonproductive asset. The candy was taking up space and doing nothing to benefit your business. Next, you needed some printing done which ordinarily you would have had to pay for with cash. Now, what have you gained by bartering?

You have taken something you didn't need, exchanged it for something you did need, and preserved your cash flow in the process. Not only have you benefited, but so has the printer. He printed your mailers during an empty time slot (also a nonproductive asset). For doing so he received candy boxes that ordinarily he would have had to pay for with cash. Here you both paid for what you wanted with nonproductive assets, and held on to your cash reserves.

WHY ISN'T BARTER USED MORE OFTEN?

You might be wondering, "If barter is this easy, and so good, why isn't everyone doing it?" Many people are doing it, but most of them are not home-basers. Big corporations, for example, have been engaging in barter deals among themselves for years: computers for land; airline seats for hotel rooms; cars for air time; sporting goods for print space. Corporate barter has always gone on, but, it's a lot like good sex: it's popular and profitable, but, for practical and personal reasons, usually a private affair. Much of corporate America conducts its barter relationships behind closed doors because if a corporation lets it be known that it will barter its products, often the assumption is "Bad times! Overproduction!" Competition wonders if it should flex its muscles. Shareholders wonder if dividends will decrease. Everyone wonders if barter will work.

Barter does work. It works for big corporations and it can work for you. If you haven't used it, it's probably because, like most novice entrepreneurs, you've been thoroughly trained to reach for your wallet or pay on credit. Most home-based business owners don't think beyond the credit or cash transaction.

Ask yourself why you haven't tried barter. Are you afraid to approach someone with a barter proposal? Are you afraid of making a bad trade? Do you feel that most business owners will not want to barter with a home-baser? Do you associate barter with lack of professionalism? Examine your reluctance, so you can learn to use this tool to better your business. Your barter exchange may result in your getting goods and services that you need directly for your business, or those that are for personal use. The end result, however, is the same: by using barter, you have reserved funds to protect your cash flow.

TYPES OF BARTER

There are several types of barter arrangements. Each has value for different situations and different products:

One-on-one barter. This is an exchange of services or goods between two agreeing parties who have found each other and are acting independently of any organization, broker, or advertisement. This form of barter can be ongoing or finite—clothing for chauffeuring, produce for pottery, art lessons for packaging help. The main thing is to locate one person, a businessperson or someone else, who has what you want and wants what you have.

Swap-meet barter. Here the search is conducted within a marketplace where everyone expects to be approached with a barter proposition. Home-based business people and private sellers set up tables overflowing with potential barterables. You display your goods, they display theirs, and negotiations begin. "I like that lamp on your table; I'm four tables down. . . ." If the lamp man likes one of the leather bags you're exhibiting, it's as easy as that: bag for lamp—provided, of course, that you both feel the swap is a good one.

Suppose you like the lamp, but the lamp man doesn't want anything on your table. What can you do? Ask him if there is something at the meet that he does want but is unable to barter for. If he wants a bushel of apples from the vendor three aisles down, and the apple vendor doesn't want anything he's showing, but loves your leather bags, you can engage in a form of "intermediate barter." You trade leather for apples (which you don't want) and apples for a lamp (which you do want). Usually cash is acceptable on this circuit too; but a barter mind-set prevails, so you can feel totally comfortable with the arrangement.

Swap-meet barter is the most basic form of barter. It worked for the settlers; it's an established form of business in many Third World nations; and it's working here today. It's the easiest way to learn to be a barterer and the fastest way to learn that product paying is every bit as respectable and revered as cash paying. Not only is the swap-meet atmosphere conducive to trading goods and experiences, but it's lots of fun as well.

Classified-ad barter. Here you can advertise what you can't easily cart to a swap meet—a horse for real estate, rare art for data-processing equipment, consulting services for landscaping. You also reach a larger audience than at a swap meet. Many national and local publications take classified barter ads. For a home-based businessperson a local classified is usually best, as it can lead quickly and easily to an inexpensive face-to-face meeting, an on-site inspection of each other's offerings, and an ongoing business arrangement.

The barter broker. Just as a real-estate broker can find the property you're looking for, a barter broker can find the barter match you're seeking. Generally barter brokers are affiliated with some organization (such as a community barter club, described below) which puts them in frequent contact with a variety of people and their needs; or they are independent agents, usually (but not always) handling big corporate trades. If you ask around within your industry, and read trade publications, you should be able to find a barter broker who's right for your needs. A good barter broker can supply two things which many home-basers can use—speed and privacy. For example, you would like to quickly and quietly unload your present inventory to concentrate exclusively on marketing your new line. A good barter broker with many contacts in many neighborhoods can accomplish in a day or two what it could take you months to achieve.

Community barter. This is a neighborhood pooling of products and skills. Community members—individuals, home-based business owners, and small businesses—provide their offerings to other community members and receive "credits" for doing so. The participants are members of a community barter club and can apply their earned credits to the offerings of any club member. There is a central recording system—usually operated by a couple of women in a community office, "Y," or church—that posts credits earned and credits used. To become a club member an applicant lists the products, services, or skills that he wishes to use as currency. An applicant is advised as to what products, services, and skills are in highest demand. If ten people are offering the same product or service, a rotation is made so that everyone gets a chance to earn credits.

Generally community barter clubs work like this. You make a barter request to the local club office (the women at central recording): "I need someone to type invoices two afternoons a week." You are referred to three persons from whom to make your choice. The "giver" of the service, and you (the "getter"), agree on credit value based upon the club's guidelines, which can vary. Sometimes credits equal cash value: 1 credit = $1. Sometimes credits equal time spent: 1 credit = 1 hour. A "giver and getter" card is signed by both parties and mailed to the community barter office where credits and debits are posted.

Here again we see how cash is preserved. Rather than laying out cash for typing services, you provide club members with merchandise which is either in surplus supply or which costs you much less cash to produce than the amount you would have to pay a typist. The dollars you would have spent to pay a typist can now be put into business-expansion activities that you would have had to save up for.

In addition to preserving cash flow, community barter ultimately upgrades the quality of a neighborhood, which is good for you personally as well as professionally. The abilities of all community members are tapped—home-based business owners, struggling shopkeepers, the unemployed, the underemployed, the inflation poor, the middle-class luxury seeker, senior-citizens, and the handicapped. This form of barter is especially good for bringing the socially isolated out of their feelings of loneliness. Ads for community barter clubs can be found in local publications and on neighborhood bulletin boards. Often these clubs are featured in local media. One home-baser found her club by talking to the manager of the YMCA. Another learned of a community barter club from her pastor. Organizations that serve a community are usually aware of operations such as these.

Commercial barter. This is a computerized pooling of business and professional offerings. This barter-club arrangement can be most helpful to a home-based entrepreneur, a store owner, a professional, or a semiprofessional person. Commercial barter works this way: Tom's Toy Shop provides the commercial barter-club members with $2,000 worth of surplus stock. For doing this Tom receives 2,000 trade units (1 unit = $1 retail). He uses his units to get airline tickets (from an airline that is a club member) and a deck built on his home (by a carpenter who is a club member). Not only is Tom clearing a large amount of surplus, but he is getting things he would otherwise have to pay cash for. Now he can use the cash he had allotted for airline tickets and deck building to purchase new stock. Also, his spending power is doubled since the inventory he puts up for 2,000 units—$2,000 worth of purchasing power—costs him $1,000 wholesale.

A good commercial barter club is both local and nationwide. It has the technology and membership to continually direct new business to its members so that trade units are always being accumulated and used. It does not have big "house accounts" reserved mostly for special members and itself, which results in a long waiting list of ordinary members for high-demand goods or services. It does not expect its members to travel unreasonable distances to use their trade units. Join-up fees usually run about $300. Annual dues average about $250. Generally 10% of the trade units of each transaction goes to the club itself.

In many ways the commercial barter club acts like a personal business broker, examining its merchandise offerings, enacting barter matches, noting member transactions, keeping members up to date on new offerings through newsletters and mailers, searching for new members, settling complaints or disputes, issuing monthy statements of members' trade activities. Many clubs have showrooms in their headquarters where members can showcase their samples to other members. Also, some clubs hold periodic swap fairs so that members can congregate in a large forum and exchange among themselves. (See end of chapter and Appendix for more information.)

WHEN TO BARTER

Barter is an excellent way to help a business, but is not a way to run one. In our economy, cash, not barter credits or trade units, is king. If cash is pouring in and your phone is ringing off the hook with orders, you're not going to say, "Please don't pay me with dollars; pay me with your products or services." However, there are many times when cash and orders are scarce and when barter comes to the rescue by enabling you to hold tight to your cash reserves and acquire retail-priced items with wholesale purchasing power or surplus stock. The best times to barter are when:

Sales are sluggish. Consumers who won't, or can't, pay cash for an item will often take it on a barter basis, thus reducing your surplus inventory.

You're cash-poor and opportunity-rich. A laid-off carpenter offers to build the shelves you've always wanted in your workroom. You have no spare cash to pay for his services. Make a barter offer: "I can't pay you with cash; but I can pay you with a combination of my framed photographs and photography lessons, if you're interested."

You're settling for inferior merchandise or services. You want exquisite art work on your mailers, but you can only afford the services of a second-rate artist. Don't rush to settle. Approach the artist whose services you desire with a part-cash, part-barter proposition. Many business people are amenable to such deals.

Your business is broke. Barter alone cannot revive a dying corporation, but it can pump a great amount of life into a temporarily down-and-out home-based business. The reason for this is that as a home-baser you don't have a huge overhead to meet. If you're "broke" it usually means you've temporarily run out of the funds necessary to enable you to try new supplies, new marketing approaches, new packaging methods. Suppliers and advertising people are not strangers to cash-flow problems. Offer a product-for-product or product-for-service deal and you may be able to stay afloat until the Christmas season, when your new ideas will catch on and your cash situation will improve.

HOW TO BARTER

If you walk into an office-supply outlet and say to the manager, "I'll give you four of my floor plants for one hundred mailing bags," it's quite possible your offer will be rejected. And, if you're a sensitive person, you might decide to reject as unworkable the barter approach to survival. Don't let this happen. Barter is a way to do business; and just as a business deal must be approached properly, so must a barter deal. The best way to approach an individual, whom you're not meeting through a barter club or barter broker, is to assume that the person is not seeking a barter match but may be interested in your offer, if it's presented properly. Follow these guidelines:

Begin with people you know. A barterer, like a businessman, does best if he has credibility on his side. You are most credible to those who know you, your products, your credentials, and your abilities. Your neighbor, who has always admired your woodcrafting abilities, will be much more likely to trade his legal expertise for your crafted items than will a lawyer in another town who doesn't know you and has never heard of your company.

Be prepared to supply references. If you want to barter with a particular person you don't know, try to search out a mutual acquaintance who will help you establish credibility. You operate a greenhouse and a landscaping service from your home. You'd like repair work done on your company truck by a mechanic whose work you've heard is excellent. You know his reputation; but what does he know about your work that will convince him to swap truck repair for plants or landscaping? If you can propose your swap and tell him that you've landscaped his Cousin Joe's yard, or sold house trees to his Aunt Mary, then you're in a good position to get the trade you want.

Deal with those who have the authority to deal with you. Propose your barter deal to the specific person who is in the position to proceed with the swap. If you want to barter for something in a local shop, speak to the shop owner or manager. A sales clerk, or part-time employee, may think your offer is superb, but he does not have the power to say yes to a swap. All he can do is sell to you for cash.

Begin with people who you're fairly sure will consider your proposition advantageous. If you operate the greenhouse mentioned above and you see a new gift boutique opening in your neighborhood, it's likely that the boutique owner can use several attractive floor plants to decorate her new shop. Visit her shop. Tell her what you do. Show her slides or samples and ask if she'd be interested in getting four floor plants in exchange for four of her pieces of pottery (or whatever else she's displaying that you want).

Approach your barter match at a quiet time. Whether you're selling your product or the concept of barter, don't expect someone to consider what you're showing or saying while he's busy with customers. Make your offer when no customers are around and when the person you'd like to trade with appears unhurried. Not only does this display good manners, but psychologically a retailer will be most inclined to barter with you when dollar bills are not filling the air.

Practice your presentation. Successful barterers are not born. They are people who recognize the importance of polishing and perfecting. The more you practice approaching someone with a barter deal, addressing responses, and explaining procedural techniques, the better you get at it. You learn to anticipate and answer questions with smoothness and sincerity.

Don't be put off by rejection. The best-planned and -practiced presentation can be rejected simply because the person to whom you're making your offer is not currently interested in what you're offering, is getting it from another source, or is hoping to get quick cash. Whatever the case may be, keep in mind that it is your offer which is being rejected, not you. A refusal to barter, like a refusal to buy, means that for this person, at this time, your offer is not appealing enough. Another person may well consider your proposition to be a magnificent opportunity and barter with you instantly.

WHAT TO BARTER/ WHAT TO ASK FOR

In order to gain the most from barter, be imaginative. If you're selling art, you may be able to barter art lessons as well as art. Or, if you're dealing with a printer, you can ask for the use of his duplicating machine during off-peak hours rather than for his printing services. You, and those you'd like to deal with, are usually in possession of more than just one barterable.

The problem most of us have in relation to barter is not a lack of barterables, but a lack of imagination. In order to overcome this, take the time to envision the things you take for granted, or even ignore, as having value to others. In addition to your art work, or art lessons, what else can you barter? How about some surplus art supplies, or storage space in your studio, or your services in judging a local art contest? In barter, as in life in general, one person's trash is another person's treasure. What you shrug off, or look upon as valueless, another might consider a great find or a wonderful opportunity.

BARTER AND TAXATION

By this time, you've probably developed a workable bookkeeping and accounting system for your business (see Chapter 8 for more on this). However, you may not be aware of the place of barter as it relates to taxation. Sometimes barter is a taxable event. Sometimes it's not.

Barter is a taxable event when it results in income or capital gain. Ordinary income, or capital-gain income, resulting from barter, must be reported the same way as cash transactions. When Tom (of Tom's Toy Shop) puts up $2,000 worth of surplus stock at the commercial barter club where he is a member, he is putting up goods which cost him $1,000. However, he is receiving $2,000 worth of spending power in the form of trade units. Thus he has increased his purchasing power by $1,000. This profit of

$1,000 is taxable as income when Tom "spends" his trade units at the commercial barter club.

A key phrase in dealing with the subject of barter and taxation is "fair market value." If, through barter, you receive goods or services instead of cash, these goods or services should be reported as income based on their fair market value. Suppose you supply four tins of your gourmet popcorn to a local café in exchange for two dinners at the café. You and the café owner have earned "income" based on the going rate (fair market value) of what you each have received. This income is taxable.

Usually fair market value can be calculated in more than one way—retail market value, wholesale market value, distributor market value. The lower the market value at which you calculate your barter income, the less tax you pay. As long as you are consistent, and reasonable, in your calculations, you will not be penalized for arranging things so that your welfare comes before that of the United States Treasury.

Under certain circumstances barter is not a taxable event. Here again we find another key phrase in dealing with the subject of barter and taxation—"like-kind exchanges." Like-kind exchanges are swaps of similar possessions of equal value, and are not subject to taxation. If you trade a truck worth $5,000 for another truck worth $5,000, there is no capital gain, and thus no tax to report.

Barter is also not a taxable event when things that fall under the category of "gifts" are traded. If you shovel your neighbor's driveway and he repays your kindness with a cord of firewood, you are not expected to report the firewood on your tax form.

Also nontaxable in the barter area are tax-deductible expenses. If you receive a typewriter for your business in exchange for installing an alarm system in the typewriter store, neither the typewriter you receive nor the alarm system the typewriter store owner receives is subject to taxation, because both fall under the category of tax-deductible expenses.

Items that fall under the category of "used goods" are also nontaxable. If you swap your office couch for your neighbor's lawnmower, no tax is payable, because the fair market value of both items is less than their original cost.

BARTER BEWARES

Barter can be an excellent business aid. However, just as you observe buyer and seller bewares in your cash dealings, so must you in your barter dealings:

Don't barter a hateable or a lovable. Don't agree to teach someone your craft if you hate teaching. Similarly, if you love your old tools, don't consider swapping them.

Don't be a poor time judge. If you're bartering your labor, or if your labor is a part of a barter transaction, make sure you correctly estimate how long a job will take.

Don't hoard barter credits or units. Continual trading is the lifeblood of all barter clubs. Also, don't wait too long in one-on-one barter to collect on your part of the deal lest you find that your barter partner is unavailable to pay up.

Don't join without checking. Is the barter club you're considering on the level? Is it glutted with members offering what you have to offer? Does it have what you want? Investigate barter clubs and also the honesty of any individual with whom you're considering bartering.

Don't barter for "hot" items. If you suspect you're being offered stolen merchandise, don't bury your head. Ask questions. Be careful with goods such as office machines, cameras, watches, furs, and jewels.

Don't get obsessed with exact-dollar swaps. Certainly you shouldn't accept a potted geranium for a pair of leather boots; however, don't try to negotiate down to the last cent. If you feel the leather boots you sell are worth "about" the same as the gold chain you can have in exchange, make the trade if you want the gold chain. Don't concern yourself with whether the leather boots would sell for $5 more or less than the chain in this or that retail outlet.

BARTER DO'S

Just as there are certain things to beware of when bartering, there are certain things you should do to make your trades as profitable as possible:

Be a listmaker. Make a barter inventory of all the items and services you can, and want to, offer. Clubs provide possibility lists to tap the memory, but individual barterers must assess their barter assets themselves. Also make a barter shopping list. What do you want in return for what you're willing to provide? Be specific on both lists; but be flexible too. If you've decided you want a suede suit in exchange for your offerings, and the closest you can come is a suede dress, don't refuse to trade without at least considering the dress as an alternative. Examine it. Try it on. You may find it serves your needs as well as a suit would.

Be businesslike. Establish parameters. Set time limits, time availability, expectations. Be exact. When appropriate, put things in writing. Don't mislead and don't let yourself be misled.

Accept barter scrip from reliable sources. Barter scrip is basically an IOU. It is currency that allows you to get something at a future date. You decorate a local beauty shop with ten of your paintings. They in turn give you scrip worth $300 which you can apply, at your convenience, to any of the services provided by the shop. The advantage of accepting barter scrip, if it's from a reliable source, is that you buy and sell at your convenience, and have something tangible (the scrip) to show that you've given but have not yet received.

Be a record keeper. You will need accurate and ongoing records to correctly calculate your tax liabilities. Also, if you barter frequently, you don't want to rely exclusively on your memory to know what you owe or are owed.

Be product-wise. Don't make a fool's swap. Mechanical objects, gems, art, antiques, coins, should be appraised before you accept them in exchange for something you're offering.

Be family-conscious. Involve your family in the giving and getting of barter. Children can store-sit, rake, shovel, package, deliver, and provide many other services which local merchants consider valuable. It will make them feel important and responsible to partake of barter transactions. Their labor can get them items which they need and which you would otherwise pay cash for. Also, when considering a barter transaction, don't think only in terms of your business or personal needs. Include our family's wants and needs in your barter shopping list.

There are about three hundred commercial barter clubs in the United States. Many of them cater to small business owners and home-basers. For information, contact the trade group for the barter industry:

> International Association of Trade Exchanges
> 5001 Seminary Road
> Alexandria, VA 22311

6

ADVERTISING, PUBLICITY, AND PUBLIC RELATIONS

Advertising, publicity, and public relations are all means of acquainting the public with what you sell in the hope that they will buy it. Advertising is the paying way to do this. You buy ad or air space from the public media—newspaper, magazine, radio space. Publicity is the free way to call public attention to what you're selling. You get mention in the media because you or your product is considered newsworthy for some reason. Public relations may or may not cost you in dollars. It is the promotion of goodwill. Your company (or you) engages in an act which benefits the community, the ultimate hope being that the act will also benefit your business. Ideally you should use all three of these techniques in order to make your home-based business grow.

ADVERTISING

Advertising can be your most difficult promotional undertaking because there are so many choices open to you and because mistakes can be costly. A home-baser should be well aware of all the wheres, whens, and how-to's before making any choices. However, many home-basers aren't. They are well aware of the value of their products but not of how best to advertise to make consumers buy their products in great quantity.

By now you've probably done some advertising. How did it go? Were you pleased by the results? Did you feel your money was well spent? Were you disappointed? Are you still hoping to find that magic medium which will bring in a steady supply of customers? You may well find it, if you approach advertising methodically and thoroughly.

Where To Advertise

For your advertisement to pay off, you must advertise in the media that are aimed at your typical customer. It's easy to avoid glaring mistakes. You know not to advertise rare books on a rock radio station or a newsletter for undergraduate students in a magazine aimed at senior citizens. But the subtle mistakes can cost you plenty and reap poor results. Before placing an ad anywhere, investigate the demographics of the population which will be reading or hearing your ad. The more you investigate, the more you will learn that there are both good and poor spots for your ad. You can choose one or more of the good spots depending upon your ad budget.

The Yellow Pages. A *small* display ad in a *small*-town Yellow Pages is affordable. Rates are high in big-city Yellow Pages, with the payment for a 2" x 3" ad averaging $135 a month. Work closely with the phone company's in-house sales force to compose the most effective ad possible. Sometimes a one-line listing is all you'll need. A good Yellow Pages ad won't bring in a flood of customers but will bring a slow, steady stream of those who don't look elsewhere.

Your local newspaper. There's more to advertising in your local paper than just coming up with a good ad. To get the most out of your advertising dollar, aim for a "tie-in"—have your ad placed near a feature article discussing items like those you're selling, or in a section of the paper (such as Fitness and Health or Fashion and Food) that ties in to what you're selling. A newspaper-account rep or an in-house agency will inform you, free of charge, about tie-in opportunities.

One of the least expensive ways to advertise in many weekend newspapers is through an ad inserted in the paper's weekly television magazine. These magazines have a one-week table life. To keep the costs low for small business owners, ads are often "zoned"—that is, your ad appears in those television supplements delivered to your town and nearby towns, rather than to distant areas.

Free-standing inserts are another way to advertise in your local newspaper. Here you benefit not from your ad being placed in any specific part of the paper, but from the delivery of your insert with the newspaper. In a sense you receive the advantages of a direct mailing without having to rent a mailing list and address and stuff envelopes. Usually what you save on postage you spend on placing the insert. But if you want to reach that population serviced by your local newspaper, a free-standing insert can be an excellent labor saver.

Regardless of how you advertise in your local paper—free-standing, television magazine, article or section tie-in—you get the advantage of short lead time. A newspaper ad, unlike a magazine ad, can be placed a few days before the publication is out.

A community, trade, or special-interest paper. These are usually weeklies or monthlies. Ads are relatively inexpensive and lead time is short. These publications provide a direct tie-in to a neighborhood or a predisposed market.

A monthly magazine. Usually your ad will look pretty and get at least thirty days' exposure plus "pass-along" value (average four readers to a magazine) in a monthly publication. Also, most magazines are demographically oriented, which enables you to key directly into your target customer. The disadvantages here are that the lead time is usually several months and ad prices, particularly for display ads, are relatively expensive.

On the air. Network advertising is prohibitively expensive for the home-baser. However, the cost of local radio and cable-television spots can be surprisingly low and well worth looking into. Many home-basers don't realize just how affordable local radio and cable advertising can be. It is not unusual to purchase a one-minute air spot for $25. What you must decide is how best to use that air spot, what time you want it to be on (some hours are more costly than others; some hours get different listeners than others), what you want to be said or shown, and, of course, the minimum number of spots you believe it would take to get the results you want. Almost all local stations have sales help available to guide you.

Community bulletin boards. Here you don't have to pay anything to place an ad. Depending upon what you're selling, and how you write your sell copy, you can get excellent results. One home-baser made up an attractive and colorful flier advertising her homemade fudge. She described her fudge in mouth-watering detail, with mouth-watering photographs, and told readers which local shops were carrying it. She mentioned that her fudge won three awards (people like prize-winning items) and that it came giftboxed or plain-packaged (people like choices). The fliers were placed on bulletin boards all over town—at supermarkets, libraries, schools, churches. Within a week the shopkeepers stocking the fudge were sold out and calling this home-baser with orders far beyond what she had hoped for. (If you're not ready for a flier, you can nail up an eye-catching business card.)

Advertising in the best media for your typical customer is a crucial part of "positioning"—of going after that segment of the buying public most likely to purchase your product. The various media will supply you with demographics information. In-house departments will provide you with lots of assistance. And trial and error will hone your placement skills. But positioning doesn't end with just knowing where to place your ads. The whens and how-to's of positioning are equally important.

When To Advertise

Just as your ad must be well placed to reach your market, it also must be well timed. If you want your advertising to really help your business grow, you should advertise when:

You are prepared to make a commitment to continuity. A one-shot ad here or there is not the way to use advertising to build a business. Wait until you have enough cash to plan an extended advertising program. Time creates credibility in the eyes of a consumer. The more a consumer sees your ad, the more he comes to regard your business as an enterprise to deal with. Your first few ads may just register your company's name and logo on the consumer's consciousness, but after this point you become a recognized establishment, a serious operation. This holds true for all businesses; but it is especially true for mail order, which has had bad press in the past and where credibility is often questionable.

You are prepared to try a media mix. Making a commitment of extended length to one medium is good; but it's not enough when we're talking about sending a business soaring. Ideally, your ads should appear in a few different media—in your local newspaper, on a local radio station, in a community publication. Stay with one slogan line and one logo. You're building a company image. You want consumer recognition; that comes from consistency. To know which media are bringing in the best responses, "key" your ads. If you have two business phones, the ads in your local paper can give one number and the ads in your community publication another. You are keyed in, or clued, as to which medium brings you a particular customer by which number you're being called on.

Your target customer will be most ready to buy your product. If you're selling to the high-school market, don't have your ad appear during finals week. First, students are usually preoccupied with passing their exams; second, those who have jobs usually work reduced hours then, so they are broke. Wait a few weeks until school is over. Students will be ready to turn their thoughts to gratifying their desires for material possessions, and they'll have had a chance to earn the money to be able to do so. Your ads should be appearing regularly, but not every day or week. This is much too expensive, and unnecessary. Keep your name in the public eye over the long haul, but intensify your ad campaigns during what you consider peak buying periods.

The season is right. While ad campaigns should be stepped up during your particular peak buying periods, they should also be stepped up during certain seasons. For example, cash flows more freely before Christmas than after. Someone who wouldn't buy your product for himself will buy it to give as a Christmas present. This reasoning holds true for the wedding season, the barbecue-party season, Mother's Day, Father's Day, Easter, Thanksgiving, Valentine's Day, and any other season or time when gift giving is popular. If your product is something that is not generally thought of as a gift item, advertise it and package it as such during these seasons. Why can't firewood be attractively wrapped and given as a gift? What newlywed wouldn't consider a month's supply of frozen, gift-boxed, choice steaks to be a pleasant departure from a plethora of toasters? (One home-baser, in the business of drop-shipping frozen meat, built a large following by going after what he calls "the newlywed, barbecue, and Easter markets.")

You have a new product. Whenever you update your line or add a new product, let the public know that now, in addition to your usual offerings, you're carrying something new. Once you build a following, each addition or innovation is greeted with the kind of interest which leads to sales.

You're planning a special sale or offer. Consumers love bargains. If you have surplus you want to sell, or freebies you can give away with each purchase, make this information known. A home-based businessman who found himself the recipient of an unwanted, large litter of kitties turned his burden into a bonus by offering "A Free Kitten with Every Purchase over $10!" Consumers turned out in good number at this man's produce stand. Most just enjoyed looking at the kittens. A few were delighted to take them home as gifts to their children. Whatever the case, sales were excellent for the two-week period this man had the kittens. New people became acquainted with him and his business. (And, perhaps nicest of all, this entrepreneur felt he had performed a humanitarian gesture.)

How To Advertise

How should you advertise to draw the customers you want? If you've done everything mentioned above, your ads are going to accomplish a lot of what you want them to. They're going to bring in new orders, new customers, and increased sales. Now you must go a step further so that good sales can become great sales:

Don't "think greedy." It's tempting to think of your offerings as appropriate to several different markets. It's quite likely that they are. However, it's also quite likely that they are more appropriate to one special market than to all others. Since you have only a finite amount of money to spend on advertising, target your copy writing (just as you should your ad placement) to that special market most liable to buy what you're selling. This means planning what your ad is going to say and how it is going to look with your target customer in mind. Others will see your ad and buy your products also; but you can't cater to the "maybes" when you know what the "yeses" will go for.

Learn the lingo. Certain buzz words and phrases have proven to be effective in ad copy: "free," "introductory offer," "amazing," "act now," "bargain," "save." These words attract people to an ad. Study how successful advertisers use them and apply them to your own copy. In addition to learning the general words which draw, learn the language of the group you're targeting. A target audience can be viewed as teen-agers, music lovers, New Yorkers, Mexican tourists, computer aficionados, or any one of a number of groups, which will help you word your ad appropriately. The closer you come to writing your ad in a fitting idiom, the more powerful your copy. One home-based candymaker set up a refreshment table at a computer fair with a large sign that advertised "Sample Bits and Bytes of Alma's Amazing Almond Fudge!" No booth at the fair was more crowded than Alma's. All the sample bits and "bytes" led to sales, orders, and reorders for several weeks. (Because Alma's fudge is a product that can be targeted to several audiences, Alma writes several kinds of copy, depending on whom she's targeting at a particular time.)

Become an insider. Learning the lingo is one way to become an insider. Learning anything which is important to your target-buying audience can help you to this end. The more you understand the mind-set, longings, and fears of potential buyers, the better. One cosmetics entrepreneur made a fortune in mail-order sales by writing her ads to zero in on the longings and fears of would-be customers. Her buying audience was middle-aged women who longed to look young and who despised fat and flab. Her ad copy was rich in words and phrases such as "taut," "fights flab," "tight," "hides bags and sags."

Take surveys. Minisurveys, taken in the right places, can provide information which helps you to become an insider and also cues you in to the current lingo of your target buyers. One home-baser who is extremely successful at selling cassettes to teens at flea markets says her booth is always crowded because of the information-drawing surveys she runs periodically at area high schools. This home-baser struck up a mutually beneficial deal with a teacher friend. She creates surveys that students like participating in, and that serve as gradeable writing assignments for her teacher friend, in exchange for the right to read through, and learn from, all the surveys. These surveys let this cassette entrepreneur know what the teens will be likely to buy, as well as some of the jargon they're currently using. This information is useful in the composition of the catchy ad copy which ultimately adorns her booth.

Write copy that repeats the points you want remembered. As long as you stay with your company slogan and logo you can vary and update your wording and artwork. However, don't drop from any ad mention of those points which strongly sell your product. For example, if you're a craftsperson who works in a medium better than that used by your colleagues, play up this fact. Do the same if you're a foodmaker who uses ony natural ingredients, a distributor whose prices are the best on the market, an artist whose works have won many awards. Regardless of how you change your overall copy, continue to stress those points which buyers will view as making your offerings superior to similar items on the market.

Use co-op advertising. On occasion tie in your ad copy with that of another businessperson—"Dora's Delicious Donuts, served free with breakfast at Dudley's Diner!" "Dora's Donuts and David's handmade donut holders—see them both, try them both, at the Marin Street Fair!" Co-op advertising reduces your advertising costs (Dora and Dudley split the cost of the ad) and enhances your offering with " association value"—now you are associated with Dudley's and David, and assuming both are worth being associated with, you benefit from their status and followings (and they, of course, from yours).

Consult the pros. Seek advice from any advertising experts you believe can help you in areas where you're weak or inexperienced. Seek and consult, but don't hire, at this point. In-house agencies provided as a service by most media, trade colleagues, journals, books, seminars are ways to get free and valuable assistance. There is nothing wrong with hiring a good ad agency when you can easily afford to do so. However, you're better off on your own than working through a third-rate advertising agency or a large agency which will consider you an insignificant client.

PUBLICITY

Good publicity is free advertising. You and your business are promoted by the media because they feel it is in their (not your) best interests to do so. People, small businesses, new products, interesting happenings, good buys, unusual offers are the stuff of which publicity is made. If you deal with the media correctly, you can get not only the equivalent of thousands of dollars of free advertising, but new customers which your ad copy might never draw. You can get an edge on your competition. You can give your business a giant boost.

Like most entrepreneurs, you know the value of good publicity, but how do you go about getting it? Why do some people seem to be getting it time and time again? What are they doing that you too can do? Let's look into how to get publicity, the kinds of publicity you should go after, and how to use publicity once you've gotten it.

How To Get Publicity

Good publicity is not a snap to get, which is why celebrities, executives, and professionals are willing to pay publicists a substantial fee to get it for them. It takes time and know-how. In busy urban and suburban areas the competition for media attention is fierce. Media people are courted and pandered to. In small towns, rural areas, and quiet communities publicity is easier to come by; but even here it must be approached properly. As a home-baser, in search of solid, frequent, and business-boosting publicity, proceed as follows:

Become a clipper. Clip out publicity pieces that appeal to you and are similar to those you'd like done about you.

Study what they highlight. Who's writing these pieces? Does he or she seem to be interested in small businesses in general, in mothers working from home, in unusual offers being made by small entrepreneurs, or in innovative products? What are the angles being pursued by the writers of the pieces you like? Note each journalist's name and the angle or angles he's pursued. Soon you will be composing publicity pieces, and this information will be extremely useful.

Read up on publicity. Many manuals, books, and articles have been written about how to compose a professional press release. You don't have to research the subject in tedious detail, but get an idea of how it's done. Examine the proffered samples.

Bone up on your writing. Whether you send out a formal press release or a letter to a lifestyles editor pitching your newsworthiness, you'll have to be able to write, not with great wit or style, but concisely and correctly—no long, repetitive sentences, no misspelled words, no smudgy hand-drafted letters (always use a typewriter).

Make a list of everything you'd like said about you and your business. Once this list is in front of you, edit it. Cross out all the things which probably won't interest the media and its followers. If you're selling mousses, on consignment, to area stores and restaurants, eliminate from your list the fact that your son is an eagle scout. If the media is interested in that much human interest, they'll ask you about your kid's achievements.

Rewrite everything left on your list in newsworthy terms. For example, if your list says "Several kinds of mousses offered," change it to read "One of the mousses offered by Magic Mousses is made especially for calorie counters" (or diabetics, or butterscotch lovers). The more unusual your offering, and the more public-interest value it is deemed to have, the greater your chance of getting media coverage. Only on a quiet day, in a quiet town, is a vague "this homemaker is selling her goodies" story going to excite an editor, journalist, or programming director.

Compose some send-out pieces. Go to your clip-out publicity pieces (see above). Following the formats of each piece (column, feature article, spotlight mention), write similar pieces with you, or your business, as the focus.

Stress those angles or points that the journalist you're writing to seems to favor. Include other important newsworthy points. Also compose formal press releases. Next make up some brief "for your information" covering notes: "Dear Ms. James: I have observed that you write about clothing designed for select groups. I manufacture a line specifically designed for the handicapped and for senior citizens which I think will interest you and your readers. Enclosed is some descriptive literature for you to examine." (You've made it easy for her to feature you by submitting usable, or easy-to-edit copy.) "If you'd like to talk to me, I can be reached at—————."

Include photos, samples, or both in your send-out pieces. The more you can put in an envelope which will convince a media person to give you publicity, the better. Depending upon what you're selling, an attractive photo or small sample may be a perfect clincher. Send a photo that will reproduce well (black-and-white glossies for newspapers, color transparancies for magazines). Do not send any expensive samples that can be interpreted as bribes.

Send your publicity package to several (local and non-local) editors, columnists, journalists, program directors. Media people are busy and can take a long time to get back to you; some will never get back to you. Don't put yourself in the position of waiting for just one response to your request for publicity. The more media people you approach, the better your chances of getting the coverage you want. (See "Kinds Of Publicity To Go After" below.)

Be personable. As a home-baser you and your business are closely linked for publicity purposes. For your business to have publicity appeal, you must also. This means that you should look and sound attractive. If you're going to meet the media, be photographed, or appear on the air or in front of a group, you have to come off well. You can't look tacky, speak poorly, or be boring. You want to come off as a credible, successful businessperson with something worthwhile to offer the public. Wear flattering clothing. Anticipate questions. Practice your answers. Do away with any "ums" or long pauses. Publicity is often a fast-track process where you get only a small amount of time to make a lasting impact.

Send thank-you notes. Whenever you're interviewed, or given publicity, write a note thanking the media person, or people, responsible for the coverage. Not only is it good manners to do this, it's good business sense. Media people, like everyone, like to be appreciated for their work.

Get to know the local media. Being interviewed is the beginning of making media acquaintances. Attend some community functions attended by the media. One homebaser went to a business seminar where a local radio announcer was among the speakers addressing the audience on new trends in radio. This home-baser struck up an acquaintance with the announcer, mentioned she was making and selling video cassettes for use in nursery schools, and gained some unexpected and very positive mention on the announcer's show. If you're shy, it's not easy to introduce yourself to media people, but it can be done in a quiet, nonpushy manner. The media wants people to spotlight just as much as you want to be spotlighted. Once you've met a few local media people, you may be in a position to give them a fast phone call with a quick update on your newsworthy activities, which they might well decide to pass on to their audiences.

Unquestionably, all of this takes time. However, the time you spend getting publicity is time which can ultimately increase your business tenfold. If need be, take time from activities that you can delegate to apprentice labor and put it into publicity-seeking endeavors. Don't put off publicity-seeking indefinitely. Often the younger a business, the more attraction it holds for the media, the more interested they are in spotlighting it and watching it grow. If they're not writing about you, they'll be writing about someone else. That someone will be doing something similar to what you're doing, and possibly his offering will be inferior to yours; however, his business will soar past yours because it will be getting the publicity your business could have had.

Kinds Of Publicity To Go After

As a home-baser you know that fantasy must be tempered by reality. You may like the thought of being featured on a major network talk show or in a major city newspaper, and that's a possibility for the future (see "How to Use Publicity" below); but for now, start a bit more modestly. You needn't start at the very bottom. You can start at middle-level publicity and work your way down, and then up, if you have to. What this means is don't turn away an interview with the editor of your church bulletin, but don't put efforts into being featured there until you've been ignored by larger local publications. Let's look at the middle-level kinds of publicity you should seek.

The Lifestyles feature. Almost all newspapers, large and small, have a Lifestyles section (the heading can differ, but content is similar) which lets readers know what interesting things area residents are doing. If you are running a home-based business, you can be a candidate for this feature, if you follow the steps covered in "How To Get Publicity" above. If one editor or journalist in your town paper seems to be ignoring your request for publicity, try, after a reasonable interval (four to six weeks), another editor or journalist. Or follow up your written publicity request with a phone call, or even a visit. Newspaper writers are busy, but they are also impulsive. Your publicity package, which landed on an editor's desk, may have been shoved aside, put on "hold," or forgotten in favor of more pressing pieces. A phone call, or visit, can spark remembrance and interest—and gain you immediate coverage.

If you've done everything possible to get your hometown paper to give you publicity and they haven't responded, for whatever reason, try the local papers of the towns bordering your town. Newsworthiness is not limited to a single town. But if these newspapers are also uninterested in giving you publicity, and you've followed all the steps discussed above, perhaps your region is glutted with home-based entrepreneurs doing things similar to what you're doing. This isn't likely, but it's possible. Or maybe so much is currently going on in your area that there's no print space available. Again, unlikely, but possible. In either case, for now, step down to a smaller publication. Send your publicity packet to the managing editor of your church bulletin, your Junior League news, or any small local publication that services your community or an organization to which you belong.

When a feature is written about you, don't get upset if it's not done as well as you'd hoped it would be. Even if it's not perfectly written, or if details you'd wanted mentioned are omitted, you're still getting publicity and the average reader is still going to be impressed. If you're dealing with the editor of a volunteer publication who is truly an amateur writer, next time around you can offer to contribute an article or column to the publication, wherein your byline and business credentials would be included for the reader to note. Once you get community coverage and recognition, local newspapers may well become more eager to write about you.

The free editorial. You've seen those magazine consumer columns with names like "Product News," "Best Bets," "Hot Tickets," where the columnist writes about items which he believes to be of interest to the publication's readers. Those items are receiving what's known as a "free editorial." They are getting free editorial space, free publicity, free advertising, because the column editor writing about them is paid to present worthwhile consumer opportunities to his readers.

A favorable free editorial in a popular publication can do more for a product than an ad of equal size (and in popular magazines most home-basers can't afford to take out ads of a size comparable to that covered by free editorials). Also, free editorial mention often includes a picture of the product, which further adds to its promotion.

The best way to get a free editorial is to send a sample of your newest or most unusual offering (if it is small), along with a clear photograph and covering letter, to the consumer column editor of a publication whose readers will be interested in learning about and ordering the item. In your covering letter present your offering as an attractive find and buy. Everything you write will not be presented to the column's readers, but your letter will be competing with dozens of others, so you want your product to be one of those to grab the editor as a "must-write-about." Mention briefly why your product is something that the publication's readers will be interested to learn about. Mention, if it's true, that nothing similar is on the market; that the product ties in with recent articles in the magazine; or that what's on the market is clearly inferior, much more expensive, or not being offered in the same fabrics (metals, woods) or colors that you're offering. Mention those things you believe will be most likely to impress the editor; presumably you've read several of his columns, and know what seems to impress him.

Seek free editorial mention from several columnists, always slanting your cover letter to hook the editor you're writing to. One home-baser got several free editorials from publications by presenting her decorative photograph albums (made with frilly, fabric covers and cover space for a photo) differently to different editors. She presented her album as: ideal for brides; ideal for gift giving; ideal for coffee-table decoration; ideal for nostalgia buffs; and ideal for new mothers. Each consumer columnist was able to envision this entrepreneur's album as particularly suited to her readers.

Another home-baser, who has developed a mail-order catalog featuring trendy kitchen utensils, had no trouble getting a free editorial in a popular, widely read column published in a chain of newspapers. She sent one of her trendiest and newest offerings, a crumb catcher from Israel, along with a letter, to the column's editor, telling why the newspapers' many lively, gourmet readers would enjoy learning about her crumb catcher. Each person who ordered this entrepreneur's crumb catcher could, of course, expect to receive a follow-up mail-order catalog. Thus this home-baser not only got excellent publicity for one of her products, but was also able to add many names to her catalog mailing list.

Sales and bargains publicity. This is similar to free editorial mention, except here an editor gives your product publicity primarily because you are offering it at a discounted bargain rate. Many consumer publications, city magazines, trade publications, and magazines whose main intent is to service the public with money-saving ideas and products, solicit information from manufacturers who are closing out a line, reducing their prices for a limited time, providing year-end specials. Of course many savvy manufacturers realize the publicity value of editorial mention in a sales-and-bargains column and here again the editor's desk is seldom free of letters and samples. However, if you have a product that you're willing to offer at sale price (or even below sale price, as a loss leader), you can compete successfully with major manufacturing firms. Seek sales-and-bargains publicity just as you would free-editorial publicity, but make sure you stress the discounted price angle above all else.

A small home-based distributor of belt buckles sent, on a whim, a sample belt buckle and price list to the columnist handling sales and bargains publicity for a well-known major magazine. He never expected to hear from the publication but was willing to try offering his buckles for just a slight profit above his break-even point in the slim hope the editor would be interested and he might ultimately gain new business and recognition. This man was surprised and delighted to receive a call from the editor requesting information on the specific dates the sale would be on, what else the company was offering, the best time for customers to visit or call. He was further surprised and delighted when his belt-buckle offer, and his company, received a prominently placed eighth-of-a-page spread. And, the greatest thrill of all was when he found himself receiving calls, inquiries, and orders for many weeks after the publicity appeared.

It is important to note here that when you seek print publicity, whether it be a lifestyles feature, a free editorial, or sales-and-bargains publicity, you, as a home-baser, must decide ahead of time whether you want the public to be given your home address, a post-office box, or just a phone number. Also, do you want the ad to state specific days and hours for consumers to visit or call? Readers and editors don't focus on whether they are dealing with someone working from home or from a retail outlet, so you must word your publicity mail-out to your best advantage. You can encourage business, yet discourage drop-in browsers (if this is what you want to do) with statements such as "send to P.O. Box 567 for free catalog"—major retail businesses use post-office boxes as a means of separating catalog requests from other consumer mail—or "Call Monday, Wednesday, or Friday for information or appointment."

Seminar publicity. Here is the publicity where you (and your business) are judged not by how you appear in print, but by how you appear in person. Seminar publicity is not limited to seminar speaking. It means speaking to any audience which has gathered for the purpose of learning about a specific topic or topics. The computer expert gives a talk to the local parents'/ teachers organization about personal computers for home use, how to get children to use them productively, how parents can deal with computerphobia. The audience benefits from his expertise and he benefits from the fact that his computer sales company is plugged in some subtle way. Not only does this man stand a good chance of getting customers and word-of-mouth advertising from the audience, but he also stands a chance of getting local press coverage, which means double publicity.

Seminar publicity can be an excellent business booster for the home-baser who makes a pleasant appearance, speaks well, and socializes easily. Potential customers sit and listen to you teaching them something. If they enjoy the experience, and feel they're benefiting from it, you're building up credibility. You haven't pitched your product, or tried to sell anything, but subconsciously you've sold yourself. After your talk you take questions from the floor and mingle with the audience. Then, those who are interested in doing business with you request your card, or an appointment. They feel they won't be buying just from a P.O. box or a face in the newspaper, but from someone they've met in person and have had a good chance to evaluate.

The best way to get seminar publicity, if you're not a recognized, fee-paid authority on a subject, is to offer your speaking services, free, to community organizations which are planning public programs where you feel you could fit in well. One entrepreneur, who operates a plant business from a greenhouse attached to her kitchen, regularly addresses area garden clubs on plant-related topics. Club members learn about such things as setting up an infirmary for sick plants, mixing plant types, growing exotic vegetable gardens, and using trailing plants in home decorating. When members who have benefited from this home-baser's talks need plants or plant supplies, they head for the kitchen greenhouse.

Talk-show publicity. Local talk-show publicity is not as difficult to get as many people believe. Program directors at local radio and cable stations need a constant stream of interesting guests in order to hold their audiences' attention. The doings of some area entrepreneurs can be of great interest to local listening and viewing audiences. Unusual entrepreneurship, combined with home-basing, is of particular interest to many people seeking to make job changes or start sidelines from their homes. Here, as with seminar publicity, the more personable and knowledgeable you are, the greater the likelihood you will be chosen as a guest, and the more likely listeners and viewers will be to contact you with consumer inquiries.

One home-baser got herself featured on several talk shows by sending out press releases that emphasized things she knew would impress program directors. This woman manufactured soft sculptures, which though popular as gift and decorator items, were not in themselves so interesting that talk shows would grab her as a guest. What was interesting was that she used a labor force composed entirely of regional senior citizens who worked from sewing machines in their homes. Not only was this home-baser employing the unemployable (and getting low-cost labor to boot), but, as she also stressed in her press release, she was making it possible for those who most needed the advantages of home-based employment to get them. This entrepreneur emphasized that she was getting quality work often very hard to come by with younger, less patient, workers. Still another point she stressed to impress program directors was that several of her senior-citizen workers were contributing product ideas, inspired by their youth, which resulted in soft sculptures especially appealing and salable to the nostalgia and the grandma markets. For this service the contributors could expect to receive special bonuses in addition to their piecework pay.

How To Use Publicity

Generally publicity creates a flurry of business which dwindles quickly, leaving only a certain amount of newly acquired long-term customers. Once you've gone through the work of getting publicity, don't let the flurry completely die. It's fine to have a complimentary feature article for your scrapbook; but that article can be put to more profitable use. It is a piece of publicity that can generate further publicity, and more new long-term customers if used properly.

Sometimes publicity itself is a self-generating phenomenon. It can breed more publicity without your having to do very much. Feature coverage in local publications can lead to feature coverage in national publications. Local seminar, radio, and television appearances can lead to major seminar offers and network radio and television appearances. An interesting feature story in *The Ossining Citizen Register* can find its way into the Westchester section of the *New York Times*. An appearance on a cable station in Marin County can land you on a major news show on KTLA in Los Angeles. Many press people look at local media for interesting events and people to report on and spotlight. Wire services tie the country together. It's not impossible for the offerings of a Rhode Island based entrepreneur to become national news overnight. This is all wonderful and it may happen to you. However, don't leave it to chance. Act as a catalyst in your own behalf.

Once you've proven to be newsworthy with the small media, the major media will look at you with, if not great, at least mild, interest. You may be dismissed, for the time being, as not newsworthy enough. Hold on, though. Eventually, with good local publicity behind you, it's quite possible that you will be considered seriously in a few prime places. And, very often, it takes only one prime piece of publicity to turn a tiny entrepreneur into a household name. What you must do is realize that prime exposure creates celebrity entrepreneurs all the time. Work to get it; and don't give up easily.

Generate all the local publicity you can. Make attractive duplicates of all public mention. Distribute these duplicates to prime people and places farther and farther away from your home base. Don't jump from town to nation. Stay within your state, and then your area of the country, until you build up a portfolio of regional publicity. Then distribute even farther away from home base. Get friends and relatives in other parts of the country to give you names of publications, press people, and program directors to contact. Ask them to make contacts for you. Go to the library and look through the *Ayer Directory of Newspapers, Magazines, and Trade Publications* for more places to contact for possible publicity. Mail out attractively-put-together publicity packets. Follow them up with phone calls. Once you have publicity packets and people and places to send them to, it takes only a few minutes out of any day to get them out. Those who get where you'd like to be are not those whose products are better than yours. They are those who persist longer than you do.

Use your publicity in your ad copy too. If, for example, you're selling imported alpaca goods and a feature article or free editorial has said your offerings are of "outstanding craftsmanship at 'must-buy' prices," highlight this mention. It's saying what you want known anyway. But what's important here is that you're not saying it. You're not touting your product. The statement in your ad copy is clearly attributed to a respected, objective, outside authority. You reap status (and ultimately sales) by association. The San Franciso *Examiner* considers "Alan's Alpacas" to be worth mentioning. Certainly, thinks the ad reader, they must at least be worth looking at.

PUBLIC RELATIONS

Public relations means relating to the public in such a way as to appear benevolent, good, human, altruistic. You, or your company, does (rather than "sells") something to bring pleasure to a group of people.

When an oil company underwrites a cultural show on public television it is engaging in public relations. The only mention of the company is in ads or announcements promoting the performance: "This show is underwritten by a grant from————————." There are no advertisements for the company or its products during the performance. Ostensibly the company is interested in bringing pleasure to the masses, not profits to its coffers.

There is nothing underhanded about public relations. In a sense it's a form of charity. And, just as there are anonymous benefactors, there are benefactors who want their recipients to know how caring they are. On a business level this makes excellent sense. Why should a business keep its generosity a secret—particularly when its competition won't? Now, let's look at how this relates to you. You're not an oil company. You don't have the time or money to donate a lot to the public. What can you do? What can your company do to generate goodwill?

Become event-minded. What things go on in your community, county, or state that you can become involved in? Don't try to think of events which relate to your business. Just think of events in general. Think of annual area events in which you can participate and where your participation as a local businessperson will be remembered by some. There are always fun events going on where the underlying purpose is to raise funds for a charitable or public organization. Get involved in one of these events. Volunteer for the event-planning committee. Or offer to judge the pie-eating contest, to sell tickets to the funhouse, or to give out awards to contest winners.

Have your company underwrite community projects. Find something your business can donate that will help bring off a community project. One home-baser donates the paints used in the store window-painting project his community undertakes every Christmas season. He also guides the preteen painters in their efforts. His company doesn't sell paints, but because he uses them in his woodcrafting business, he is able to get them at wholesale prices. In the newspaper announcements notifying area residents of the window-painting project, this man's company always receives mention as a project sponsor. Subconsciously, the fact is implanted in parents' minds that the sponsoring company is public-spirited.

As a home-baser attempting public relations, don't put big burdens on yourself. Just direct a bit of your attention to being a part of, or having your business be a part of, something that adds to the public good. Just as you want to sell to the public, you also want to relate to them in a less selfserving, more humane manner. Only take on the kinds of public-relations ventures where you'll have a good time personally, not where you'll feel put upon. A busy home-based manufacturer of whimsical stationery supplies makes up dozens of extra sample packets each year. They are given to the administrators of local schools for use in any way the officials wish (as prizes, learning aids, etc.). School budgets are almost always too tight. This homebaser is donating luxury supplies to a budget-conscious sector. It is a public-spirited goodwill gesture—nothing more. However, all the administrators know the name of the benevolent company, should they ever have more funds or be in a position to recommend a good supplier. Even though this home-based stationery supplier wouldn't mind profiting financially from her largesse, she finds herself profiting personally because her samples are always received and used with such delight. Though her rewards are not financial, she regards the pleasure she generates as a worthwhile kind of payment.

Advertising, publicity, and public relations are all ways to put your business in the public eye and help it stay there. Sometimes the line between them can be fuzzy. However, the ultimate aim of all three is company recognition. Advertising accomplishes this in a controllable, continuous, long-term way. Publicity creates a periodic flurry of attention which you can capitalize upon. Public relations creates the kind of goodwill where the public feels you have given to them and they want to give back to you. Any one of these techniques, used over a period of time, will have cumulative effects that will boost your business. All three, used in combination, will produce super cumulative effects which will make your business grow.

THE SIMPLE SAMPLE

Samples, properly used, can be the soul of success for an entrepreneur. They should be a major part of advertising, publicity, and public-relations endeavors—a significant way for a home-baser to acquaint the public with his offerings. Put some thought and time into producing quality samples. We all know that samples sell things. But keep in mind that they can sell things spectacularly well.

People love free samples. There's a tiny voice in us all that says, "If it's not costing anything, try it!" Major manufacturers know this. When they're ready to introduce a new product, they flood potential buyers with freebies. A new diet punch is coming out. You receive a sample packet in the mail; it's enclosed in one of the manufacturer's regular products; a lady hands out small cups of it in the supermarket.

The free sample is a proven and highly cost-effective way to bring in new business and increase sales to established customers. A small, simple sample, properly packaged and presented, can skyrocket sales and profits. But it can also be a costly fiasco, if not handled correctly. One woman makes chopped liver in her kitchen, brings samples to local supermarkets, grocery stores, delicatessens, and restaurants and ends up with a $3 million-a-year international business. Another woman handcrafts attractive wooden plaques with cute sayings calligraphed on them in fluorescent colors. She brings free samples to twenty gift shops within fifty miles of her home. One shop orders three pieces. The rest thank her for her samples. Twenty costly samples result in one tiny order. What is the chopped-liver lady doing right? What is the plaque lady doing wrong?

What we see here is the difference between what can be called a "simple sample" and an "ample sample." A simple sample has these characteristics:

- It is easy to produce in large quantity.
- It is inexpensive to produce in large quantity.
- It doesn't take long to make a lot.
- It can be small in size.
- Distribution channels are many.
- It's a "natural" for sampling.

The chopped-liver lady did well partly because her product was delicious, priced to sell, and targeted to the right buying audiences, but also because she had a product which fell perfectly into the simple-sample classification. Her product was relatively cheap and easy to produce in large quantity. In one afternoon she was able to make and freeze over a hundred samples. Within five miles of her home there were fifty potential outlets for her product. The nature of her product lent itself to fast response. Over 25% of her prospective distributors tasted the chopped liver in her presence and gave her an order on the spot. This is not atypical. Food is a fast-reaction, rather than think-about, item. People will sample food and make a decision immediately, whereas other items, such as plaques, often require think-about time.

The plaque lady did not fare well with her samples because plaques fall into the ample-sample classification. An ample sample has just the opposite characteristics of the simple sample.

Unlike the simple sample, the ample sample is not easy to produce in large quantity. It requires a lot of labor. Whereas one woman working alone can produce over a hundred samples of chopped liver in an afternoon, one worker can not handcraft a hundred plaques in an afternoon. The ample sample costs a lot to produce in large quantity. If the plaque lady wanted to produce a hundred samples in one afternoon, she'd have to hire helpers, which would be expensive. If she didn't want to bear the dollar expense of hiring helpers, she'd have to take several days to make her samples, which would be costly in time.

Part of the reason the ample sample is more costly in time than the simple sample is because ample samples are larger and more detailed. Compare the size of a tablespoonful of chopped liver with a plaque.

Another disadvantage of the ample sample is that distribution channels are not plentiful. Within a five-mile radius the chopped-liver lady had fifty potential product outlets. The plaque lady had to cover fifty miles for twenty possible outlets. The more potential markets, locally and otherwise, the greater the prospects for soaring sales.

Finally the poor plaque lady lost out because items such as plaques don't lend themselves to immediate orders. Ample samples usually require a lot of think-about time. They are not "naturals" as samples. They elicit wait-and-see responses.

Does this mean that ample samples are no-no's as sales boosters? No. They have a definite place in the marketing of your product—agents and product reps use them to promote your line; you use them when you visit a department-store buying office; they are used in consignment selling; you give them as gifts to prized customers; they are displayed at trade shows and home shows. But, unlike simple samples, ample samples should never be used as casual, bulk giveaways. It's unprofitable and counter productive to do so. However, all is not hopeless for the ample sample as a bulk giveaway. First let's look into those products which lend themselves best to the simple-sample classification; then let's see what can be done to modify an ample sample so that it can be used like a simple one.

Good Simple-Sample Products

Food products. All sorts of food products can be made up into quick and easy distribution samples. Be it chopped liver, homemade chocolates, cakes, fudge, popcorn, quiches, or cookies, a little bit of effort goes a long way.

Cosmetics. Have you heard of Indian Earth—that unique product that can be used as makeup and nail color, blush, and eye shadow? It's sold as a powder in small, corked crockery jars and responds to individual body chemistry to create a unique color for each user. It was a hot seller a couple of years back. Posh department stores made great money on it. So did several home-based cosmetics manufacturers who learned that Indian Earth is nothing more than a mixture of chemically pure iron oxide (rust) and talc. These home-basers bought iron oxide and talc in large drums, at low cost, from chemical supply houses and made up hundreds of samples which they distributed with excellent results. Most cosmetics ingredients are inexpensive when purchased in bulk, and are easy to make into sample packets. Large cosmetics companies have been capitalizing on this knowledge for years.

Printed goods. Once you've drafted one sample, for a small investment in printing a thousand samples can be quickly run off. Many products that can be reproduced through the printing process are "naturals" as simple samples. Newsletters and paper products fall into this category. So too do many low-cost printed plastic, cloth, and tin items. Manufacturers of plastic pens often distribute imprinted pens as simple samples. One home-baser made a small fortune on "logo laces." He began by custom imprinting shoelaces and distributing thousands of samples at sporting goods and premium and incentives trade shows. Another home-baser did the same with signs and emblems.

Novelty items. Assuming that you don't make them yourself but purchase them from a wholesaler, novelty items ranging from costume jewelry to kitchen gadgets make good simple samples *provided* your cost is no more than around forty cents per sample, and your markup is at least 200%. Novelty items such as cloisonné earrings, Disney character balloons, and dried flowers, should definitely be distributed as simple samples. Not only does the public purchase these items on impulse, but so do many vendors who deal with home-based distributors. A homebaser who brought in five hundred pairs of cloisonné earrings from Mexico distributed a few samples to flea-market vendors good at selling costume jewelry. The earrings quickly sold for twice what the woman paid for them in Mexico. The flea-market vendors knew that even with another 200% markup tacked on, they would have little difficulty moving the earrings.

Food products, cosmetics, printed goods, and novelty items are the basic categories of simple samples. Clothing, handicrafts, small markup wholesale purchases, and any items that are time-, energy-, or dollar-expensive do not fall into the simple-sample category. However, there are modifications that can be made so that products which fall into the ample-sample category can reap the sampling advantages of products which fall into the simple-sample category.

Modifying An Ample Sample To Simple-Sample Size

A plaque sample cannot really be presented the same way as a chopped-liver sample; but it can be presented so as to reap a lot of the same results. A chopped-liver sample is a tiny, appetite-whetting example of exactly what a retail customer can expect to receive if he places an order. The chopped-liver lady writes up the order, goes back to her kitchen, fills ten or fifteen half-pound containers, and brings them (or has them delivered) to the customer who placed the order based on her tasty sample.

The plaque person also wants to whet retailers' appetites. She wants retailers to order dozens of plaques; but she can't afford to distribute a costly supply of ample samples. What she must do is distribute "replica samples."

A replica sample is an incentive that is used like a simple sample; but it is not *exactly* what a retailer can expect to receive if he places an order. For example, the plaque person makes up colorful, cardboard copies of each of her offerings with her entire pitch (wood types, colors, print styles, prices, phone number to contact) spelled out on the back of each replica. She then has these replicas run off as printed goods and distributes them as simple samples.

Don't put off making up replica samples; the time it takes is time well spent. Replica samples, if they're attractive, can maximize sales possibilities. You can distribute hundreds, or thousands, of samples—a feat which would be financially disastrous using simple samples. Here, for example, the plaque lady, rather than working twenty shops within fifty miles of her home, could cover hundreds of shops all over the country. She could distribute a huge number of her replica samples through trade shows, reps, direct mail, in less time than it would take her to make up twenty ample samples and distribute them locally.

Plaque replicas, and many replica samples, will not bring in the ordering numbers that simple samples will. But don't worry about this. The profits from these products can be as good as profits from products which fall into the simple-sample category, with many fewer pieces ordered. A twenty-dollar plaque, for example, brings in a ten-dollar profit; a two-dollar container of chopped liver brings in a one-dollar profit: in terms of profit, ten chopped liver sales equal one plaque sale. Although the percentage markup is the same in both cases, the dollar profit per piece (per plaque or per container of chopped liver) is ten times greater with one product than with the other.

Variations Of The Replica Sample Principle

Plaques lend themselves well to replica sampling. So do most items produced in one medium, such as wood, but which can be attractively reproduced in another medium, such as cardboard. Basically the replica sample is a *big* improvement over the picture or flier. There are two variations of the replica sample principle which produce excellent results and can be used in addition to, or even instead of, the replica sample:

The pizzazz piece. The pizzazz piece of a product is that part which has the most grabbing power. Not every product has a pizzazz element, but many do. In the case of plaques, for example, the pizzazz element may be the wood of which they're constructed, or the texture of the fluorescent paints used on them. In order to increase the sales-boosting potential of the replica sample, the plaque vendor can distribute her cardboard replicas, along with plaque chunks, so that potential customers will have secondary samples to induce them to buy. Now the potential customer has both a replica plaque and a visually attractive piece of a real plaque to handle and mull over.

One savvy home-based manufacturer combined replica samples and pizzazz pieces to amass a tidy sum for himself. This man made ornate wooden boxes in several shapes and sizes. He took his offerings to the New York Gift Show (a huge trade show visited by buyers from all over the country), where he set up an imaginative and crowd-pleasing display. His booth was smaller, and cheaper, than those around him, but it drew many more lookers and on-the-spot orders. Here's what he did:

On one side of the booth he exhibited ample samples of all his offerings—tiny and huge, beautifully handcrafted and handpainted, wooden boxes. On the wall of the booth behind these samples were clear, colorful, blown-up photographs showing his boxes being used as containers for all kinds of items, as small decorator tables, and as footrests. On the other side of the booth were four baskets set out on a table. One was filled with wood pieces similar to those the boxes were made of. The second contained multicolored stones, beads, and other little objects that were used to add interest and sparkle to the boxes. The third basket was low and flat and filled with paints and glue. The fourth was stacked with detailed replicas of the exhibited ample samples.

A browser at this manufacturer's booth was encouraged to play, to create a fanciful wood chunk, and to take his creation home in a little cardboard replica box. Many of the browsers did just that; and while they created, curious onlookers were drawn to the booth. The upshot was that buyers were asking if they could order this look, or that look, and holding up their little chunk creations. Orders flowed in; some for three or four boxes, some for three or four dozen. Buyers who weren't ready to order were pleased to have replica samples, pizzazz pieces, and their little creations to take away from the show. It was clear that many orders would be forthcoming.

This is an example of how one home-baser used the replica sample and the pizzazz piece together. Pizzazz pieces can also be used in place of replica samples. These pieces can make economical and dynamic sales boosters. One woman who tripled her net profits in one year is sure that her swatches did the trick. Her business is bags; a spare bedroom in her home is the bag factory. In addition to containing a desk, filing cabinets, and an industrial sewing machine, the room overflows with dramatic fabric samples. Quite by accident this home-baser discovered that people love to use interesting swatches—those of an unusual material, design, or color.

Whenever friends visited this lady's workroom, they were immediately drawn to her fabric collections. They pleaded for a swatch of this and that because the color was so vivid, or the texture was so sensual. She learned, with amusement, that the swatches were being used as patches on jeans, to make cloth picture frames, to wrap small gifts, for dolls' clothing, and for several other purposes. An idea was born. She would use swatch samples as silent salesmen. She made up small swatch kits of her most appealing fabrics. In each kit was inserted an illustrated "what to do with swatches" sheet. She attached these little kits to her promotional literature and sent them to several retailers. A short time later she was delighted to hear many of her new customers saying things like "Every time I looked at the leather patch on my son's jeans, I remembered I must order some pocketbooks made up in that fabric" or "I used the delicious-looking lavender swatch in your kit to giftwrap a pair of lavender barrettes; do you think you could make me up a dozen disco bags and belts in the same color and fabric?"

The plethora piece. The plethora piece is not a piece of your product. It is the whole product; but it is an overrun, an extra, an irregular. A businessman who sells awards, trophies, medals, ribbons, and plaques from a workshop in his garage always has a supply of plethora pieces on hand. This man cannot comfortably afford to distribute hundreds of specially produced samples. However, because he is a think-ahead person, he always has a supply of plethora pieces which have cost him almost nothing. How does he come by these plethora pieces, this surplus stock which he is able to sell or give away as samples? In two ways:

1. He buys up wholesalers' overruns, closeouts, and auctioned lots for a tiny fraction of their worth. Some of these pieces he resells and some he uses as samples. A track coach who received one of his samples, a "plethora medal," from a track event held in another state, decided that the medals he was going to use weren't classy enough. He spent an extra $50 and had medals made up that looked as impressive as the plethora sample he had been sent. This awards supplier keeps current in his field through trade journals, industry shows, visits to manufacturing plants, so he knows exactly where to shop for his giveaways and what to bid.

2. He has extras made up with every order. Though it can be costly to order ten or twenty sample ribbons or medals, it is usually not costly to add this amount to a large order. The extras from all the orders this awards supplier has made up serve as excellent samples of what he can offer customers, of what he has done for his customers, and of who his customers are. Also, in the spirit of promotion, whenever this entrepreneur sends a big order to an athletic coach, he has a special "Coach's Medal" made up for the coach to enjoy wearing on the day of the meet.

Plethora pieces can also be irregulars which are purchased solely for sample giving. A home-based designer and supplier of high-quality stationery with features such as raised lettering and sketches, refuses to make up hundreds of expensive samples. Instead she contacts printers and offers to pay for their mistakes—that is, a misspelled name or a color used by mistake on high-quality stationery. This way buyers have an inexpensive means of seeing and feeling the difference between luxury stationery and dimestore stationery. Some of the printers contacted are willing to give the stationery designer their mistakes in the hope that she will one day use their services to process some of her orders. Those printers who sell their mistakes to her sell them for very little. This stationery designer has amassed a large, lovely, and still-growing inventory of lush samples.

How To Distribute Samples

No matter how many samples you have, or how easily and cheaply you may be able to acquire them, if they're not distributed correctly, they won't do you enough good. Samples should go to potential customers, to those people who will be most likely to order, reorder, display, and talk up your merchandise. The best ways to distribute samples are:

Through trade shows. These industry-wide events are excellent arenas for putting your samples into the hands of those immediately interested in placing orders. Professional buyers not only get your samples to take home, but they meet you and talk to you personally, though your base of operations may be 3,000 miles away. You literally "put" your samples into their hands, and buyers like this opportunity.

As stuffers with current orders. The awards supplier always includes a couple of carefully selected samples in shipments to his customers, "Just," as he writes on the plastic bag he puts them in, "to give you some ideas for the future."

To those retailers with the power to order. Only certain retailers have the authority to place an order. A store clerk may love your offerings, but, unless he really has the ear of his boss, it's unlikely his love will do much for you. The chopped-liver lady, for example, knew not to bring a sample to the boy behind the grocery-store register. She found out when the store owner would be available and brought it in then.

Through sales agents. The most loyal sales agents you can have are probably your own sales force. However, a sales force is costly and not necessarily the fastest or best way to have your products seen by scores of retailers nationwide. If you can find (through a trade organization or industry contacts) a reliable, respected professional agent who is enthusiastic about your line and willing to rep it throughout the country, try him. Professional reps know to whom to distribute samples and which samples work best in which markets. A 10% commission on goods sold can be the best money you pay out—if you get a rep who works hard to show your samples and if this rep is able to write up lots of sizable orders. Of course, don't sign any contract with any rep unless you've read the contract carefully and agree to all the stated terms.

Through the mail. Not all samples lend themselves easily to mail distribution (chopped liver doesn't, custom-designed stationery does); but many of those that do can be sent out bulk-rate, and, if targeted properly, can boost sales substantially. One home-baser who created her own hair-thickening shampoo and conditioner did what the big cosmetics companies do. She had hundreds of samples packaged in sealed foil and mailed them, along with her brochure and price list, to select markets—to students on college campuses, subscribers to teen magazines, young mothers. This lady's diligence in buying and collecting good mailing lists paid off well. (See Appendix for a representative list of mailing-list brokers.)

Through friends. Friends travel. Friends live all over the country. They belong to clubs and organizations. They know potential markets in distant parts of the country that you might never hear about or have access to. If your friends like your products, and want to help you expand your markets, they may be more than willing to distribute your samples and talk up your offerings. If they want to do it on a regular basis, pay them as you would a professional agent, or give them some merchandise, if they prefer that.

Through community mixers. Today many areas have community mixers where home-basers can get together with each other, and with small shop owners, to discuss common problems, hear guest speakers, and showcase their products. These mixers, often listed in the business and other sections of local newspapers, are good places to distribute samples, receive instant feedback, and network in general.

Through talks and seminars. The shampoo lady mentioned above speaks at women's club meetings on issues relating to hair care. She never pitches her products during her talks; but after she's finished, and after the question-and-answer period, she distributes her samples, along with ordering sheets, to audience members.

At flea markets, crafts fairs, fundraisers. These festive events are good places to give out samples and sell your products simultaneously. One woman averages $500 a weekend selling her "secret recipe" cheesecakes at a flea market. Customers try samples of her chocolate, strawberry-swirl, peach-glazed, and nut cheesecakes and are hooked on the spot.

Through barter clubs. As discussed in Chapter 5, the showrooms of these clubs can be good places to display and distribute samples, provided you are prepared to trade for goods and services as well as sell for cash.

Simple samples, replica samples, pizzazz pieces, plethora pieces—they all can multiply sales many times over for the home-baser on a modest advertising budget. In addition to the inherent sales-spurring quality of samples in general, the fact that a home-baser makes and distributes professional samples and price lists brings credibility and customers to his enterprise. Local buyers are impressed. And often nonlocal buyers, such as those obtained through trade shows, sales agents, mailings, and the like, automatically assume they're dealing with a well-established corporation and feel comfortable placing sizable opening orders. If your samples are appealing, and your accompanying literature is persuasive, your business will grow quickly as you accumulate steady customers.

7

DIRECT AND INDIRECT SELLING

As a home-baser you can engage in direct selling, indirect selling, or both. Direct selling simply means selling directly to the public—from your home, in their homes, at flea markets, etc. You make ten types of fudge, set up a fudge shop in your home, and sell to fudge lovers. Indirect selling means selling to the trade. You make ten kinds of fudge, set up a fudge exhibit at the Fancy Foods Trade Show, and sell to buyers who sell to fudge lovers. As a direct seller you are a retailer. You, personally, meet the people who will be using your product. As an indirect seller you are a wholesaler. You do not meet the people who will be using your product. You meet the middlemen who will sell to these people.

There are four basic types of direct selling and four basic types of indirect selling. There are others; but these are the major ones for home-basers:

Direct Selling

1. the home shop
2. flea markets
3. multilevel sales
   (also called direct sales)
4. mail order

Indirect Selling

1. trade shows
2. store buyers
3. sales agents
4. corporate buyers

It's quite possible that when your business is soaring you will find it most cost-effective, profitable, and enjoyable to go exclusively with just one of these eight types. But, for now, you should use a mix of direct- and indirect-selling methods. Later, you can streamline—drop those types of selling which aren't working well for you, and concentrate on those that are. This concept, called "multi-marketing," was introduced in Chapter 3.

DIRECT SELLING

Most home-basers start off with one form of direct selling. Rare is the home-baser who begins by using all the forms of direct selling or by using middlemen. This is fine; a home-baser can build confidence in self and product by selling to friends, neighbors, and the public. However, once a home-based business is established, if it's just plodding along, other forms of direct selling should also be used. So should some forms of indirect selling. Let's look at the four types of direct selling and indirect selling to encourage you to try some combination of them simultaneously:

The Home Shop

Many consider a home shop small-time stuff. How much money can Betty Jo make selling baskets and bowls from a shop in her garage? You'd be surprised how much Betty Jo can make, if she runs her business well—not a fortune, but probably a lot more than if she ran her business from a high-rent mall location.

Home-shop selling can be a good way to begin and a good way to go on. If your home is well located for customer traffic and you have ample space, you're in good shape. If your product can be tied in with a service, so much the better. Betty Jo can make money selling her baskets and bowls. She can teach people the craft of basket or bowl making if she wants to make more money and bring in more customers. There are many books and articles on the how-to's of setting up a moneymaking home shop—how to organize it, stock it, advertise it, maintain it, teach classes from it, use student labor, and so on.

The home-basers with home shops usually net a few thousand dollars a year. The problem begins when a home-based shop owner wants more than a few thousand a year, has done all that can be done with a home shop, and still doesn't have enough customers. This is when the owner must think of the home shop as part of a sales program, not as a business in itself.

Flea Markets

Flea markets have now become part of the American landscape. Buyers go there for bargains, for treasures, for the unexpected. And they get what they're after. It's usually the sellers who don't get enough of what they're after—money. Most flea-market vendors are home-based manufacturers or distributors who dream of going home with an empty station wagon and full pockets. Sometimes this dream is realized—there are some savvy vendors out there—but usually it's not. Competition is stiff. Many flea-market shoppers are jaded, or want to get something for nothing. Flea markets are weekend events—a vendor has only two days to draw his customers.

There are other negatives to flea-market selling. But there are positives too. As discussed in Chapter 3, flea markets, when approached properly, can be excellent places to test the public's reaction to a product. They are low-cost learning grounds, where you can build experience in the art of negotiation and salesmanship. They are a way to observe and check out your competition. One vendor of multicolored and -flavored jelly beans learned from her flea-market vending experiences that just selling her jelly beans in attractive canisters wasn't enough. Decorative canisters worked okay from her home shop, which she set up during holiday seasons. But they didn't work well enough at flea markets, because many people didn't want to pay for a canister; they just wanted a couple of ounces of jelly beans, in a plain bag, to munch on while wandering around the flea market. This jelly-bean lady added a scale and several scoop-out bins to her canister exhibit and tripled her flea-market sales. She also helped her home-shop business. Not only did she realize that what worked in her home shop didn't work well enough at a flea market, but she discovered that her home-shop business could also be increased by offering customers the opportunity to buy by the bag.

Selling from a home shop and selling from a flea market are two types of direct selling which can be carried on simultaneously. You can double and triple your number of customers, and your income, while you learn that things from one kind of selling can be profitably applied to the other. Even in *Successful Flea Market Selling,* I encouraged the reader to try related methods of selling and not just stick to flea-market vending.

Multilevel Sales

Multilevel sales (also called "direct sales" by the trade) are very big today. Many people are making small bucks from it; and a few are making very big bucks. Unlike the home-shop or flea-market vending, multilevel sales seems to offer home-basers the possibility of reaping a fortune in a relatively short time. But many home-basers, or would-be home-basers, fall into multilevel sales without truly understanding what it's all about.

If you're in multilevel sales, or if you know anyone who is, you know something about it—or the company names, like Mary Kay, Amway, Shaklee, Sarah Coventry, may be familiar to you. The big money comes from finding and motivating recruits to sell what you're selling. Then they find people to sell what they're selling, and so forth. You earn commissions on your sales, your recruits' sales, and the sales of their recruits, and their recruits' recruits, down to several levels (thus the terms "multilevel" marketing and selling). You work out of your home, keep your own inventories and records, and if you're successful in recruiting and training other serious salespersons, your business will soar and your income will skyrocket.

It sounds very easy. You get a few friends or relatives to arrange gatherings in their homes (party-plan selling is the traditional basis of multilevel sales), and give them free merchandise for their efforts. You sell your products, and recruit others to do the same, thus setting up a chain of buyers and recruits. But if it's so easy, why aren't the millions of people involved in multilevel sales owners of home-based business empires?

It *is* possible to make it big in multilevel sales. Unlike chance events, such as winning a lottery, where you have no control over whether or not you make a fortune, here you have control. However, there are several factors which will determine just how far your control will take you. To strike gold you must:

Be a super recruiter. If you can find several people with time, ambition, and good sales potential, and motivate them properly, you may very well be able to build an empire. Yet finding the right people can be difficult and time-consuming. You can't rely exclusively on small party plans for sales and recruits. Use them, but think also in terms of the large "party." Those few who build a giant home-based business from multilevel sales are always drumming up large groups to address. One crackerjack saleswoman of skincare products convinces women's-group leaders, beauty-school managers, sorority presidents, and dozens of other organization heads, that their groups will benefit greatly from her presentations. She is persistent, but not "naggy," in getting these organization heads to commit themselves to a date. Once she has it, she puts on a great show, and encourages her audiences to try her products, and to ask questions about them and about skin care in general. She comes off as informed and sincere. She is amusing as well. This businesswoman reaps a very large number of orders, reorders, and recruits. And, to top it off, the groups to whom she speaks are grateful and often recommend her to other groups.

A dynamo of a man, who makes thousands a month from the sale of vitamins, uses another sales method that also goes well beyond small party-plan selling. This man, with computer aid from his multilevel corporation, searches out areas which are not vitamin-and health-saturated. He gets talk space in these areas either by convincing community centers, schools, libraries, that he is performing a community service; or by renting it from a local motel. He then places a box ad, offering a "free health seminar," in highly visible spots in area newspapers, and goes on to address the twenty to fifty people who usually show up. He talks to them on the pros and cons of vitamins, how to use them for the best results, how to combine them with body-building exercises. He distributes informative handouts and samples, and uses visual aids to enhance his performance. Because this man looks and sounds healthy, and speaks in a polished, inspiring, "you can do it" way, his listeners are eased into buying what he is selling. And, like the skin-care lady, he always has an eye out for candidates who might make excellent recruits.

Like selling, talking, and making presentations to groups. It's hard to be a super recruiter if you're shy, lacking in confidence, or unable to deal with rejection. If this is the case, it's possible that multilevel sales may not be for you. However, it may be just the thing to bring you out of yourself and build your confidence. Many people in multilevel marketing claim that the process has not only been financially beneficial, but socially beneficial as well. There's no question that whatever social skills you have, or develop, will very definitely influence your success in multilevel sales and in life in general.

If you are shy, lacking in confidence, or unable to deal with rejection, don't think in terms of the large party plan for a while. It may do you in. Fortify yourself first by selling at small parties, or, even easier, at flea markets, where potential customers will approach you. The better you get at meeting and greeting, at dealing and "spieling," the more your business will grow, the bigger the steps you can take. But remember, take it slowly. No amount of money is worth forcing yourself into a spotlight position that you find torturous.

Have a super product. It's much easier to be a super salesperson when you have a super product. A super product is one for which there is a genuine repeat need. If the product you're promoting is a gimmick or fad, it's unlikely your business will ever truly soar, even if you have a great personality for sales. A super product is also one for which you have strong enthusiasm. It's almost impossible to pitch a product which leaves you cold, and not feel like a fraud. It's also great if your product has excellent holiday gift-giving possibilities (one strong Christmas season can pay a lot of bills).

Be right for the product you're selling. You'll find it very tough to sell a diet product if you're grossly overweight; or a fashion product if you have no fashion flair; or a skin-care product if your complexion is poor. With many multilevel sales products the salesperson has to be a walking endorsement of his product. If you don't look as though the product you're selling is doing you great good, people will be negatively influenced.

Getting testimonials from successful users of your product can be tremendously helpful, particularly if they've done better with your product than you have; however, people will be the most influenced if *you* look as though you've benefited greatly from your product. They will not only buy your product, but recommend it, and you, to others.

One woman who sells tins of a diet and health product, and has dozens of recruits working for her, for an income of over $70,000 annually, began by being fat and lethargic. She tested the diet and health product on herself for three months, lost weight quickly, felt strong and energetic, grew the long nails she always wanted, and developed a glowing complexion and shinier, stronger hair. This woman took "before," "along the way," and "after" photographs of herself, and proved that not only can a picture be worth a thousand words, but many thousands of dollars. Customers who weren't interested in becoming recruits recommended potential recruits to this lady in numbers which skyrocked her income.

Be energetic. To be happily successful in multilevel sales you should have a lot of physical stamina. Are you willing to work odd hours, travel, lug, pack, unpack, set up, and clean up? This is a part of multilevel sales whether you're selling through small party plans, party-plan-type gatherings, or at flea markets.

Some feel that the appeal of party-plan selling is that you don't feel as though you're selling. However, most parties are given nights or weekends, which you may not regard as a plus if you're tired at night, or like to relax on your weekends. Also, substantial traveling is frequently necessary to get to a party site, as is the lugging, packing, unpacking, and setting up of samples. And there is clean-up time. You cannot leave a hostess's home in messy condition. Once you have your recruits in good shape, you can slow down, enjoy the commissions from their sales, and sell to your customers from a part-time home shop. But it takes time, as well as energy, to get to this point; so be patient.

Have a price structure and a commission structure which work for you. Even if you have a super product, it must be competitively priced. This is particularly true if similar products are available in the local marketplace for substantially less. Also, your multilevel marketing corporation must have a good commissions system. Even if you're mathematically adept, a commissions system that is difficult to calculate is difficult to sell to recruits.

Feel free to become involved with more than one multilevel marketing corporation. Don't let yourself be bound to one multilevel organization. If it is to your financial advantage to stay loyally bound to one corporation, fine. But understand that once you've become skillful in multilevel selling, it is often your skill which has great value, more than the particular product or line which you are handling. This means that:

1. If your product has exhausted itself, or been shot down by a better product, you don't die with the company. Similarly, if another multilevel company is dying, you can "rescue" their reps. Approach them as potential recruits.

2. Once you've learned the ins and outs of multilevel marketing, you are a free agent in a good position. If you feel you can do better with another multilevel corporation—maybe their product is more timely and less competitive, or you have the opportunity to get in with a new and expanding company—switch over. Or, if you have a few good recruits, you may want to stay on for a while but concentrate your major efforts elsewhere. Or you may be able to sell your business. Many multilevel organizations have provisions for the transferring of customers, recruits, records, from one businessperson to another.

3. You can work with more than one line. One homebaser doubled her income in months by taking on a second, related product. She was moderately successful selling, and recruiting others to sell, a cosmetics line; but it wasn't until she combined her cosmetics line with a jewelry line that her income became substantial. Now she presents both lines together. Sales of one spur sales of the other. She feels the additional labor required is more than compensated for by the large amount of extra sales.

4. You can create your own multilevel company as well as handle a line from a multilevel sales corporation. One apartment-based shoe and boot importer decided that the presentation and sales of her footwear would be enhanced by taking on a clothing line. Her first instinct was to import clothing the same way she was importing footwear. She changed her mind when she discovered a multilevel sales organization marketing clothing that went nicely with her shoes and boots. By selling footwear and clothing together, through party plans and flea-market fundraisers, this woman's income went from about $5,000 a year to over $25,000, in just two years. By having women in her audiences model her shoes and clothing together, she not only stimulated sales of each, and found good recruits for her clothing line, but she also found women who were eager to represent her footwear line. The latter was something she hadn't anticipated, and which has turned into a nice bonus business. This lady is now the owner of a small, but profitable, multilevel shoe-marketing company, as well as an independent dealer for a large multilevel sales clothing corporation.

Following all the above "musts" will help you strike gold in multilevel sales. Knowing the following caveats will ensure that the gold is not "fool's gold":

Beware of pyramid schemes masquerading as multilevel sales companies. The main difference between the legitimate multilevel marketing company and a pyramiding scam is that in a legitimate company, money is earned based upon the sale of products. In a pyramiding scam money is earned not through the sale of products, but by signing up new members who pay to get into the pyramid. The problem with the latter is that pyramids crumble because they are mathematically impossible to maintain and legally impossible to justify. Only the scam's originators (the people on the top of the pyramid) make money. The majority of recruits not only don't make a profit but lose their original investments as well.

Beware of multilevel marketing organizations demanding large initial investments. If a company is asking you to put up more than $50, examine carefully what you're getting for your money.

Beware of multilevel sales organizations where help and training are not readily available. A good multilevel organization will train you in the sale, and, when necessary, the use of its products, as well as in the recruiting of new salespeople. Make sure the company has literature which explains the basics, that you are compatible with your recruiter and his values, and that you are not joining up with a cultlike firm.

Beware of companies with long deliveries and poor guarantees and return policies. A worthwhile organization delivers quickly, refunds easily, and guarantees all its products.

Know that though multilevel sales is part of homebasing, there is also a distant homebase involved over which you have no control. A diet consultant who had worked hard to develop a repeat market for her diet supplement, and built a network of reliable recruits, watched helplessly as her business dwindled because of a barrage of negative media coverage about her product. Carefully investigate any multilevel marketing company you're considering joining. Don't rely exclusively on the testimonies of seemingly devoted personnel or customers. Contact the local offices of the Better Business Bureau, Small Business Administration, Postal Inspector, Attorney General, Federal Drug Administration, the National Association for Multilevel Marketing, or any other agency which might have a good handle on fraud, pending investigations, shady histories. (See Appendix for representative list of multilevel marketing companies.)

Again, as with home shops and flea markets, don't feel you must limit yourself to multilevel selling. It can fit in beautifully with other types of direct selling.

Mail Order

Mail order, like multilevel sales, is a type of direct selling that entices many home-basers with the possibility of raking in fortunes. It's ideal for the person who dislikes face-to-face selling. However, here too the fortunes may not flow in. Mail order can be a business in itself, or it can be one of several ways to increase sales of a product. It is primarily the latter that we're discussing here—using mail-order marketing as one means of making your home-based business soar.

Your aim in using mail order is to have a mailbox

frequently filled with checks for your product. This can really happen, but it takes know-how, patience, and persistence. Many home-basers have the following disillusioning experience with mail-order advertising: An ad is placed in a national tabloid. The hope is to receive enough orders to cover the cost of the ad and to net a few hundred dollars as well. Instead of receiving orders, the home-baser receives offers—offers of all kinds from people who build mailing lists based on classified listings. One home-baser placed a classified ad for a ski guide and found her mailbox filled both with solicitations for her to advertise her ski guide in other publications and with chain-letter inducements ("buy the first item on this list, put your item on the bottom, mail this letter to ten addresses you've found in classifieds"). She didn't receive a check for, or even an inquiry about, her product. Not one! Does this happen often? Yes, and to intelligent and honest businesspeople like yourself, who half-believed the hype they'd heard about millions being made in mail order.

It is not at all unthinkable for a home-baser trying to increase sales to place a small classified here or there. The process is simple; the risk is minimal. The problem here is that because of the ease of ad placement and the small financial risk involved, many do not give serious thought to the wording of the ad, to where and when it is placed, and to the total process of building a mail-order clientele. Attention to these details is crucial to the success of the ad. When an ad is produced in a hit-or-miss fashion, the results are usually dismal, and the mail-order approach to business boosting is abandoned.

For mail order to increase sales, you must start small and work up. A good overall plan for the entire process of building a mail-order clientele is to:

Begin with a small classified ad in a publication widely read by your potential customers. If you want to sell a watch for skiers, for example, place your ad in a widely read skiers' magazine. Similarly, a pattern for a soft-sculpture doll should be advertised in a popular needlecrafts publication. If you're not sure which magazines are best for your offering, go to the library and read reference directories such as *Standard Rate and Data* and the *Directory of Magazines with Classified Ads* to learn all the publications in the country which take mail-order ads.

Begin your ads in test-proven good months. January, February, September, October, and November are the best for most products. Place your ads far enough in advance so that they appear in the issues you want.

Read how-to books on mail order and word your ads the way they advise. There are proven attention-grabbing words and phrases. There are phrases which create confidence ("satisfaction guaranteed"), and others which stimulate action ("don't wait!"). There are ways to say a lot in a few (and thus inexpensive) number of words.

Upgrade slowly and cautiously. Once you begin to show a profit using classifieds, you can upgrade to display ads, or try your ads under more and different classified headings in a greater variety of publications. The important thing is not to squander your ad budget. Test each ad. Note the response it brings in. Then consider your next move. Don't place ten ads simultaneously until you're sure of your ads, of the publications you're using. Even then proceed with care. Once you've saturated a particular market, it's often wise to wait several months before reinserting your winning ad.

Build a mailing list. If a customer buys from you once, and is pleased with his purchase, there is a good possibility that he will buy from you again. Keep a list of everyone who buys or inquires.

Print inexpensive fliers or catalogs and send them out periodically. Once you've built a list of mail-order customers, keep them buying by sending out regular mailings of illustrated specials and new offerings. Always include an order form in your mailings for easy response. Eventually you should consider offering credit-card buying privileges on your order form to encourage easy spending.

Rent mailing lists. When you've begun to show a good mail-order profit, or when you're sure which groups of people will be most likely to buy what you're selling, rent mailing lists that are best for reaching them. A flea-market vendor of kitchen novelties for gourmets was initially surprised to learn that her best customers were male homosexuals. Her surprise turned to delight when she rented mailing lists with names of affluent gay males and ultimately found herself with a post-office box flooded with checks. (See Appendix for representative list of mailing-list brokers.)

Computerize. When you're on your way to becoming a mail-order Midas, you'll find that processing orders, keeping inventory control, and addressing mailing labels is much less time-consuming if you have computer aid. Take time to research the computer market to find the hardware and software that is best for your particular needs.

This is an effective overall plan for building a mail-order clientele. However, it will work only if you have a product which lends itself well to mail-order sales. Many seemingly unlikely products have turned out to be mail-order winners, particularly when marketed by people with good sales backgrounds; however, certain products are ideal for the mail-order beginner.

The ideal product for the mail-order beginner is one that is:

Unique. If you have a product that no one else has, that is not easily obtainable through flea markets, discount stores, and catalogs, you are off to a good start. It may be a product that you have invented, or that someone you know has invented and is allowing you to market. Or it may be an item that you're importing from a supplier you've found off the beaten path.

Some examples of products that people have originated and sold successfully by mail are educational activity cards and cassettes; joke sheets; winning sheets (contests, chess, backgammon); naturejewelry (made from stones, shells, and nuts); instructions on growing prize-winning fruits, vegetables, and flowers; toys for pets; travel toys; executive toys; garage-sale packets (containing how-to pamphlets, signs, and sample ad copy); baby chickens; novelty inventions such as personalized metric converters, dolls' clothing, and fur fabric swatches; pamphlets on stretching exercises for joggers, on eye exercises for tennis players, on how to negotiate when fired from a job, on how to write a will.

Among the biggest mail-order best sellers are various kinds of kits—beer-brewing kits, rug-design kits, vinyl-repair kits, stitchery kits, yogurt-making kits, candle-making kits, toy kits. Regional relics and souvenirs often do well (pieces of Mt. Saint Helen's spill brought one mail-order seller dozens of orders). Make-it-yourself formulas (bug-ridder formulas, nail-growing formulas, hair-growing formulas) have wide appeal too.

Needed. If your product meets a genuine need that no one else has met, or is meeting, or is approaching as a "need-meeter," mail-order ads can lead to a tremendous increase in sales. One clever entrepreneur came up with a small digital clock that flashes time, day, and month, called it Spot O'Time, and marketed it through the mail as a device to be attached to a bathroom mirror. Though this man did not invent the clock, he invented an ingenious use for it (made it a "need-meeter"), and consequently sold many thousands of Spot O'Times, first through the mail, then directly to corporations which have used them as premiums.

An impulse item. Mail-order and impulse buying go well together. An armchair buyer often orders items he never knew he wanted simply because they strike his immediate fancy and mail order is convenient. If your product has whimsical appeal, either for personal use or for gift giving, a well-worded and -illustrated ad targeted to potential buyers can bring in a flood of checks. This is especially true if your ad is timed to correspond to a gift-giving season such as Mother's Day, Christmas, or Graduation.

Well made. Whether selling by mail order or any other way, quality merchandise brings in repeat orders and customer referrals. You must be exceedingly scrupulous when selling by mail, as mail order does have something of a shady past (within the last fifteen years the Direct Mail Marketing Association, which represents the mail order industry in many ways, has done a lot to change that), and does intimidate some buyers. If a customer, particularly a mail-order customer, feels deceived, he will not buy from you again, will not recommend your merchandise to others, and will often go to great lengths to bad-mouth your product. Then it becomes almost impossible to build a good mailing list.

Reasonably priced. Kits for building an MG convertible, costing over $10,000, have been successfully sold by mail-order ads. However, the ideal product for a mail-order novice is one that is inexpensive and quickly recognized as a good buy. Generally, if someone has not done business with you before, or is not familiar with your company, he will be reluctant to lay out a lot of money, regardless of the merit of your offering. This is true whether you are using classified ads, display ads, sending out product literature, or are using any combination of these three. It is particularly true for classified ads which do not invite the potential buyer to send for "free details," but ask him to send a check for $29.95 outright.

Mail-order buyers will easily put two or three dollars in an envelope for something they want. They will send out a check for ten or fifteen dollars for something they want and haven't seen elsewhere. And they will send away for free information or free details. However, generally they will not send large sums through the mail to strangers.

Small and sturdy. Packaging and shipping are important parts of mail-order selling. If a product is poorly packaged or shipped, it may well be destroyed by the time it reaches its destination. Good packaging materials and shipping services don't have to cost a lot, but they do cost something. In general, the larger a product, the more costly (in time and money) it is to package and ship. If you're new to mail order, and have a few good mail-order possibilities, begin by marketing the smallest and least fragile one. Later on you can experiment with the larger-sized ones.

The following are mail-order tips and caveats.

Choose classification headings wisely. If in any publication you notice only one or two offerings under "Pamphlets" week after week, and many under "Moneymaking Opportunities," it is correct to assume that the latter heading is the bigger buyer draw. If you have a product which could fit into either classification (an entreprenuerial pamphlet, for example), place it under "Moneymaking Opportunities."

Be a good imitator. Once you get into the habit of examining classified ads, you'll find that certain ads are repeated frequently and others appear once or twice and never reappear. You can be sure that the ones which keep appearing are drawing the dollars. What are they selling? How are they worded? Are you selling something similar to what they're offering? If you are, imitate the ad-copy style, and place your ad in one of the publications where the winning ad keeps appearing.

A home-based publisher of a "singles" newsletter noticed a recurring ad for a will-writing pamphlet in several publications. Since will writing was one of the topics that had been covered extensively in his newsletter, he decided to recycle his research through mail order. He created a kit containing various necessary legal documents and instructional forms, and placed a small classified ad for a will-writing kit in one of the publications where the ad for the will-writing pamphlet frequently appeared. The ad netted him over $200, was the first of many more similarly profitable ads, and ultimately led him into a profitable offshoot mail-order business. Now, whenever information appears in his newsletter which he feels has pamphlet or kit-making possibilities, he repackages it and gets double mileage out of his initial research. Recently this home-baser made over $2,000 on a divorce kit he put together based on information he had researched for his newsletter.

The advice about imitation that applies to classified ads also applies to direct mailings. What draws you in a direct mailing? What do you consider junk mail and throw out immediately? What mail ads do you hold on to, consider, file away, or order from? Certainly a lot has to do with the particular item being offered and your needs of the moment. But the wording of the ad, the print, the illustrations, and whether or not a prestamped order form is at hand are also important. Analyze the direct mailings that have impressed you or have gotten you to buy. Query others on the direct mailings to which they have responded. If you're marketing your product by direct-mail advertising, as opposed to, or in addition to, placing a small classified, here again find good ad copy that is pitching a product similar to yours and imitate it. Don't imitate it word for word, or idea for idea, or illustration for illustration, but come reasonably close. Those whom you're imitating are already in a position where they can deal with you as an imitator—the same position you will be in when you're making it big and a novice imitates your copy!

Provide fast delivery. It's good for repeat business. Also, there's a Federal Trade Commission ruling that mail-order goods must be delivered within thirty days unless otherwise stated in your ad. If you can't deliver within thirty days, you must notify your customer of this and give him the opportunity to withdraw his order. This is a bother and certainly does not boost sales.

Keep records. Do this for your own information and also for income-tax purposes. When you're just starting to use mail order as a sales booster, you don't think of it as something that will ever mushroom into a solid offshoot business. Because of this many home-basers don't bother to set up a detailed mail-order bookkeeping system. Make sure, from your very first mail-order ad, to keep records of when you place your ads, where you place them, how much they cost, how many you place, and the results of each ad. Mail-order record keeping should be an integral part of your overall bookkeeping system.

Observe mail-order rules and regulations. You don't need a federal permit to sell mail order, but some localities do have laws which all businesses must follow. You can find out if legal authorization is necessary by contacting your nearest business licensing office. This may be your town hall, or a county government office, or your state licensing bureau. If authorization is required, you will be informed as to what costs are involved and what forms must be filed.

Never place misleading or exaggerated ads. The Federal Trade Commission and the Postal Inspector's office have policing power and can impose penalties. The Direct Mail Marketing Association can discredit you in the mail marketing business.

Learn about the mathematics of mail order. It is crucial that you know where you get the best return on your advertising dollar. This is figured by dividing the cost of an ad by the number of orders the ad brought in (cost per ad divided by the number of orders cost per order). You must key your ads in order to know which publications are bringing in your orders. Otherwise you can't figure out where you're getting the best return on your advertising dollar. Dept. M, for example, could be the key in your mail-order address that means "order via ad in *Mechanics Magazine*."

Make your prices simple and appealing to handle: $3,

for example, is better, in mail order, than $2.75 because many people feel more comfortable placing three singles in an envelope than writing out a check for $2.75. (A surprisingly large number of people are willing to send cash up to $3 through the mail.) Also, learn how to package and ship so that you use the mails cheaply and efficiently. Thickly padded mailing bags can be superior to boxes. United Parcel Service is usually cheaper and faster than the postal service.

When using direct mailings think in terms of "sample stuffing." A good sample (see "The Simple-Sample" in Chapter 6), stuffed into a direct mailing, will often extend interest, keep your direct mailing out of the trash can, and act as a silent persuader. A home-based distributer of jean patches tripled his unimpressive mail-order income when he began stuffing sample patches into his mailings. Though his ad copy was well done, it didn't have the same pitching power as attractive ad copy plus an attractive freebie. Similarly, a home-based distributor of colorful "corporate pens" skyrocked her sales by not only including a freebie pen in each well-targeted direct mailing, but also by having each pen personalized with the name, address, and phone number of the company that was receiving the pen. Marketing managers bought hundreds of her corporate pens for their salesmen to distribute to customers and potential customers.

One of the major benefits of all types of direct selling, as opposed to all types of indirect selling, is that you can get fast feedback from those you're serving. Because there are no middlemen between you and your customer, you learn quickly what you're doing right and what you're doing wrong, and what your customers like and don't like, or are tiring of. One mail-order millionaire installed an 800 number "hotline" phone just to encourage customers to call him with their comments, criticisms, complaints, and questions. Though this hotline service is not cheap, it more than pays for itself by permitting this man to be directly in touch with those who are actually ordering and using his products.

The chance to adjust *quickly* to the needs and demands of customers, in what is almost always a buyer's market, is very important. It is a bonus that you do not always reap from indirect selling, since you need agents to keep you in touch. The better and faster they serve you, the better and faster you can serve your public, and the better your sales will be. But because you don't want to be at the mercy of agents for all your information, it is wise for you to combine at least one or two types of indirect selling with at least one or two types of direct selling.

INDIRECT SELLING

Indirect selling is generally regarded as more professional than direct selling. Here you're dealing with the "trade," not with Jane or John Doe. This is fine, but it doesn't mean that you're necessarily going to make more money than by dealing with the public. Sometimes a homebaser gets caught up in "image":"Oh, I don't bother with flea markets; my reps bring me in enough business." If your reps are really bringing you in enough business, great. And if you're more interested in image than in earnings, okay. But if you really want your business to soar, and you're like most home-basers, you should get used to dealing, for now, with both the public and the trade. This means selling to both simultaneously and letting one help you to better understand and deal with the other. But how do you best go about this? Macy's isn't going to deal with you for long if you're selling both to them and at the flea market a few blocks away. A sales agent isn't going to bother with your line if he finds that you're selling it through multilevel sales and he has to compete with several recruits in his territory.

There's no problem in combining all four kinds of direct selling—the home shop, flea-market vending, multilevel sales, and mail order—if you have the time, energy, and desire to do so. But in order to combine direct and indirect selling to maximize profits, you must proceed wisely. Now there are people to answer to.

Chapter 4 discussed the four kinds of indirect selling—trade shows, buyers and buying offices, sales agents, the corporate market—and how to go about selling to each. Now let's analyze how to correctly and profitably coordinate these with the four forms of direct selling.

Trade Shows

Trade-show selling is one of those forms of selling that by itself can make your business soar (as opposed, for example, to the home shop, which, used by itself, will usually not make a business soar). However, rare is the home-baser who starts with trade-show selling, uses it exclusively, and retires rich. One of the best ways to strike gold at trade shows is to sell simultaneously at fleas. Trade shows and flea markets have a lot in common. A carnival atmosphere prevails at both. A booth, or exhibit, is set up at both. Masses of people are in attendance. Buyers approach vendors. Negotiating is common. The main difference is that at trade shows you sell to the trade and at flea markets you sell to the public.

Another difference is that it costs much more to set up at a trade show than at a flea market. This means that each time you exhibit at a trade show, you want to be sure you are selling a product which the public is willing to hand over its dollars for. What sells well at a flea market is likely to sell well at a trade show; so think of using these two forms together—as a " sales program." If you have a good product, you can use just these two, of the eight types of selling, and your business will soar. Here's how one home-baser successfully uses this "sales program":

Lisa sells stickers (children collect them, trade them, and use them for decoration) and friendship beads (tiny multicolored and -shaped pieces of plastic which children collect, put on safety pins, and give as gifts to their pals, who wear them on their sneakers, clothes, hair). She makes and distributes rolls and rolls of different kinds of eye-catching stickers and dozens of styles and shapes of friendship beads. She sets up her rolls of stickers and her bins of beads at flea markets and trade shows all over the country. The flea markets serve three purposes:

First, they give Lisa a way to see for herself which stickers and beads child buyers are most drawn to, which are perennial good sellers, and which are beginning to be rejected for newer versions. This helps her decide what to take to her next trade show and what to consider dropping from her line.

Second, they let her see what her retail competitors have come up with. If they seem to be doing well with new ideas she hasn't thought of, she now considers adding them to her trade-show exhibits.

Last, they provide her with a means for unloading surplus. In addition to using flea markets as testing grounds Lisa uses them as dumping grounds. When she finds that trade-show buyers are no longer interested in certain stickers or beads, she often sells them off to the public at trade prices, which are perceived by the public to be bargain prices (remember the trade always pays less than retail, even flea-market retail). Though this surplus may not move at her regular flea-market prices, there are always enough people around, children and their parents, who will buy because her price makes the offering a "steal."

Just as the flea-market part of Lisa's sales program serves three purposes, so does the trade-show part of the program.

First, trade shows provide a means for checking out the competition, and for acting fast. Do some of the pros know something Lisa doesn't, or have a hot new offering? If they do, they alone won't benefit from their knowledge or offering for long. Even if it's old news by the time she gets to her next trade show, it may well be hot at her next flea-market exhibit. For example, at one trade show Lisa got the idea of displaying friendship beads on color-coordinated barrettes, an idea which resulted in landmark sales at a junior-high-school flea market.

Trade shows are also where the big orders are placed. Lisa loves "fleaing," but it's the wholesaling that gives her her major profits. It's as easy for her to manufacture ten thousand stickers as to manufacture a thousand, so why not sell ten thousand if she can?

Finally, they're where mutually beneficial trade alliances can be struck. For example, at a variety merchandise trade show Lisa met a sneaker manufacturer who decided that some of her tiny "sparkle stickers" would look wonderful on his monotoned sneakers. He bought her entire sparkle sticker exhibit, for less than wholesale, at the close of the show. He used her stickers as premium giveaways to retailers, who used them as buying incentives in their shops. Lisa not only made a fast profit (even with discounting her wholesale price), but her stickers received unanticipated promotion (in shoe stores) which ultimately led to new markets and increased income.

Buyers and Buying Offices

What if you don't like the excitement and carnival atmosphere of fleas and trade shows? Or suppose you don't sell a "crossover" product that can move easily from one industry to another and thus be exhibited at dozens of different kinds of trade shows annually? Visiting buyers and buying offices may be an answer for you. But this alone is usually not enough of an answer. Even the biggest manufacturers seldom rely exclusively on this type of selling. Instead, think in terms of a sales program that includes the use of sales agents and running a part-time or seasonal home shop. The use of sales agents will permit your company to receive exposure in many sections of the country. A part-time or seasonal home shop will provide you with not only a good testing ground but a good outlet for what the trade doesn't want.

Paul, the home-baser whose pottery "people pieces" have collectible appeal, does very well combining buying-office selling with agent and home-shop selling. His business, which now nets him over $30,000 annually, began to take off when he realized that he would never do as well as he wanted to just by selling to buyers and buying offices in his state. He found a sales agent who liked his work and had experience representing potters. This agent now represents Paul in sections of the country that he can't afford the time or money to visit.

Paul has also turned his garage into a home-shop which his wife manages most of the time. Not only is this home shop a profitable outlet for his work (customers like visiting his shop and studio and buying directly), but when Paul fills in for his wife in the shop, he takes time to talk to customers, listen to their comments, answer their questions, and consider their criticisms and requests. Their input influences his output. He has learned that "trade contacts aren't enough for an artist; you've got to talk to the people who are going to be putting your work in their homes."

Agents

As we've seen, agents can represent you in places where you can't, or don't want to, represent yourself. Several successful home-basers have agents who represent them at trade shows in distant parts of the country. They also use these and other agents to show their work to buying offices and store managers that they don't wish to deal with. This is fine if you can find reliable and capable agents who want to represent your work. However, if you want your business to soar, don't rely exclusively on agents. Use them with another type of indirect selling. How about representing yourself at a few not-too-distant trade shows? Or why not talk to some shop owners and get them, if not to purchase your products, at least to try a few on consignment? As long as you're not competing with your sales agent, it's fine. Again, try to reach your buyers directly. Agent selling often goes well with mail-order selling. You're not competing with your agent, and you're reaching for a market segment that he would probably never bring in. So while your agent is building you a trade clientele, why not build yourself a mail-order clientele?

The Corporate Market

This market, consisting of corporations and institutions, is seldom approached by home-basers or their sales agents; and it's almost never approached by home-basers as a "first stop" on the way to success. It's okay if you don't try this market as a first step. Even though it often turns out to be quite a friendly place, it can seem formidable to a home-baser still building her sales skills and confidence. But the fact that the corporate market is very often *never* approached as part of a sales program is sad.

Should little Lenore try selling her lithographs to Corporate America? Consignment at a local shop, a home sale, or a flea market, yes, but the corporate market too? Why not? A local corporation may well decide it can use some of Lenore's lithographs for decoration. A local bank may view them as good gifts for new accounts. And, it's quite possible that a local flea market may be the wrong outlet for them and Lenore won't make a dime.

Corporate-market selling and multilevel sales can also go beautifully together. One home-baser made a mint in one year by selling her handmade lampshades to a timesharing corporation. The corporation used the lampshades in all its model condominiums and its furnished units. This woman might never have thought to approach the timeshare market had she not had a handful of women marketing her lampshades through multilevel sales partyplan selling. A lady at one of the party-plan gatherings turned out to be the wife of a timeshare developer. She fell in love with the lampshades and recommended them to her husband. It was that simple. This home-baser has since successfully approached other real-estate developers and hotel and motel managers with her lampshades.

Corporate-market selling, flea-market selling, multilevel sales, and mail order can all be successfully combined to form a powerful sales program. One very rich home-baser sells his custom-developed vinyl-repair kits to corporate purchasing agents for use on company chairs and couches, to flea-market buyers, to a group of recruits engaging in party-plan selling, and through mail-order classifieds. This man is doing so well now that he's decided to drop fleamarket vending, which he doesn't enjoy, from his sales program. He plans to concentrate on his other three selling methods, which give him greater, and more pleasurable profits, with less effort.

The point of this chapter is to encourage you to combine different types of selling. Try the likely and the unlikely together. One type of selling will work; another may not. One type may help the other. One type used alone may not give you anywhere near enough money to send your child to college or to retire on. A sales program consisting of two types of selling may make it possible for you to fulfill your dreams in style. Always be willing to experiment until you find the combination that pays off for you.

> Big shots are only little shots who keep shooting.
> —Christopher Morley

8

GETTING EXPERT HELP

You've been encouraged in this book to seek guidance from successful home-basers, to consult with trade associations, to consider sales aid from reps and agents, to look into barter clubs, and to get assistance from in-house agencies in placing effective ad copy. These are some ways of bringing expert help to your business. Any "pro input" that can save you from costly mistakes should be sought and heeded. The more you get in the habit of consulting competent and honest experts, the more you learn how critical it is that you continue to do so.

Just as there are general experts whom all home-basers should consult (these are covered below), there are special experts whose help is valuable, and who should be consulted for aid within a given industry or for heading your business in a new direction. If, for example, you're selling food items that you want to have a long shelf life, a good chemist might be able to tell you what preservatives to consider using and which you should avoid. Similarly, if you're considering exporting your products to foreign markets, a professional export agent (see Chapter 9) can save you problems and bring you profits. Or if you're a photographer interested in installing a color darkroom in your home, an experienced lighting technician might be able to give you advice that goes well beyond what's available in the trade publications.

Often it's tempting, and simple, to bypass the pros and follow your own instincts. Don't yield to this temptation. You can always use your instincts, but do so only after you've checked around, after you've consulted several experts. Consulting not only enables a home-baser to avoid expensive errors and gain useful help and information, but it can also result in beneficial operating changes which otherwise might never come about. A home-baser who designs and markets silk flower centerpieces consulted an importer for a list of Oriental suppliers. The importer couldn't supply her with any names better than the ones she already had and was using. However, he offered her the name of a supplier of flowers made from wooden shavings. The home-baser had not considered substituting wood for silk, but when she saw samples of the delicately crafted "shavings flowers," an idea was born—silk and wood combined! The idea worked well and increased sales for this lady who asked for names and ended up using new materials that delighted her.

In addition to getting help from special experts working in areas related to your field, you must also seek advice and help from the masters of the game—from the financial and legal sources who know all about businesses soaring and sinking. Let's look at these sources and see what they can do for you.

BANKERS

Bank loan officers can lend you expansion capital. They can give you a loan to purchase inventory or equipment. They can advance you money on past-due accounts. Though they are not the only source of financing you can turn to, they are a major source, and one that you should investigate if you need funds to try activities which you believe will ultimately boost sales and profits. If you do turn to bankers, you must be able to do so in a way that will get you what you want. What does a bank look for in granting a home-baser a loan? Why will one home-baser secure a $50,000 loan while another equally talented home-baser will be denied any funds?

What Banks Want

Banks, particularly commercial banks, want to lend money. They make money by lending. But they don't necessarily want to lend money to you. Given a choice, they'd prefer to lend it to collateral-rich corporations that don't really need it. However, they're not always given a choice; and when they are, they're not often given enough choices. They need the business of small companies and entrepreneurs. They want promising loan applicants, large and small. In the actual process of loan processing they specifically want:

To be sure you can repay the loan. Even if you have good collateral, banks won't be eager to lend you money if they aren't convinced your business will succeed according to your predictions. They don't like to have to foreclose on loans, go after co-signers, or cash in on collateral. They want to feel that your business is such that you will be able to repay their loan from company income.

To hold collateral. Though they don't want to have to use it, they want it for safety. The more convinced a bank is of your company's future growth (remember it wants you coming around when you're big-time), the less demanding they are about the specific types of collateral they'll accept. Collateral that falls into the "prime" category are: a savings account, bluechip stocks and bonds, a home mortgage, a chattel mortgage (based on possessions), the cost value of a life-insurance policy, and a guarantee by the Small Business Association. However, other collateral is often considered acceptable. So don't be reluctant to offer as collateral the signature of your affluent spouse, a piece of property you own, or some precious gems or collectibles.

To see evidence of your being able to help yourself. You don't have to be willing to cash in on your retirement bonds to finance the color darkroom you want. But you should indicate that you intend to invest some of your savings in whatever project you're planning to undertake. A bank wants to help an applicant who shows that he's prepared to help himself. Make it clear that you're committed to investing your funds and your time in expanding your business.

To see entrepreneurial spirit combined with organizational and managerial skills. If you can put up some cash of your own to finance your undertaking, a loan officer will be favorably impressed. However, your character must also make a favorable impression. An organizational and managerial personality ranks high. Are you successful at organizing time and tasks? Are you good at managing people and money? Do you have evidence that supports these claims? If you've worked for a company where these organizational and managerial skills were demonstrated, provide this information. Do the same if you've worked for a volunteer organization or have been involved in community projects. To what extent have these skills been demonstrated in the creation of your own home-based business? Have you outlined your future plans in detail, with a strong eye toward organization and management? (See "Have a Prepared Business Plan" below, and the "Self-Assessment Questionnaire" in the Appendix.)

To see a community, or local, need for your product. As a home-baser you may be shipping your products all over the country, and possibly to different parts of the world; nevertheless, banks still feel most comfortable lending money to small businesses that can prove a neighborhood need for what they're selling. If the nation and the world likes what you're selling, great. But try to show that you're also meeting a need close to home. Banks like to think of themselves as public-spirited institutions improving the lives of the communities they serve. If, for example, you're manufacturing cosmetics that are selling widely in sun-drenched sections of the country, try to prove that there is also a market for your offerings in your blizzard-battered community. Even if your goods are selling locally only to beauty schools that are buying your surplus at discount, this is still a local market, so play it up. If applicable, present your company as not just a nationwide supplier, but as an "educational supplier" on the local level.

To give short-term loans. Banks don't want to lend a home-baser money for more than five years. They feel it is safest, and most profitable for them, to lend you money at the highest interest rates of the moment. If you've proven a good loan risk, they can then retrieve this money quickly, and relend it to you in the future at interest rates that will probably be higher. Their ideal situation is to lend you money for less than a year. The longer you want a loan for, the more collateral banks require, and the more restrictions they try to impose on your operations. If you need a short-term loan to stock up on additional inventory for a busy season, or to keep up your cash flow while your accounts receivable are dripping in, you are in the best position. Longer-term loans can be obtained, for heavy equipment, fixtures, and even leveraged buyouts of other small businesses; but you will need strong collateral, guarantees, or personal assets to back these loans.

Putting the Loan Odds in Your Favor

There is a lot that you can, and should, do to get what you want from a bank. Never walk into a bank on a whim, just to see what's available to you. Carefully think out what you need in the way of funds and terms, and then go about setting yourself up for success by doing the following:

Choose a local bank friendly to small businesses. You're best off dealing with a neighborhood bank that has demonstrated its interest in aiding local enterprises. Often local business organizations and merchant friends can head you toward the right lending institution. So can your local newspapers. Articles frequently mention area banks sponsoring a local event or providing financing for a neighborhood venture. Make note of the banks that receive this sort of positive press. They'll be more likely to be responsive to your needs than banks that are only written about in relation to huge overseas ventures and massive undertakings.

The ideal situation for you is to have already built a relationship with an area bank. If you haven't, you should start to. Banks are most responsive to their regular customers. Keep several of your accounts, and your mortgage if you have one, at an entrepreneur-friendly local bank. Build some clout, even if it's only a little clout, with this one bank. Get to know the people who work there. Seek their advice on commercial issues. In addition to giving money, banks can give good advice. They have the advantage of research facilities and information services which you don't have. They have easy access to statistics that can sway you in one direction or another. Banks like to provide regular customers with information—it's a good customer service.

Bring in your accountant. If you can convince your accountant to accompany you when applying for a bank loan, do so. If having your accountant accompany you means working around his busy season, work around it. His presence can be extremely valuable. Just the fact that an accountant is with you (if he's known locally, so much the better) gives you and your company a good shot of clout. Add to this the fact that loan officers frequently like to talk in buzz words, or use terms unfamiliar to the average home-baser, and a jargon-savvy accountant becomes still more valuable. No need for you to squirm when the loan officer asks whether you'd prefer a "revolving line of credit" or a "term loan." Your accountant can answer such questions with complete calm.

Seek a loan at least three months before you think you'll need it. Seldom are commercial loans granted quickly to home-basers. The process takes awhile. Credit investigations are made. Often a loan committee has to convene to vote on your worthiness. Patience is required, and if you start to appear anxious or desperate, you can easily blow your chances of getting what you want. Advance planning is a must here.

Sell before you tell. Sell a loan officer on lending you money before you tell him the amount you want to borrow. Once the bank views you and your company as credit-worthy, negotiating specific sums becomes a simpler task. Do all you can to convince the lending institution that you are running a credible, credit-worthy enterprise. Depending upon your particular operation, you can invite a bank representative to visit your base of operations, and/or you can bring in samples of your work, photographs, literature that supports the need and positive outlook for a venture such as yours, references from bank-respected local citizens—anything which helps to establish you as a good loan prospect.

Ask for more than you need. Banks are conservative institutions, particularly where home-basers are concerned. It's quite likely that whatever you ask for, you will be answered with an offer for less. If your figures show that you need $15,000 in order to proceed comfortably, ask for $20,000.

Don't be a supplicant. For some reason inexperienced loan seekers and small entrepreneurs often view banks as potential favor bestowers. A bank isn't doing you a favor if it lends you money. It is doing business with you. You are a loan customer paying for the money you are borrowing. If anything, you are doing the bank a favor by giving them your business instead of taking it elsewhere. When you approach a loan officer, approach him as a business person interested in purchasing a service, not as a needy novice pleading for his aid. You'll bring your dreams to life and make your business soar with or without his help. If you don't borrow money from his bank, you'll get it elsewhere. And you'll remember those who helped you, and those who didn't, when you're big-time and everyone wants to help you!

Don't lie and don't conceal important truths. Banks have enormous resources for finding out what they want to know. If, for example, a loan officer asks if you've been rejected for a loan by another bank, don't think you're saving face by saying no if the answer is yes. Loan applications, rejected or accepted, are filed in credit reporting bureaus to which all banks have access. So are many other facts related to your credit-worthiness.

If one bank turns you down, try to find out why and use this information to your advantage in applying to another bank. Banks are influenced by each other's rejections, but they are competitors, and they are also influenced by honesty. "Yes, First Nationwide turned down my application. They claimed they didn't have any funds left for inventory loans such as I'm requesting. This may be partially true, but I think the loan committee was negatively influenced by the fact that my spouse is ultra-liberal politically." By answering questions frankly, and supplying a bank with information that it will learn anyway, you're establishing yourself as trustworthy. Now let the bank officer ask you if you feel your husband's politics should have any bearing on your being granted a loan. (Of course you've prepared for this question and have the perfect disclaiming answer on hand.)

Have a prepared business plan. All of the above is crucial to your success in getting the loan you want; but this is the clincher. Be prepared to submit a carefully worked out, detailed business plan for the bank's examination. Ninety-five percent of all home-basers don't submit detailed business plans, and coincidentally, ninety-five percent of all home-basers don't earn more than $5,000 annually even when they do manage to eke out small loans from neighborhood banks.

A prepared business plan is a blueprint for your future success. It forces you to think through every detail of your operation. Supersuccessful home-basers, whether they're applying for a loan or not, almost always work from blueprints. They are meticulous and realistic planners who outline strategies for their businesses' immediate and long-range futures. There is no one way in which a business plan should be written (typed, actually). However, the Small Business Association has pamphlets available which describe the basic elements of a business plan and how to write one. They also provide outlines for loan proposals.

Following is a general list of what to include in a business plan accompanying a loan application: *an overview of your company* (what is your business all about? what does it do?); *an inventory list* (what stock and equipment does your business own?); *a personal résumé* (what qualifies you to run this business, and especially, to make it soar?); *business references* (what respected notables or local citizens are dealing with your company?); *a projected balance sheet for the next three years with a projected operating statement* (including projected cash flow and payroll expenses); *projected sales assumptions*.

All of these things should be prepared with the help of a good accountant who has research statistics on operations similar to yours and can provide you with a realistic breakdown of your projections. By providing the bank a well-thought-out, professionally prepared business plan, you're giving it something solid to examine in processing your loan request. Inevitably the bank will be impressed by the fact that you're a responsible, reliable credit risk. The loan odds swing to your favor.

THE SMALL BUSINESS ADMINISTRATION

The SBA is often talked about as the place to turn if you're turned down for a bank loan. It is this, to some extent, but it is also a lot more. The SBA is a federally financed government agency whose primary interest is to strengthen the national and local economies by aiding small business owners. SBA experts will consult with you, free of charge, on issues ranging from financing to franchising to exporting. They can provide you with more than five thousand pieces of literature on every imaginable aspect of small business building and maintenance. You can write for a publications list from which you can order free business guides, or you can visit your local SBA office if you wish to consult personally with local small business authorities. While there, you can pick up dozens of useful pamphlets and sheets free or for a very nominal fee. They are an excellent resource library for any home-baser—an expert source of business aid which almost all supersuccessful home-basers have used, and use frequently. The SBA's address is:

> Small Business Association
> P.O. Box 15434
> Ft. Worth, TX 76119

In addition to providing consulting services, and a vast store of literature, the SBA sometimes provides financial services in the way of loan guarantees and loans. The SBA may come to your rescue if you've been denied bank financing. This rescue could be in the form of guaranteeing a bank loan for you, acting as a co-loaner with a bank, or granting you a direct loan. However, the SBA is not eager to give home-basers, or any small business owners, expansion capital—regardless of how promising a business appears, or how good its potential for soaring seems. It is a nonprofit organization. It does not make money by lending money and it simply does not have a lot of funds to give. During some political administrations the SBA gets more allotments than during others, but it is never overflowing with handout reserves.

You can qualify for SBA loan consideration by providing evidence that you've been refused bank financing and by submitting a good business plan, personal credit record, and references. If you get an SBA loan, you'll get a better interest rate than a bank will give you, and you may well get a longer-term loan. SBA loans are usually, but not always, limited to those businesses which can show that they in some way serve national or local interests. If, for example, you are requesting funds to go into exporting or to increase your output by hiring unemployed minority workers, you will fall into an SBA loan priority category. You will stand a reasonable chance of getting an SBA loan of some sort. It is important to stress here that whether or not you qualify for SBA loan assistance, you always qualify for SBA advice and you should get into the habit of getting it whenever you need business information. Don't think of the SBA as primarily a lending institution. To do so is to do yourself out of some valuable expert help.

LAWYERS AND LEGAL EXPERTS

Getting a lawyer, or expert legal aid, will not help your home-based business grow, but it can keep it from shrinking. You might ask how much legal help a home-baser really needs once his business is set up and running. The answer is probably not a lot. However, we live in a nation of existing laws, changing laws, new laws, and lawsuits, and it's crucial that you know your rights and obligations regarding any law affecting your particular business. If you fail to comply with certain laws, either because of neglect or ignorance, you can end up in jail and/or paying a fine up to $25,000, to say nothing of losing your business entirely.

What can a home-baser do that can possibly result in a $25,000 fine? He can distribute certain piecework to other home-basers and be in violation of the Fair Labor Standards Act. He can innocently sell a product that is deemed to be dangerous. One home-baser was sued and fined for selling cloisonné jewelry that was judged to be radiation-contaminated. Or he can employ helpers on premises that are deemed to be unsafe. Acts such as the Consumer Product Safety Act and the Occupational Safety and Health Act, for example, include thousands of regulations which can very much affect a home-baser. Does this mean you should hire an attorney to see if your operation is in any way in violation of these and other acts? You can do this if you have good reason to believe you might have a problem. It's easier than spending countless hours of your business time poring over legalese which you might or might not understand. However, it's also very expensive. Your best bet is to first seek assistance from your trade association. There are usually legal experts within every trade association who keep up with the legislation affecting members of their trade. Or it's quite likely that your membership dues in an organization related to your interests entitle you to consult with special attorneys (usually for a small fee) who are well versed on legislation that applies directly to people in your trade. Or you might consult with your insurance carrier if you have questions about your legal safety. Again, the SBA can be a good source of legal aid in many instances.

If you don't already have a lawyer and decide you want to hire one to answer specific questions, perform specific tasks, examine the rules and regulations you must obey, or give you preventive legal advice, make sure you hire wisely. You'll need an attorney who specializes in small businesses and has a reasonable familiarity with home-basing. If he is familiar with your particular business, and enthusiastic about it, so much the better.

One home-based potter was granted a commission to do a complete line for a large dinnerware company. Though she was delighted and knew it would mean a substantial boost for her business, she was worried about taking on helpers and whether her premises were occupationally safe for outside labor. She also felt unsure signing the lengthy contracts she had been given. She wanted legal assistance. A craftsmen's organization that she belonged to put her in contact with a lawyer who was experienced in working with craftspeople and who enjoyed doing so. The lawyer was so enthused about this home-baser's pottery that when she questioned him about his fees, he countered her questions with a barter offer. He would give her the legal assistance she wanted in exchange for some of her pieces. A deal was struck. Both parties were satisfied, and the potter went on to larger commissions and barter deals with her lawyer, who became a devoted patron.

If you can find an entrepreneurial-minded lawyer interested in representng small businesses (most lawyers aren't), who wants to barter with you, or who is willing to consider a barter arrangement, by all means deal in this manner if it is to your liking. However, you may not fall into such a situation. It's more likely that you'll have to discuss fees. If this is the case, do so in a businesslike manner. Try to find a young, new, local lawyer who is eager for business and well recommended as capable and honest. Interview him to see how much he knows about homebasing and about your industry (ask ahead of time if he charges for an interview; don't assume that he does or doesn't). If you like what you see and hear, negotiate fees thoroughly and specifically. Make sure you indicate exactly what you want done and what you don't. Payment per job is usually preferable to payment per hour.

Don't waste your money hiring a lawyer to do simple tasks that you can do yourself quickly and easily. One home-baser hired a lawyer to get him a resale license. The lawyer was honest enough to tell the man that it was only a matter of filling out a simple form. Nevertheless, this home-baser wouldn't listen. The lawyer had his secretary obtain the license and he billed his client $100. The client was outraged; but it was his own fault. Lawyers don't come cheap and it's foolish to use them for tasks that don't require legal expertise.

It's equally foolish, and very costly, to call in a lawyer at the zero hour. If you suspect you might be heading for trouble, don't wait until after the fact to get legal help. Plan well ahead. One home-based publisher knew her work was going to be plagiarized, was advised by her trade association to have a lawyer issue a cease-and-desist order on the would-be plagiarizer, and still she procrastinated. After her plagiarized work appeared in print she became furious and decided to sue. A capable lawyer agreed to take on the case but advised her that there was a good chance she wouldn't get any compensation, that the case could drag on for a long time, and that her legal costs would be considerable. The publisher decided to let the matter drop, to take revenge in petty ways, and four years later she is still seething about something she could have prevented quickly and cheaply.

ACCOUNTANTS AND BOOKKEEPERS

You need them! Good record keeping is a must. Poor record keeping can prevent your business from growing even more than poor marketing can. You need a clear and accurate picture of what's going on financially to guide your business decisions. Unfortunately, the more a business grows, the more complex its bookkeeping becomes. If, at the very beginning you used cash-basis accounting, and did all the bookkeeping yourself, you no longer can. Increased inventories, orders from wholesalers and retailers, and quantity purchases have forced you into credit financing and accrual accounting. Though you haven't yet built your financial empire, a paper empire is forming quickly. The temptation, when things are humming, or when you're expansion-motivated, is to temporarily push aside the paper and concentrate on business. Yet, ironically, by pushing aside the paper, you're doing just the opposite. You can't concentrate on your business without concentrating on the paper it generates.

It is crucial that you always have a complete and updated record of your company's financial health. What is your current inventory? your current accounts payable (what you owe)? your current accounts receivable (money owed you)? your payroll expenses? loans due? taxes due? What is your current cash flow (actual cash in hand to pay what you owe)? If sales are up and orders are coming in, or if you're working on making this happen, you probably don't have a lot of time to devote to all this. Or you may hate record keeping. Whatever the case, if you're not doing it, someone reliable must be—and you must be overseeing them and understanding what they're doing. (See Chapter 11: "Figurephobia.")

Whether you do your own bookkeeping, use a bookkeeping service, an accountant, or some combination of these, should depend upon your particular business and its changing needs as it grows. By this time your business is well beyond a nickle-and-dime hobby/enterprise and you need a certified public accountant working for you—even if only to file required tax reports and represent you in a tax audit, if necessary. He will set up your records to show that though your business is home-based, it is a serious operation with profit-making intentions and not in any way a hobby or pastime. (If the IRS views your enterprise as a hobby, losses are disallowed.)

Your accountant should be someone who is able to take a combination of recorded figures (sales, purchases, income, taxes) and present them to you as financial facts—facts from which you can make business-boosting decisions. "Margaret, your accounts receivable show that Calico Creatures waits months and months to pay your invoices, despite repeated requests, and when they do pay, the payment is always followed by a large reorder, which again goes unpaid for several months. If this continues, your cash flow can be damaged to the point where you'll have to take out a high-interest inventory loan to fund their tardiness." With information such as this you can decide immediately how to deal with Calico Creatures. (You might offer them a discount incentive for orders paid within thirty days; you might offer to ship COD and not bill them UPS charges; you can request partial payment before shipping; or you might pursue one of several other possibilities.)

If you don't already have a good accountant (or you have one you don't like), seek out recommendations from your trade association, from business acquaintances, from friends. You need someone who is experienced with small business accounting, who is sympathetic to your goals, and who likes to explain things to his clients. Beware of mystery men who do nothing but send you forms to sign and bills to pay.

The right accountant, giving you the right advice, can save you his fees many times over. He can point out where your true profits lie, pitfalls you're unaware of (for example, you may be concentrating your promotion efforts on favored items which allow you only a small markup and ignoring items which provide a much higher markup), and penalties that could be forthcoming if certain changes aren't undertaken. He can keep your taxes to the lowest legal amount, advise you of the financial consequences of new decisions (one home-baser was warned that paying a certain major supplier early in order to get a discounted price and avoid interest charges would destroy her cash flow), inform you about changes in tax laws, help you to get loans, and show you how to formulate a realistic budget and projections.

Having quality financial advice from a good accountant is invaluable. But it is not enough. You need expert bookkeeping help also. An accountant needs complete and updated bookkeeping figures from which to work. How much bookkeeping help you need depends on the nature of your business and on your personal nature. Do you have a good head for details? Are you inclined to record all figures and transactions promptly, or do you tend to keep financial facts juggling around in your head? If you have recordkeeping talents as well as marketing talents, you have a dynamic duo going. You can save yourself bookkeeping expenses by keeping your own daily records—by recording daily sales, expenses, and billings. And you can get your sales soaring: remember, it is your daily and weekly journal and ledger entries that your accountant will use to make up the income statements and balance sheets which will give you the overall picture of your business's financial health and permit you to make ongoing business-building decisions.

If you don't have the time, or inclination, to do daily bookkeeping, you must hire a capable part-time bookkeeper. In addition to keeping your records current, she can keep your billings current (the faster you bill, the faster your accounts-receivable payments, the better your cash flow). If your books are a mess or you need a new system, you may be able to get free assistance from SCORE (Service Corps of Retired Executives), which is an SBA-sponsored program intended to guide small business owners in managing their operations with maximum effectiveness. Regardless of how much bookkeeping aid you get, or how much you hate being responsible for the financial recording of your business's activities, never let a great gap grow between what you're doing for your business and how others are recording your actions on paper. You don't have to do posting if you hate it. You don't have to fill out forms if it pains you to do so. But you are the boss and you must always keep a watchful and knowing eye on your company's fiscal portrait. The more your business grows, the higher your taxes (up to 50% of income!), the better the IRS likes you, and the more closely they watch you.

In recent years computers and computer software have made it easy and inexpensive for accountants, bookkeepers, and business owners to prepare financial reports and keep neat records. Data can be entered, changed, and manipulated by just pressing a few keys. "What if" projections can be made. Facts can be called up instantly to make comparisons or check the results of a new procedural plan. One home-baser who runs a Dial-a Cookie bake shop used her computer to help her decide if she should add a dial-a-brownie service to her operation. The computer showed her the circumstances under which it would and would not be a profitable move. Another home-baser used his computer to help him decide whether or not to offer customers credit-card privileges. If your business has reached the point where it can profit from computerization, look into it.

A computer-comfortable accountant (and most are today) can guide you. He can show you how to use a computer to make business decisions such as the above and to keep everyday records. It is not hard to learn how to feed information into these machines or how to get the output you want. Don't let machinephobia (again, see Chapter 11) keep you from computerizing if it will save you time, money, and work.

INSURANCE AGENTS

Consulting insurance agents is seldom among the top priorities of home-basers. Insurance is neither interesting nor business-boosting. If anything, it's dull, bothersome, and costly—easy to put off thinking about. Getting help from an expert insurance agent is something you "intend" to do. Every home-baser agrees that as his business grows he'll have to look into getting insurance, or more insurance than he already has, or finding an experienced and honest agent. However, it is generally a put-off activity.

Getting expert insurance help is usually put off until one of two things occurs: either you suffer a financial loss that could have been avoided had you been properly insured or an acquaintance in a business similar to yours suffers a loss or is forced into bankruptcy because of lack of adequate coverage. Now what usually happens is that instead of maintaining a "put-off" stance, you adopt a "must-have" attitude. This would be okay except that here you're also vulnerable. You're frightened and you're eager—an easy target for a self-serving insurance agent.

Don't put off getting adequate coverage and don't rush to get it either. Buy calmly, carefully, and from a position of strength. If you don't already have an excellent agent and solid, comprehensive, coverage, get both. Your trade association and business acquaintances can make recommendations which you can follow up on. However, the best recommendation is often from people who have dealt with a particular agent or his company *after* a loss has been suffered. Most agents and insurance companies are friendly enough before any damage occurs, before they have to make good on a policy or pay out anything. What you should know is how do they come through when you need them? Do they find a lot of fine print that brings their obligation to a pittance? Do they take forever to process claims, leaving clients not only anxious, but with rapidly shrinking cash flows? You want an insurance agent and an insurance company who are good after the fact, who have proven loyal and reliable in time of need.

What else should you have in an insurance agent? You want an agent who is a good "explainer." Beyond the standard policies available, there are others you should be aware of as a home-baser. Your agent should be more than a "tell and sell" man—"Ms. Jones, I will tell you what you need and sell it all to you under one nice umbrella policy." You want someone trustworthy, experienced in dealing with entrepreneurs such as yourself, and interested in taking the time to understand your business and give you a few options. He should be willing and able to explain the benefits and drawbacks of each kind of insurance, and let you decide those that would be best for your particular operation. If you choose to go with inferior coverage, he can voice his opinion, giving you specific reasons why you should rethink your choice. But the final decision, of course, must be yours.

There are those who will tell you you're best off dealing with a large agency which handles all forms of insurance. The reasoning is that you have access to several specialists all employed by one company, and that you're considered an important customer because this one company is selling you *all* your policies. There are also those who will advise you not to deal with a large insurance company, but with an independent agent. The reasoning here is that an independent agent doesn't work for just one company and can get you the best deals from several different companies; additionally, as an independent agent, he is a small businessperson, sometimes a home-baser, like yourself, and thus more in tune with your personality. There are still others who will tell you not to deal with one large company, or with an independent agent, but to combine—deal with a couple of large companies, a couple of independents, or a large company and an independent. Here the reasoning is that you're best served by having the differing opinions and information of more than one insurance expert. Also, by combining, you can use one carrier to review the policies and prices of the other, thus keeping both on their toes and eager to please you. All of these positions have merit and should be considered.

Whatever position you agree with, you'll want an agent who has taken the time to meet proscribed professional standards—preferably an agent who has earned the titles that certify him as learned and competent in the insurance field. Such agents have abbreviations after thir names: CLU (Certified Life Underwriter), CLCU (Certified Liability and Casualty Underwriter), or both. They're usually proud of these credentials, take them seriously, and maintain a required professional code of ethics. Generally, professionals of this caliber keep current in their field and will keep you current if you keep after them to do so. They pay attention to detail and change, and as your company grows and the areas of potential risk increase, they are in a position to advise you of your new needs and new options available to you.

As a home-baser interested in boosting your income, you're probably used to cutting corners. While this can be good in such areas as purchasing supplies at closeouts or booth sharing at trade shows, it is not a good idea where insurance is concerned. When you cut corners by under-insuring your business, you're gambling. You're taking dangerous risks. Make sure that any agent you consider is able to cover the following kinds of insurance. You needn't take them all if they're not relevant to your particular business, but you must know about them all and about the consequences of not having them. Certainly it's foolish to overinsure; but it's reckless to underinsure!

Casualty. Casualty covers your business in the event of severe hardships such as fire or storm damage. There are lots of loopholes, so read the fine print.

Liability. Here you're covered if someone is injured on your premises or, in the case of "product liability," if someone is injured by using your product. Product liability should be particularly considered by home-basers making food products, as users sometimes sue for food poisoning whether or not manufacturer or product are actually to blame.

Malpractice. Consider this if you're in a position where a customer is likely to sue you for acting in error. One home-baser who sells crushed scents made of herbs and dried flowers was sued by an allergy sufferer who claimed he was not advised that the product could be harmful to people with allergies. With all products you should protect yourself by issuing any warnings pertinent to the product. However, this isn't always possible, so question your insurance agent about situations similar to your own where malpractice insurance has been proven to be necessary.

Key man. A lot of home-basers don't know about this valuable insurance. Basically it insures you or any employee valuable to your company (such as a star sales rep responsible for a majority of your orders) in the event of death.

Partnership. If you have a partner, look into this. It can be very important should your partner die.

Theft. Think of this in terms of customer theft, intruder theft, and employee theft.

Equipment. Major pieces of equipment should be insured against malfunction or breakdown. If, for example, you have a company truck, make sure it (and whoever is driving it) is adequately covered.

Business interruption. Here's another valuable type of insurance unknown to many home-basers. Suppose your business is temporarily stopped or slowed down by hurricane damage to your home, or by hurricane damage to a major customer who won't be purchasing from you for the three months it takes to rebuild his shut-down premises. Your business is interrupted, but your normal business expenses are covered during the crisis.

Bad debt. This insures you if a customer goes bankrupt before paying you money owed or, under certain circumstances, if a customer can't be forced to pay his debts to you. Instead of having to write off a delinquent account as a loss, you're covered for the bad debt.

Workers' Compensation. If you have employees, make sure you have this. If an employee is injured while working for you, you are responsible. Your liability can be great, so don't take any chances.

Life, Medical, Employee benefits. These are three different types of insurance, all self-explanatory and all well known. They are grouped here because if you have a few employees working for you, you may be able to benefit from group rates—it might be financially advantageous for you to purchase these policies through your business rather than as an individual. Check with your agent.

These are the major types of insurance you should look into. However, there are others. Today there are numerous types of insurance available and new ones coming out periodically. Different companies and different agents offer different plans, combinations, and umbrella policies. If one agent can't tell you all you want to know or meet all your needs, take the best he has to offer and go further. Not only will insurance protect you and your business, but you won't be granted a bank loan without certain types of coverage. Make sure you get whatever you need—insurance is not a business booster but it's very definitely a business safeguard. Some insurance policies are remarkably inexpensive; always ask prices and comparison price shop. In all cases *read the fine print before buying. As wonderful as your agent may be, he is still your adversary in a sense*. In the case of loss, damage, destruction or disaster he and his company are going to want to pay you as little as possible; and you, and your business, are going to need and want to get as much as possible.

BUSINESS CONSULTANTS

These experts get both good and bad press. You've heard the saying, "Those who can, do; those who can't, teach." This is how some view business consultants—as "experts" who give advice to entrepreneurs, but who have no entrepreneurial abilities or successes themselves. They are regarded as little more than overschooled formula faddists dispensing packaged solutions to free-wheeling doers and risk-takers.

Business consultants are also viewed positively. They are seen as students of small business who have the know-how to skillfully guide a small enterprise to financial fame and fortune. They are not scorned as professional advice givers, but are admired as experts on what makes a business succeed or fail and on what constitutes the entrepreneurial personality.

There is no one "right" view. Some business consultants aren't worth much; and they don't usually go far in their careers. But some are excellent. They have analyzed dozens of entrepreneurial successes and failures and have come up with solid, applicable conclusions. They have learned how to zero in on trouble spots and create turnaround situations quickly and efficiently. Sometimes they have had the nuts-and-bolts experience of building successful enterprises of their own. Consultants of this caliber can be worth their fees many times over, and their services should be sought when traditional approaches haven't produced adequate results.

One home-based manufacturer of toys for slow learners consulted several in-house advertising specialists, public-relations people, and her accountant, in an attempt to shoot some adrenaline into her business. She got some good results and her sales did increase; but it wasn't until after she spent a few hours with a well-chosen business consultant that her enterprise really began to move. The consultant was able to look beyond standard product promotion and budget-trimming techniques. She advised her client to try *really* out-of-the-way, untapped, possibly high-potential markets, and to increase prices and charge interest on late payments.

Here was the reasoning: The toys for slow learners had been advertised in all the "right" places. The press had cooperated in doing some features on the home-baser and her unusual offerings. The business had trimmed all fat and was operating on a conservative budget. Close analysis of the business indicated that a new low-cost marketing approach had to be tried, and that the business's cash flow had to be increased by an aggressive, not a budget-trimming, move.

The new low-cost marketing approach began with an ad in a *"really* out-of-the-way" publication for health-food believers. The ad, which cost $15, brought in sixty inquiries and eleven sales for a total of over $400. The business consultant had figured correctly—a new marketing approach was needed—and she had guessed correctly—many people who were into health foods and "pure" living were into the best kinds of toys possible for their children who weren't performing up to par. More ads were placed in this and other publications aimed at spiritualist readers. The responses were excellent, sales figures multiplied, and, as a bonus, the home-baser found herself doing business with unusual characters whom she truly liked.

The reasoning behind the aggressive pricing move was that many of the people and institutions who had been buying this home-baser's specialized toys were used to being extended exceptional courtesies and often took months to respond to invoices. This led to cash-flow problems which the consultant felt must be met with increased prices and interest charges on late payments. Again her advice proved excellent—the slight price increase went unnoticed and the usually delinquent payers paid more promptly.

This toy manufacturer was fortunate to find an innovative consultant who was perfect for her needs, who was able to think successfully beyond the advice of standard professional experts. It is not easy to find the perfect consultant; however, it can be done.

The best way for a home-baser to find the right consultant is through the "seminar approach." Business consultants are frequent speakers at the many seminars and courses aimed at, or given for, small business owners. As a home-baser you should be attending these events regularly and asking questions of the speakers during the question-and-answer periods. Sometimes a problem that is troubling you can be quickly solved on the spot. And sometimes you will find a speaker who you feel is right for your needs, someone you'd be willing to pay for a few hours of consultation. Here you've had the chance to see and hear the expert in person. Now approach him and see if an appointment can be set up. Business consultants often speak at seminars and give courses in order to drum up clients, so don't be afraid to offer them your business.

Another way to find a suitable consultant is through the publications they write for or the books they write. If you read a column, an article, or a book by a business writer who addresses problems such as yours in a manner you find appealing, write to the consultant, in care of the publication, and see if you can avail yourself of his services. Again, many business consultants write in trade and other publications in the hope of acquainting readers with their approaches and attracting clients to their private practices. Like yourself, they are home-basers who use public forums to establish themselves as authority figures, acquaint the public with their offerings, and build their incomes.

One home-based mail-order seller read a book written by a mail-order millionaire (beware of those who tell you how to make millions but haven't done it themselves), found the book extremely helpful, but found there were a few questions not answered there that perhaps the writer could answer for her. She wrote to him, stated her questions, and asked if it would be possible for her to pay for a half-hour's consulting time over the phone. (The writer lived in a distant city.) Within a week the home-baser received a three-page letter, gratis, answering all her questions, and wishing her great luck with her business. Apparently this expert didn't need to build a client roster, but was nevertheless interested in having a good public image.

Another way to find a business consultant is through special-interest organizations offering aid to individuals who fall within a certain classification. One home-baser, for example, read about a Dialing for Answers service set up primarily for female entrepreneurs with urgent business problems. Run by the American Woman's Economic Development Corporation, it was described as a telephone hotline consulting service "staffed by management consultants, entrepreneurs, professors, and retired business people ready to answer any business questions" between 10:00 A.M. and 5:00 P.M. EST. For $5, a caller could ask one ten-minute question and bill the call on a major credit card or pay in advance by check. More difficult problems could be handled by a related telephone or in-person counseling service. (For information, phone 800-222-AWED; in New York state, call 800-442-AWED; and in New York City, Alaska, or Hawaii, call 212-692-9100.) This home-baser, in just a few minutes, and for a tiny sum, was able to receive the answers to questions that had been bothering her for months.

In purchasing the services of business consultants, or any other experts, don't ever feel bound to the services of any one of them. Shop around if you're not completely satisfied. Get bids on specific jobs or time allotments. Let those experts you're considering see what you're presently getting for your money and compete for your business. Remember, you want the experts so that your business will grow and they want you so that their businesses will grow. You may be a small account now, but you won't be for long, and many experts are clever enough to want to get in on the ground floor of a growing enterprise. Deal with these professionals as you do with your suppliers—aim for the best service at the best price.

9

EXPORTING MADE EASY

Does the thought of exporting your product to foreign markets seem overwhelming? Does it seem like a complex, costly concept requiring knowledge of dozens of detailed how-to's? The reality is that exporting abroad can be as easy for you as filling domestic orders. You should, however, make sure that there is an overseas market for your products. If you're handling any of the following (or similar, related) items, read this chapter carefully: healthcare products, medical products or equipment, cosmetics, perfume, environmental equipment, clothing, electronics equipment, sporting goods, chemical products, scientific instruments, do-it-yourself kits, low-tech consumer products, high-tech consumer products, long-life food products and additives, tools, audio accessories, automotive equipment, cleansing products, component parts, simple machinery, and books or specific supplies suitable to the climate, culture, and sophistication of specific foreign nations.

If you don't handle any of these products, your prospects of finding overseas representation are not currently strong. But the economic situation changes quickly; products for which there is presently little need abroad may find a strong market there in the future. For example, there is currently a demand in Third World countries for automotive equipment and for audio accessories; this demand did not exist several years ago. So if you don't presently handle any of the products mentioned, hold off on approaching the export market for now, and keep it as a future business-building opportunity.

Exporting *can* be easy—provided, that is, that you delegate the technical aspects of the sales process to an intermediary. It is not recommended that an inexperienced home-baser take on the entire task of exporting. This would be direct exporting, where you find the overseas market for your product and ship the goods there yourself. It involves considerable know-how as well as heavy detail work—market research, paper work, special shipping, learning legal aspects—and is not for the novice.

However, indirect exporting is another matter. Here, no more demand is put on you than in selling to home markets. The reason for this is the accessibility of the export management company. An export management company will take over the entire task of exporting for you. It will purchase your goods at a discounted price (about 15% beneath wholesale) and sell them to foreign markets for a profit. All you have to do is be able to mass-produce, find an export management company that specializes in what you're selling, and see if a mutually lucrative deal can be struck. You don't have to do anything more than you're doing now, yet your sales and profits can increase dramatically. Let's look at exactly what export management companies do, what you should look for before affiliating yourself with one or more of them, and what you can do to reap the best possible results from this form of indirect selling.

EXPORT MANAGEMENT COMPANIES

These companies are market-driven organizations—they research the needs of the marketplace, and seek to meet these needs by buying high-demand, low-cost, quality goods from several sources and selling these goods to those select foreign markets where they get the best prices. All their energy is devoted to acting as intermediaries in international trade. They are the specialists for companies that want export profits, but do not have the facilities, interest, or experience needed to sell abroad. An export management company doesn't care whether you're operating from a family room or a factory as long as your products can be profitably sold overseas. Almost all export management companies:

Represent several manufacturers of allied, but noncompetitive, products. Some companies represent as few as four companies, others as many as fifty. Often the larger firms have several divisions, each division specializing in a field or industry. This product specialization permits them to concentrate their efforts in circumscribed areas, so they can become strong forces in those areas. Consequently the firm's needs and yours are well served.

Provide a complete range of client services. This includes affiliations with overseas distributors and reps, exhibition of client merchandise at international trade shows, continuous analyses of traditional and new market needs, billing and financial services, advertising, legal, packaging, labeling, shipping, and documentation services. All a client has to do is fill the orders.

Are sociologically alert. They deal with overseas accounts in the appropriate foreign tongues and with an awareness of foreign customs and beliefs. Certain countries, for example, don't like specific numbers or colors. In Japan, four is considered the number of death. In much of Africa, red is associated with witchcraft, Satan, and death. In Taiwan, triangular shapes represent difficulties.

Regularly monitor their overseas contacts and overseas economic and political conditions. A seemingly minor insurrection can mean the end of a relationship with one local agent and possibly the beginning of one with another.

Cover specific sections of the world. Most export management companies concentrate their efforts in a few countries to the exclusion of others. One company will have major inroads in the Latin American countries. Another will specialize in Asia and Africa. If you find yourself doing well in the export market, you may decide to work with more than one company to gain greater world coverage.

Require you to sign a contract with them. This is reasonable. If a company is going to devote its efforts to expanding your markets, they want to benefit from their groundwork, at least for the two- or three-year duration of a contract.

Extend credit privileges. Most export management companies today extend credit terms up to six months to well-established foreign customers. These terms attract overseas buyers, as they enable them to sell their purchases before paying for them. A foreign buyer is induced to buy your offerings, yet you don't have to worry about letters of credit, prolonged accounts receivable, or delinquent accounts. You are paid promptly by the export marketing company—a procedure much preferable to having to invoice customers yourself.

How to Find an Export Management Company

These companies are not hard to find, but neither are they located on your neighborhood Main Street. An excellent way to quickly contact several export management companies is to write to:

The Federation of Export Management Companies
P.O. Box 7612
Washington, D. C. 20044

Your letter should be brief, stating simply that you're interested in exporting your products and are enclosing a dozen product brochures for inspection by member companies. Your literature will be distributed to regional members who will determine if your product may be profitably taken on. Those companies who feel they may be able to do well with your offerings will contact you to set up meetings. They will have a chance to meet you and examine your products. And you will have the opportunity to check them out.

Another way to gain quick access to several export management companies is by contacting NEXCO:

National Association of Export Management Companies
200 Madison Ave.
New York, N.Y. 10016

This organization has over one hundred member companies and will refer you to those members who handle products allied to yours. Here all you need send is a short letter stating your interest in exporting and the product you manufacture or distribute domestically. When you receive a list of appropriate companies to contact, you can send them your product literature with a covering letter.

In addition to contacting the Federation of Export Management Companies and NEXCO, see what expert advice and leads you can get from trade specialists at your nearest Commerce Department District Office, from your trade association, from your bank, and from the local office of the Small Business Association. Often these sources can also give you details about a company's principals.

In October 1982 the Export Company Trading Act was passed by Congress. The overall aim of this act was to boost exports of American goods worldwide by permitting competing firms to form Japanese-style export trading companies (without fear of prosecution under U.S. antitrust laws) and by allowing bank holding companies to own or invest in these companies (thus helping to finance the relatively small American export trading company industry). This means that there is now concrete government interest in finding international channels of distribution for small businesses. So far, that interest has been directed toward major corporations rather than small businesses. However, the interest will filter down to small businesses and the home-baser will be able to capitalize on it. Many more export management companies will appear in this country in the near future. Existing ones will become more diversified. Home-basers will then have the opportunity to get wider and better representation in the global market.

How to Select an Export Management Company

There are about a thousand export management companies in the United States. Almost all of them will search for buyers for clients' goods, package and warehouse, prepare documentation, arrange for transportation and insurance, and service buyers after sales are made. Many will do much more. However, only a limited number of these companies will be right for your needs. There are certain things to look for in selecting an export management company and specific information you should have before making any commitments or signing any contracts:

Is the company handling competing products? It is not in your best interests to deal with a company that is handling a competitor's products in foreign markets. It's generally not a good practice, and it's particulary not a good idea for a home-baser whose goods will not get the same attention as the goods of a larger competitor. Always find out what other companies the export management company represents before finalizing an arrangement.

Who are the company's clients? In addition to ascertaining that the company is not handling the products of a competitor, a check of its client roster will give you an idea of the businesses it does represent. Are they similar to yours? Are they large or small? Are they successful? Do they have good reputations? What kinds of products do they produce? Are they product-minded more than service-minded? If you're selling cosmetics, for example, you are better off being represented by an export management company experienced in handling perfume than by one that sets up technical advisors in underdeveloped nations.

How large is the company? How big is its export management sales staff? What is the ratio of sales personnel to clients? Is the sales staff large enough to offer a new client adequate representation? What kind of sales volume has the company produced for its clients? Don't rely solely on the company's answers; check with the clients themselves to see how satisfied they are with the representation they're receiving.

What is the company's overall performance record? What is its financial status? How many countries does it cover? What is the nature of its representation in these countries? Do representatives travel frequently to covered areas? What is the procedure for introducing new products into these areas?

Who's running the company? Get the names of the company's principals and as much background information on them as you can. This information can be obtained from The Federation of Export Management Companies or NEXCO; but very often a preliminary résumé can be gotten from company literature.

How to Get the Best Results from an Export Management Company

Let's assume you've answered all the above questions and you've selected a handful of possibilities. Now, in order to get the best results you must:

Narrow the field to the one or two companies that can do the most for you. This means writing to each of the names on your "good possibilities" list. Describe your product in detail. Indicate what you'd like done and why you believe they might be able to do it. If, for example, you're manufacturing a special formula sunscreen that you believe would get a good reception in a certain South American country serviced largely by the company, indicate why you feel your product would sell particularly well in that country; and make it clear that you're writing this company because of its strong contacts there. Send a few samples and some supporting literature. If the company, and other companies you write to, are interested, they will get back to you with their specific requirements. You'll then be able to further narrow the field.

See and speak before you sign. Visit the export management companies that you're seriously interested in working with. Discuss with them what they believe to be the sales potential of your product, how they would handle it, and how long it would take for you to see results. Find out exactly what kind of contract you'd be expected to sign. Will the company buy outright from you and bill their overseas customers (which is becoming a popular operating method today), or will you be responsible for invoicing customers (which is less preferable) and paying sales commissions? Sometimes the former can be negotiated if it's not offered. Does the contract include a cancellation or renewal clause which permits you or the company, or both, to terminate the arrangement after a few months if it's not working out? Often an export management company will want to confer with its foreign representatives before taking on a new line. Product evaluation by the people who will actually be selling your products in their countries is important. It is to your benefit, as well as to the management company's benefit, to have this third-party opinion before any papers are signed. Be prepared to supply literature and samples to the export company for examination by its overseas agents.

Make it clear that you're flexible. Once you've decided upon a certain company or companies, let them know you're prepared to cooperate with them in making product modifications which they feel will increase sales. Many overseas markets, for instance, insist that a product's packaging or container be reusable. If your product is slated for sale in Africa, and the export company thinks it will help sales to use cylindrical packaging, try cylindrical packaging at least for those goods that will be going to Africa. (Certain African countries are attracted to products packaged in cylinders, because they use cylinders as measuring cans.)

Let the export management company know that you're interested in working with them in developing marketing strategies for your goods. Often the more involved you're willing to become in product promotion, the more the company will give priority treatment to your products. If, for example, the export company is renting a booth at an international trade fair in a country you'd like to visit, (and can visit inexpensively) let them know that you're willing to make an appearance at the trade fair to demonstrate your product, hand out product literature, or explain the fine points of your product. They may welcome your help—particularly if you've had experience exhibiting at domestic trade shows or if you speak the language of the country the show is being held in.

PIGGYBACKING

Although export management companies usually do the best job of finding and attracting foreign buyers for small businesses, piggybacking is another good exporting method of distribution that can work well for home-basers. If you are selling certain kinds of merchandise, you can link up (piggyback) with a large domestic manufacturer of related products who has established export outlets. Such a manufacturer may be very willing to assume responsibility for the overseas distribution of your goods through its sales branches in foreign countries, if your product fits easily into its foreign marketing setup. Suppose, for example, you manufacture Colonial dollhouse kits. A toy manufacturer might be interested in acting as an export distributor for your line and in promoting it along with its line of tiny dolls. As long as the company sees profits without problems, it's to their advantage to take on your kits. The manufacturer buys your kits on its own account and then resells them to its foreign accounts.

In piggybacking, your relationship to the exporter you link up with is similar to the relationship you have with any domestic wholesalers to whom you sell. There are advantages and disadvantages: on the one hand you're freed from marketing problems, but on the other hand, you've relinquished control over your product. Once you've sold your product to an exporting manufacturer your role is a passive one. You don't have to worry about how or where your goods are promoted. For a small business person this passive role is usually advantageous. No energies or resources need be devoted to developing foreign markets. However, it could be unsatisfactory if you have products with strong sales potential in overseas markets, and you want to see this potential fully developed. In this case, a more active role (such as finding and employing foreign sales representatives who work under contract and by commission) on your part would be needed.

The best way to locate manufacturers with whom you can piggyback is by contacting Department of Commerce trade specialists, and trade associations and publications. They will be able to put you in touch with those companies that are active in overseas markets and interested in distributing related goods through their foreign sales divisions. Or, if you know of a large company already engaged in piggybacking activities, and you have a product you think they'd be interested in, write to their overseas sales manager and enclose your product literature.

Assuming you have found an appropriate means of overseas distribution for your offerings and you're ready to sign on the dotted line, now is the time to put down your pen and make doubly sure that your answer to the following two questions is a strong *yes:*

Have you explored all your domestic markets? By all means increase your business through exporting. However, do all you can locally first. The stronger your domestic base and the more marketing experience you've had, the more appeal you'll have for an overseas exporter. You will get your best representation from export marketing companies and exporting manufacturers if you come in with a polished product and presentation.

Can you afford to discount? Be sure you can profitably sell to an exporter at wholesale less a discount of about 15%. As a home-baser with low overhead you may be able to carry this off. But if you're selling an item where there's only a slim margin for discounting, you're not selling a good export item. An ideal export item is not just one that is needed in foreign markets, but one that all sellers—you, the exporter, and the foreign retailer—can make a decent profit on.

Presumably you've explored all your domestic options and the degree to which you can comfortably discount before considering exporting as a business-boosting technique. However, often in the process of searching out foreign distribution channels, previously untapped domestic opportunities present themselves or become apparent—markets where you don't have to offer a 15% discount to an export agent. Pause and think before you sign any export agreements. One home-baser was so flattered by a piggyback offer from a company exporting farm equipment —this large manufacturer was interested in her highly cultivated plant vitamins—that she was willing to sign a contract where she would barely break even. Fortunately she consulted her dispassionate accountant, who correctly pointed out that if she was willing to settle for a 25% profit there were several domestic outlets that would grab her offerings—outlets that had already expressed a great interest in her plant vitamins. This woman had failed to see that she was ready to sell overseas for a profit she wouldn't consider domestically.

COMBINING EXPORTING AND IMPORTING

Exporting and importing both involve the use of foreign countries for domestic profits. You sell your plant vitamins to those countries that don't have them but need them; or you buy jewelry for resale from those foreign wholesalers who will sell to you for less than will domestic wholesalers. In either case you benefit—whether from your business relationship with foreign buyers or with foreign sellers. It is also possible for you to benefit from a relationship with *both* foreign buyers and foreign sellers. Either exporting or importing can increase your profits. Used together, your profits can be increased still further.

Once you seriously begin exporting, whether through an export management company or a piggybacking arrangement, you'll find yourself thinking, I wish I could net more from these export deals. It's not that you're greedy. It's just that because of the additional middlemen and the additional modifications often involved in the export process, profits are less than you receive, for example, from home-shop selling or mail-order sales. Importing is the way to up your export profits. *You can import part of what goes into your final export product and, by doing so, reduce your production costs.* Suppose you're selling plant vitamins to the Ivory Coast. Following the advice of your export management company, you're packaging these vitamins in cyclindrical containers (remember we said that many African nations reuse these containers as measuring devices) rather than in the plastic bags used for domestic sales. The domestic manufacturer from whom you're purchasing these containers is charging eight cents per container. Why not import your containers and pay five cents apiece if you can?

Special export packaging can often be purchased more inexpensively from foreign manufacturers than from domestic manufacturers. And packaging isn't the only thing you should consider importing to reduce your production costs on exports. Many component parts can be profitably imported. One home-baser exporting patchwork-quilt-making kits learned that her South American buyers, unlike her home buyers, preferred circular patches to square patches. She enjoyed designing special quilt patterns to please her foreign buyers, but found that her American textile suppliers couldn't inexpensively supply her the same high-quality patches in circular shapes that they could in squares. While on vacation in Mexico she was able to strike a deal with a textile supplier whose fabrics were excellent for quilts. He was willing to supply her all the circular patches she wanted for a fraction of what she was paying domestically for inferior patches.

If you know, either through advice from your export agent or from your own research, that your product will receive a greater welcome abroad if you make modifications that are domestically unnecessary, don't be kept from making them because of the high cost of certain American packaging equipment or component parts. Find foreign suppliers who will enable you to increase your export profits by supplying you needed low-cost, quality imports.

How To Import

As with exporting, you're best off, at least in the beginning, if you let someone else worry about the procedural details of getting goods from foreign dockside to your door. Eventually, if you wish, you can learn the ins and outs of customs regulations, labeling, packaging, shipping, financing, and fumigation requirements. But for now, find professional importers who will do the work for you. Just as there are preferred ways for a home-baser to export, there are also preferred means of importing.

The easiest way for a home-baser to import is to tour a few trade shows. Dozens of importers exhibit at these shows. Some represent a single multi-national exporter. Others are agents for several foreign manufacturers. Here, under one roof, you have a chance to comparison shop among several importers and domestic manufacturers. You can compare selections, quality, and prices. Should you find a product you wish to import, all you need do is place an order. It's no more complicated than buying locally. The importer will make all arrangements necessary for getting the goods to your home. If you have acceptable credit references you will be billed with your shipment, or shortly after its arrival, and have the standard thirty days within which to pay. If you do not have acceptable credit references, or if you are dealing with importers who do not use traditional billing procedures, your merchandise will be sent to you COD.

A less convenient, but sometimes better, way to import is to locate a foreign exporter on his turf, not through import agents, and make your own arrangements with him. You can do this while on a trip or through friends abroad. By dealing directly with a foreign manufacturer you eliminate the import agent's cut and thus further benefit from foreign prices. The negatives to this form of importing are that the financing is usually through a letter of credit, which involves a certain amount of paperwork and bank involvement; and that it may fall upon your shoulders to check with U.S. government agencies to make sure there is no problem in bringing in the imported goods, there are no high duty costs, etc. A letter of credit is a letter arranged by your banker, authorizing a foreign bank to issue your funds to a foreign exporter once his goods are at dockside, waiting to be shipped to you. This procedure does become simple once you become familar with it.

If you deal with a foreign manufacturer who is knowledgeable about the rules and restrictions regarding exports, who is savvy about packaging and shipping rules and customs regulations and has the cooperation of his local government, all you'll probably need to concern yourself with is payment. The exporter will get the goods to your door once a letter of credit is arranged.

A third way to import is to go to a well-stocked library and open a copy of the *American Register of Exporters and Importers*. This book, available in many library reference sections, lists dozens of companies importing all sorts of products. Get the names and addresses of those importing goods that interest you and write for their product literature and price lists. If you find an importer who seems to be right for your needs, send for product samples. Should you decide to do business with the importer, the procedure will be the same as if you had located him through a trade show. (Some Yellow Pages also contain lists of importers.)

BECOMING AN IMPORTER

Building an importing business and using importing to increase your export profits are two entirely different things. This chapter is about the latter, about exporting. However, in the process of exporting, or importing packaging materials or component parts, you might find yourself intrigued by the thought of becoming an importer. While you like what you're presently making and marketing, you'd like to become an importer also. Perhaps, for example, you're making clothing and you'd like to sell shoes along with your outfits. Or maybe you're making pottery and you'd like to sell dried flower arrangements for use in your fired goods. Or maybe you're making Christmas wreaths and Christmas dolls and you'd like to add tree ornaments to your line. Whatever the case, now we're talking about importing a finished product for the purpose of profitably reselling it in this country. If there's an American market for the product you want to import, you may substantially increase your profits. Just be aware of the following:

You won't get the same government support in importing that you will in exporting. The Department of Commerce and dozens of government agencies are interested in helping small business owners export their goods and in protecting U. S. manufacturers from foreign competitors. They are not interested in fostering an already thriving import economy. Though there are plenty of resources available for getting information on importing, you won't get the same encouragement and hand-holding help you will when seeking information and assistance in exporting.

Foreign government trade offices will help you locate exporters in their countries. Many countries have U.S.-based trade offices set up to assist American importers. A call or letter to the embassies of these countries will put you in touch with these offices. It is much more in the interests of an exporting nation to assist you than it is in the interests of this country.

It is essential you choose those imports which will appeal to a product-glutted American market. Wants, needs, and whims change quickly here. If you have an instinctive sense of what will sell at a given moment, you can do well. If you don't, you may get stuck with a lot of imported bargains that no one wants even at bargain prices.

Competition in the import business is stiff. American entrepreneurs are attracted to the import market not just because of cheap prices, but also because of the appeal of doing business with exotic countries, learning local customs, and meeting foreign business and craftspeople. However, many of these entrepreneurs discover that they are not only in competition with each other, but also with importers who have an arm here and abroad. This kind of competition is hard to beat. They have an edge, as they know exactly where to go for the best prices and the newest products. One home-baser who sells comfortable and beautiful sportswear has in-laws based in Bolivia and a husband who visits them frequently. She is constantly coming up with new, well-priced, attractive alpaca sweaters, skirts, capes, hats that few other small business owners are able to find. Her husband and his family know several out-of-the-way suppliers who are not accessible to foreigners. This type of competition is common today as more and more immigrants are finding it profitable to use their contacts back in their native countries to supply unique offerings to a receptive American buying public.

It is extremely helpful to speak the language of the country you're importing from if you are importing directly. If you like to travel and want to deal directly with foreign tradespeople, craftspeople, or business owners, you must speak their language. You'll be less likely to be regarded as exploitive or to be exploited. Don't believe that money speaks for itself or that money alone is an international language. The ability to communicate person-to-person is very important.

Customs regulations, quotas, and duties are constantly changing. Stay on top of these things, particularly if you're importing directly. What is a good buy or a fast delivery in the fall may be a poor bet the following spring. If you're serious about importing, visit a local U.S. customs office and collect all the literature you can. Read books and articles on the how-to's of importing. Attend seminars given by business organizations and export/import associations where you can learn how to deal with customs brokers, keep current with govermnent controls, and keep your overhead expenses down.

You need planned outlets for your imports. You get your best buys with imports, as with all products, when you purchase in bulk. (A Colombian glove exporter isn't interested in selling you three pairs of gloves.) However, if you're going to purchase in bulk, you must be able to resell everything. When buying American goods you can often return or exchange unsold items. This is not usually true (particularly for a home-baser) when purchasing imports. This means you must get orders, through samples or catalogs, *prior* to ordering your imports, so that you're not stuck with unsalables. Whether you're selling your imports to retail outlets, institutions, or private buyers, make sure you have a definite commitment and, if possible, a deposit. One home-baser who travels frequently to Europe and imports from overseas friends such gourmet delicacies as chocolate jam and Irish shortbread, frankly explains up front that she requires a 25% deposit to continue offering low prices for her unique specialties. She uses one room of her posh city apartment as a showroom. Retail buyers stop by, taste her offerings, chat a bit about what's currently going on in Europe's commercial kitchens, and place their orders. Many protest that they're not authorized to pay out deposits, but those sincerely interested ultimately come around. They understand that once the goods arrive in this country they have to be more than just honor-bound to take them, lest their supplier find herself unable to profitably stay in business.

THE "ONE WORLD" CONCEPT

Commercially we are not a world of hundreds of independent nations. The more you do business internationally, the more you come to embrace and enjoy the "one world" philosophy. You realize that other countries want and need our goods, that we want and need their goods, that there are honest and dishonest businessmen here and abroad, and that everyone is interested in bottom-line profits and increased sales. You begin to see that despite cultural differences and government attitudes, international entrepreneurs have a lot in common and can easily cross international boundaries.

If you have any desire or reason to deal internationally, don't be put off by the fact that you're a small home-baser. You're part of a large international business community. Many entrepreneurs throughout the world are small home-basers. Multinational companies are buying from, and selling to, small home-basers. Some of the world's greatest entrepreneurs started out as home-basers and are still home-based. Just like taking any new professional step, be it setting up at a trade show or placing your goods on a barter exchange, exporting and importing can seem a bit frightening at first. But once you get into it and get good at it, you'll feel you've taken an exciting and cosmopolitan step toward making your home-based business grow.

10

AVOIDING COMMON HOME-BASED BUSINESS MISTAKES

When a home-based business fails to grow it is seldom because its owner is making a glaring mistake. It is usually because simple mistakes are being made over an extended time. If your business isn't growing because of a glaring mistake, chances are you know about it. People would tell you if your quiches tasted disgusting, or your clothing fell apart, or your cosmetics caused a skin rash. But they wouldn't tell you if something more subtle was keeping your income low. They couldn't. The subtle mistakes are ignored or undetected by customer and owner alike. Following are the most common home-based business mistakes—mistakes that go uncorrected either because they are not recognized as mistakes or because they are not recognized at all.

Sideline thinking. Home-basers too often look upon their businesses as sideline ventures—as sources of supplemental income that could never mushroom into anything big. "Sure it would be fantastic," says Francine, "if I could net $40,000 a year selling my fudge, but be realistic!" The thought of Francine's Fudges netting more than $5,000 a year is unrealistic to Francine. She regards it as a dream that could never come true. And because she does, she will make sure it never does come true!

The main reason this self-fulfilling prophecy occurs is that currently there are not a lot of successful home-basers around to serve as encouraging role models. For the reasons discussed in the introduction to this book, this will change. However, for now there are few entrepreneurs living solely on homebased profits. There are few examples that you can point to and say, "If he or she is doing it, so can I." And you regard those few who do exist as exceptions to the "rule" that big money cannot be made at home.

The dearth of successful role models is a strong deterrent to the "I Can Make It" thinking necessary for taking a home-based business from a sideline to a main line. There is a natural instinct in all of us to believe that if it could be done, it would be done; and if it's not being done, it can't be done. You look around at most of the home-basers you know and they're earning basically what you are. Why should you be any different? Why should your luck be better than theirs?

Luck has little to do with it. Nor does the belief, "If it could be done, it would be done." Nor is there any rule that says big money cannot be made from home. It can and is being done, but not by most home-basers—because most of them think small, identify with the average person, and believe that when something big happens to an average person it is because of luck. What they fail to see is that most of the time these average people *made* their luck happen. They started by truly believing it could, by believing they deserved to have it happen, by believing that if it could happen to even one rare John Doe, it could happen to them too. To this extent the "average person" wasn't so average—and you shouldn't be either.

How do you get yourself thinking this way? How do you rise above sideline thinking? By doing these three things:

1. Think about the fact that most store-based or office-based entrepreneurs earn very little. They may be earning a little more than you are because, in recent decades, our economic system and beliefs have fostered out-of-the-home businesses. However, their earnings are still small and their enterprises not impressive. Basically success comes from how you think, not from where you're located.

2. Envision yourself as already successful. Today lots of psychologists are advocating "envisioning" in relation to everything from being thin to being popular. And though it may sound trendy and questionable, it does work. The idea is to relax, free your mind, and concentrate on your behavior as *that person you want to become*. What are you doing? How are you acting and reacting to people and

situations? Here, again, is the self-fulfilling prophecy at work, except here it's working for you rather than against you. Much has been written about this sort of productive imagining. Read up for more detailed information.

3. Commit yourself to being a professional. You've already begun to do this by reading this book. Rare is the entrepreneur who just stumbles into great wealth. It happens when you're willing to take those steps that will help it happen. The amateur may have fun. He'll set up his wares at a flea market because that's what his friend is doing, make a few bucks, and come home satisfied. This is not how a sideline is turned into a main line. Think like a serious student on the way to becoming a master. This means working harder and more skillfully than the amateur who's really just playing around, and is not determined to do much more than he's already doing.

Failure to delegate. The average home-baser is uncomfortable delegating authority to subordinates. It's part of the "No one can do it as well as I can" syndrome. It's associated consciously or subconsciously with losing control over your operation. Many home-basers, realizing there is a limit to how far they can stretch themselves, hire domestic help to relieve them of household chores so they can devote more time to their businesses. This is a good move when your business is starting to grow. But once it becomes apparent that what began as a small, informal operation is rapidly expanding into a truly profitable company, just having domestic help is not enough. You need regular business help as well. *If you don't let others share your business chores, your company will stay small.* You must relinquish some control to capable and reliable employees. Don't be running to UPS with product shipments when you should be conferring on new and important promotional strategies.

In order to channel your energies most effectively, hire and train workers who can free you from donkey labor and routine tasks. And, once your company grows still further, hire assistants who can help you with selling and managerial tasks—personnel you can motivate to go after new markets, design new products, etc. The more you delegate short-term details and small decisions, the more you can concentrate on your company's long-term directions. Initially, being the "boss," not just of a business, but of employees, may make you edgy or nervous, but by proceeding slowly and carefully, you'll get used to it and realize that it's an inevitable (and ultimately pleasant) part of owning a big business.

Becoming used to delegating authority is part of preparing your business to soar. You must also get good at it. Determine the number of employees you need at each stage of development and make it clear what you want each person to do. Either hire people who can do what you need done or hire people who can easily be trained. Make sure you hire people you feel comfortable working with. Create a work environment where your employees feel relaxed enough to communicate honestly with you about what they feel you may be doing right or wrong. Reward top workers and sales agents with bonuses and solid, open-ended commissions.

Measuring time unrealistically. Chapter 1 discussed effective time management. Time measurement is a part of this. You can prioritize chores, delegate the distasteful ones, coordinate difficult tasks with peak energy periods, and divide big tasks into little tasks, and still be in bad shape if you incorrectly estimate how long it takes to complete specific tasks. Home-basers are frequently unrealistic here. They believe they can fit either much more or much less into a morning than is actually possible.

If you're planning to work at home doing a job you've done many times, you can pretty well estimate how long the job will take—you know you can sew, or paint, or construct, or cook so many items in so many hours. You're experienced here, and barring any unusual interruptions, you can measure time realistically. The problem arises when you're estimating the time it takes to do a task that you don't regularly do, or when you're estimating the time it takes to accomplish a job where other people are involved, where how fast you finish is related to how fast they work.

When measuring the time it takes to complete a task regarded as pleasurable, there is a tendency to estimate that the task can be done more quickly than it actually can. Beware of this. You may love the thought of gift wrapping, for example; however, to beautifully gift-wrap the fifty samples that you're sending to choice customers can take a few hours. It's not a chore that can be knocked off in thirty or forty minutes before "getting down to real business." Similarly, if you're dreading the thought of doing something, and find yourself procrastinating, chances are you're putting off the chore because you believe it will take you much longer to finish than it actually will. Cleaning some dirty equipment, for example, may seem like a chore that will take forever and keep you away from more pressing and pleasant responsibilities; however, if you stop thinking about how much you hate cleaning equipment and just get out your supplies and start scrubbing, chances are you'll have the job completed and out of the way within an hour (and it might even be an hour that you enjoy if you scrub while chatting with a friend).

When estimating the time it takes to complete a job where you are dependent upon the cooperation of other people, realize that most people are not going to move as quickly as you'd like them to. Traffic can creep, people can arrive late for appointments, conversations can drag. Don't think that you'll polish off 1, 2, and 3 on your list right away and come home and do 4, 5, and 6. It's more than likely that 1, 2, and 3 will take you all day, or will exhaust you. Double your time estimate. Plan on just completing 1, 2, and 3. If things move quickly, you can attend to tasks that you thought would have to wait, and feel ahead of the game. But don't set yourself up for disappointment and stress by underestimating how long it takes to accomplish things when several people's schedules have to coincide with your own.

Allowing stress damage. Stress cannot always be prevented, but its damaging effects often can be. You cannot prevent a late delivery or a power failure or an employee getting ill, but you can prevent these occurrences from damaging your health and consequently your business. Because they're trying to run a business and a home simultaneously with too little help, too little money, and too little time, many home-basers permit stressful events to nibble away at them. They don't realize that though they can't prevent all stressful events, they have the power to protect themselves from being done in by the events.

As a home-baser you will face small, but persistent,

problems that because of their frequency can cause you more stress damage than can a major crisis. Make yourself stress-resistant not by trying to avoid these problems, but by confronting them whenever possible and using them to your advantage. If there's a power failure while you're using your electric typewriter, take advantage of the time you can't type to stuff and stamp envelopes, or to do some other chore that doesn't require electricity. In this way you are controlling your stress, rather than allowing it to control you.

Though a stressful event can mean a temporary change in plans, remember that you are not helpless in the face of this event. You can *act* and undermine its intensity, rather than *react* and let it keep you from functioning properly. This sort of behavior modification takes a bit of practicing, so don't be discouraged if even after working on stress control you find yourself twitching because your delivery truck breaks down en route to an important customer. You'll always need some stress to keep you on your toes and able to deal with the world; but use these three techniques to keep stress from crushing you:

1. Pinpoint those specific and recurring situations that tend to bother you the most and plan for them. If you find yourself frequently upset because you've run out of component supplies, don't try to stretch supplies to the bitter end. Order in larger quantities.

2. Choose the stress that you'll allow yourself to react to. Some stress is more important than other stress. Bang your walls and scream your head off, if a situation warrants it. But don't let a trivial event get you going. It's healthy to release anger over something big but damaging to do so over every little inconvenience.

3. Build your stress resistance through exercise. Exercise increases mental as well as physical strength. It puts a stress shield around you by reducing general mental tension. If your head aches, your legs feel crampy, or you're experiencing indigestion, your body may well be telling you it needs some concentrated workouts.

Networking nonchalance. Most corporate executives are well aware of the benefits of networking. Those who are good at it increase their contacts at geometric speed and greatly accelerate their career climbs. For some reason, home-basers don't approach networking with the same zeal as do corporate executives. It's not a case of denying the positive effects of networking. It's just an indifference to the whole concept. You're so busy making and marketing your products that you can't be bothered figuring out and acting upon an effective networking program. If someone calls you and says that there's a Craftspersons' Conference, a Women Working Home meeting, or an Entrepreneurs' Get-together at the local community center, you may attend. You may even take notes, phone numbers, etc. But will you seek out these events? Will you travel a couple of hours to attend them? Do you scour trade publications for possible networking opportunities?

Don't let networking be a casual, occasional, "if it's convenient" event. Most networking opportunities are not extremely local. You may or may not be notified of them or specifically invited to attend. Generally you'll have to seek out and follow up on these events. Often it will cost you some money, time, and effort to partake of them. But don't let this keep you from active involvement with people and groups that can ultimately bring increased sales and profits to your business.

One home-based writer and publisher had to be pushed by his wife to attend a publishers' conference in a nearby city. His wife had heard about the conference on the radio. The man was sure there'd be nothing at the conference for him, that it would be populated by big-name publishers eager to mingle with each other and not at all interested in the few self-help books he published annually from his garage and sold through mail order. It turned out that this home-baser couldn't have been more wrong. Yes, there were big names at the conference. There were also a lot of small publishers, a few helpful workshops, and many people very interested in what he was doing. Ironically, it was one of the big publishers who took his literature and some samples and put him in touch with a book packager who gave him a good contract. The book packager introduced this home-baser to other people in the field of professional publishing who were also impressed with his work and ability. These contacts resulted in further business and more contracts.

Underestimating the power of the press. Just as the power of networking is underestimated by many home-basers, so too is the power of the press. One feature article in a local newspaper can bring in ten new customers who will bring in ten more new customers, and so on. Some successful entrepreneurs have traced the turning points in their businesses to magazine or newspaper stories that had repercussions beyond their wildest dreams.

Several home-basers who are earning big dollars and are periodically featured in local media claim they always forget just how powerful the press is in bringing in new business. A home-based potter and ceramics teacher who is periodically featured in her local newspaper finds that each time an article appears she is deluged with calls from would-be students who want to take her classes and from local businesspeople who want to display the work of local artisans. She says that between articles she tends to forget how strongly impressed and influenced people are by press pieces. This potter doesn't really enjoy being "the celebrity of the moment," but she does enjoy her growing business enough to "put up with those who would probably ignore my work if the press didn't play it up."

When seeking press coverage bear in mind that the press's power is such that it can have a negative as well as a positive effect on your business. If you have reason to believe that a particular writer or publication will give you negative, or even mediocre, coverage, keep away. Don't believe that any coverage is beneficial. Poor coverage can harm your business. It's only beneficial to a publication looking for a story, positive or negative, that will interest its readers. Think in terms of restaurant reviews. A good one usually brings in lots of new business. A rave one brings in even more. And a bad review not only doesn't bring in new business, but it often drives away existing business.

Failing to combine service selling with product selling. The potter mentioned above gets more publicity than do many artisans because in addition to selling a product she sells a service. She teaches people how to make their own creations. As a potter and a teacher she is considered more newsworthy than she would be if she was just a potter. Journalists feel that by writing about this woman they're not just plugging her products, they're informing their readers that ceramics classes given by an established professional are locally available. And it is not only journalists who keep this home-baser in the public eye. Her students talk about the classes they take with her. They buy her work and encourage others to do so.

If your business is such that you can easily combine service selling with the product you're selling, do it. You don't have to give a lot of classes, but, unless you hate teaching, you should give it a try. It can bring you into the mainstream of your community, call attention to your business, and ultimately bring you new customers. In addition, you will be paid for your teaching, which is still more income for you.

Of course, not every product business combines realistically with service selling. If you're selling imported leather boots, you'll have to go a ways to come up with a realisically related course you could offer. However, in many cases the connection is a natural one. If you bake, cook, construct, write, knit, sew, photograph, or paint in the manufacturing of your product, you're an expert and have the makings of a good course. Focus on the particular aspect of your craft that can be easily taught to amateurs and that you'd like to teach. Study up on effective teaching methods. Read articles and books on planning a winning adult-education course. Attend a few classes that are in keeping with what you're considering. Practice teaching (and making your mistakes on) a few friends and relatives. Then get started. Place your ads, put up your notices, enlist the word-of-mouth aid of friends. Your first class may be small, and more than likely, you'll make some mistakes; but within a short time you may well find yourself with a long waiting list and a greatly expanded business as well.

Shutting out family. Family labor can be wonderful. Many successful home-basers owe much of their success to a spouse who happens also to be a lawyer, accountant, business consultant, or some sort of professional with skills or contacts that helped build the business. Similarly, parents, children, and siblings have been directly responsible for helping a home-based business to soar. No awards are given for going it alone. Yet many home-basers feel that there is something noble about not involving one's family, about keeping family and business separate. This is nonsense. Tap family members for all the help you can get. Involve them in the various aspects of your business. Seek their advice. And, when appropriate, pay them (particularly your children) for their input.

One rep, selling a diet supplement manufactured by a multilevel marketing company, felt "a bit uncomfortable" about asking her eighteen-year-old daughter if some of the students in her dorm might be interested in buying her supplement and in becoming recruits. Though she was enthusiastic about her product, she didn't want to push her daughter. As it turned out the daughter brought up the subject and ended up bringing in enough sales and recruits to relieve her mother from the burden of paying her college tuition.

Though your children should not be permitted to use your office as a playroom, or to undermine your professional facade, they, and other family members should be consulted and made to feel needed. There is nothing unprofessional or compromising about getting assistance from those whom you love and who love you the most. One day, if your business becomes a major company, you may want to pass it on to your children, so why not include them in it now?

Run-of-the-mill advertising. It is not easy to come up with creative, winning advertising methods. Large corporations pay big dollars to advertising agencies to create campaigns that will attract great numbers of new customers; yet often the campaigns are duds. If large advertising agencies, with all sorts of talent, experience, and resources at their disposal, can make mistakes, you may wonder what chance the ordinary home-baser has.

You have a good chance, if, like the large corporations and their agencies, you're patient and persistent. Try a series of low-cost or no-cost ad campaigns and eliminate those that don't work for you. Just like the large advertising agencies, you'll make mistakes. Certain campaigns, ads, or methods won't bring you in the increase in sales you're looking for. But eventually you'll find that unique ad, offer, or medium that does what none of your other attempts did.

One home-based frame maker placed some typical ads

in run-of-the-mill places and got a good cumulative response over the long haul, but she felt that there was some form of advertising she had yet to hit upon that would produce a more dramatic response. After unsuccessfully trying a few affordable techniques, she discovered coupon advertising. A local ad packager rounded up ten community businesses, had each one make up a one-page ad with a coupon offer, polished them up, photo-reduced them, and mailed them to select area residents. The coupon mail ads didn't produce miracles for any of the participants; but they worked exceptionally well for the framer. She got an astonishingly high number of new customers for little effort and a cost that was far less than direct-mail advertising would have been.

Sometimes run-of-the-mill ads bring in good results, but for home-basers more imaginative means are often required to get a business really going. Experiment with several atypical, inexpensive advertising techniques. Don't make the mistake of settling for the easiest, most traditional methods. Your products may be exceptional, but chances are your sales won't be until you try new methods of reaching your prime market.

Trying to create new demand rather than capitalizing on existing demand. Speaking of your prime market —do you know what it is and are you going after it? Many home-basers make the mistake of ignoring an existing market that has a genuine need for what they're offering. They identify a group they believe wants and should be using what they're selling, and target their advertising energies toward that group. What happens is that this group, though possibly fascinated with the offerings, doesn't spend in sufficient numbers to have a strong impact on profits, and the prime market that might spend in big numbers doesn't because they're not being reached.

One home-baser almost destroyed his business with this mistake. Carl invented a tiny, portable burglar alarm that a person can carry in his pocket and set off easily if accosted by a mugger. His device received a fair amount of press, and Carl received several inquiries and orders, particularly from senior citizens residing in certain high-crime areas. You might think that Carl would aim his ads at senior citizens in these high-crime areas and then branch out to senior citizens in other high-crime areas. Instead, he made a mistake that many home-basers and novice entrepreneurs make. He assumed that the senior-citizen market would seek him out without much advertising and decided to promote his invention among young women frequenting bars, late night parties, etc. His idea wasn't bad, but he failed to distinguish between interest and need. The young women thought his portable alarm was an interesting idea. If given to them as a gift they probably would use it. But they didn't feel enough of a need for it to purchase it. Consequently many good ad dollars devoted to creating a market among young singles were wasted. Sales were sluggish and Carl's cash flow was sinking.

Fortunately a business-consultant friend saved Carl by getting him to quickly detour his energies and ad dollars to the senior-citizen market that had an immediate and strong need for his product. However, many home-basers are not saved in the nick of time. They blow their ad budgets by acting out a dream—the dream of making their own private markets for their products—and ignoring the solid realities. By all means go after new potential markets, but not until you've thoroughly courted and conquered your existing prime markets.

Counting on volume sales. In pricing their products many home-basers make the mistake of counting on volume sales for their profits. It would be lovely if you had so many customers that you needed only a small markup to reap large profits. Lovely, but not likely until your business starts soaring. And your prices must reflect this fact. For now, price as competitively as you can, but price high enough to bring in a good bottom line with only a moderate number of customers.

As your business grows, you can offer a good discount to those customers who purchase in quantity. Eventually you may be able to knock emerging competition off the market by undercutting their prices and maintaining exceptionally low prices. But don't anticipate volume sales, price accordingly, and price yourself off the market. If strong competitors undercut your prices, don't fight back by engaging in a price war. You can't afford one at this time. Modify your product, upgrade it, or offer special services or incentives to hold on to your customers. But don't price precariously.

There may be moments when you feel thoroughly disillusioned and ready to throw in the towel because you see someone offering a product just like yours, or even nicer, for less money. If your product is reasonably and competitively priced, don't let this upset you. It happens to all businesspeople at times. The lower-priced product may be being used as a loss leader. Or it may be being offset by other products in the seller's line that are overpriced. Or the seller may not know what he's doing. Or there may be other explanations. Remove your product from a negative comparison by underplaying the price angle and highlighting other angles. Many successful entrepreneurs get around price comparisons by concentrating strongly on what their competitors are not offering—color selection, home delivery, special wrapping, name engraving.

Unrealistic pricing. Though you should price for profit, and you shouldn't price precariously, you must price to sell. Home-basers, particularly those engaged in crafts production, often have an inflated or unrealistic idea of what their goods will sell for. One home-based glassblower puts a great deal of work and time into each of her creations. She feels that based on her input, she is entitled to the prices she is asking. By objective standards, she is. She is figuring in her cost of materials, her overhead cost per piece, and a per-hour salary for herself, and doubling that figure. This is the way craftspeople and others are often advised to price. It's an acceptable formula—except it doesn't always work. In this glassblower's case, it doesn't work mainly because her work is mediocre. Were it magnificent, she might be able to get her asking prices and more. Her prices are fair; the problem is that they are unrealistic. People won't pay what she's asking; and unless she lowers her prices or upgrades the quality of her work, her business will sink.

You may love what you're selling and the company you're building. You probably are putting a great deal of time and effort into all aspects of your business. But from the customer's viewpoint this is inconsequential. If you want your products to sell, know the pricing formula most appropriate to your field; but adapt that formula to take into account the quality and rarity of your product, the current demand for it, and the economic means of the people to whom you're targeting your goods. You'll do a lot better saying to yourself, "My work is good, but not really great; since there are similar products around, I'll have to price modestly" than proudly proclaiming, "I've put my heart and sweat into these pieces and if I can't get the prices I'm asking, I'd rather not sell them!"

Occasionally you'll find yourself in the delightful situation where you think you're pricing realistically, but learn to your surprise that you're pricing too low. One woman who usually sells quilts at rural flea markets found this true when she started taking her work to pricey crafts exhibits. Another home-baser knew that he couldn't get more, locally, than he was already getting for his home-made tools, but discovered that he could double his prices when selling his tools through upscale mail-order catalogs. Obviously, having your pricing unrealistically low is as self-defeating as having it unrealistically high. Guiltlessly raise your prices if the former is the case and hold on to the fact that the time may come when a reverse procedure will be necessary.

Leaving home base. Pricing is not the only place where home-basers are often unrealistic. Many home-basers have made the mistake of leaving home base and renting an outside business address, only to suffer unprecedented losses and great disillusionment. What usually happens here is that a business starts to boom. Sales are better than ever. New orders are flowing in. There is a lively public interest in the company. The future looks good. And home base begins to look inadequate—too small, too tacky, too unbusinesslike. The environment that gave birth to the fledgling enterprise, and saw it emerge into a profitable company, is suddenly inadequate. All that will do now is a commercial location.

Be wary of this sort of thinking. When working from home base you're pleased when orders are flowing in and business is booming, but you don't have to agonize during slow periods. Your overhead is predictable and manageable. This is not true once you've left home base. Sure, you've estimated needed sales and new expenses before making the move. But even with the most realistic and comprehensive estimates there is a "what if" stress factor that you don't have at home—what if some unforeseen competition emerges? what if the economy turns around and sales estimates don't materialize? what if the rental space is broken into or leaks or is robbed? what if it turns out you were happier working at home?

Be certain you're not moving out prematurely and that you really want to and have to leave home base. Consult with several objective financial advisors. Just as many growing families are finding it more convenient and economically sound to add to their existing homes rather than to relocate to new neighborhoods, you may find it better to add to your work space, to add a room, shelves, desks, rather than to move either to an affordable semidump or to an expensive rental that will have you fretting over every lost penny. If the time comes when your company is so large, by your estimate and professional estimates, that it must be quartered elsewhere, you'll have to move; but until then, strongly evaluate your motives for wanting to move, and do all you can to stay where you are.

Pettiness. Once there is a clear indication that a neighborhood home-baser is doing well, other neighborhood residents frequently decide, "Gee, if Joan is doing so well selling her brownies (or paintings, or knitted goods), why don't I do the same thing? I can bake (or paint, or knit) too." This may be how you got started—you were inspired by a local success story. Or, your newest competitors might be people who were inspired by your success.

During the "inspiration stage" everyone is usually ostensibly friendly. Sometimes the established home-baser, if she's really supersuccessful and secure in her success, even becomes the encouraging mentor to a newly inspired, and almost worshipful, would-be home-baser just a few streets away. There is an unwritten and moral understanding that once the new home-baser is ready to begin her business, she won't go after the markets of her inspiration, but seek out her own markets.

Unfortunately many home-basers who start out well intentioned abandon all unwritten and moral codes when they discover that it's not easy to sell, that it takes time to acquire repeat customers, that there's a limited market for most products. They begin to enviously eye their inspiration's customers, and sneakily pursue them—even if their inspiration is someone who was generous enough to act as an encouraging mentor. This is not something shocking. Big corporations do it all the time. Though it's not considered genteel, it's regarded as necessary and considered par for the course by the business community.

Yet what may be acceptable for big corporations is petty and nasty when practiced by neighborhood home-basers. As a home-baser, you're also Jimmy's parent, and Betty's next-door neighbor, and the nice person who shops at the local supermarket. Your image is more than just that of a business shark intent on commercial survival. Beware of underhandedly pursuing a neighbor's customers. If you do this, you will dent the human part of your image, compromise your local reputation, and, even if you manage to succeed in pulling away customers, you will run the risk of initiating an unhealthy competition that can come back to haunt you and possibly terminate your enterprise.

Does this mean that you can never expect to share, or win over, another home-baser's customers? Not at all. It just means that you shouldn't go after your neighbor's slowly and honestly acquired markets with a concealed slicing edge. By all means compete for local customers after you've tried to develop as many of your own markets as possible. But compete openly and fairly. Make your products and services publicly known through advertising, exhibitions, etc. Interested parties will comparison shop and possibly decide to detour part or all of their business to you. But never try to lure away a neighbor's customers by using petty tactics such as calling up known customers and implying that your product is superior to your neighbor's, or that your neighbor is this, that, or the other thing. Establish the fact that you have a business which you're interested in expanding. Make your products and services as attractive and competitive as possible. But don't let yourself be tempted into pettiness—don't stoop to business behavior that you know to be socially unsavory.

Sometimes neighborhood home-basers, selling similar items, are able to help themselves and each other by banding together. For example, if you and your neighbor five streets away are both selling baked goods and giving baking classes from your homes, you may decide that one of you will give baking lessons exclusively to children and all adult students will belong to the other. Or you may agree that you will stop baking brownies, which are her favorite, and concentrate on your other offerings, and she will stop offering breads, which are your specialty, and concentrate more on her brownies and her other products. By cooperating, you are both carving out distinct niches for yourselves. You are also preventing direct competition and the hard feelings that may result. And you're creating a mutually beneficial situation where each of you can happily recommend the services and products of the other, consequently paving the way for your own business's expansion.

Thinking all debt is bad. From the time we're little, we're usually raised to believe that debt is bad. You don't owe people money if you can help it. You save up for what you want and then proceed to purchase. This sounds right, but it's only partially true. Even though it goes against all we're taught to believe, debt is sometimes good.

There are basically two kinds of debt—consumer debt and investment debt. Consumer debt is what you incur when you borrow money to finance your vacation or to buy yourself a new watch. This kind of debt is undesirable in that it leads nowhere and leaves you paying high interest rates. However, investment debt is another story. Here you're not borrowing money to gratify an immediate want, but to create eventual wealth.

Once your business has reached a certain point, and you've developed a substantial degree of expertise, you may feel it's time to expand. Maybe the time is ripe to buy some high-tech equipment, to add to your work area, or even to leave home base. If after careful evaluation and financial consultation you're sure, for example, that by purchasing a certain computerized printing machine, you'll be able to greatly increase your output and bring in new business, then you shouldn't wait to acquire the machine. It may take you five years to save for it—five years where your business is stagnating for want and need of it. Go into debt. Get the best terms you can, and borrow the funds to finance the machine. In one year, as a result of having it, you may increase your business several-fold.

Don't make the home-baser's classic mistake of thinking, I'll wait to expand until I can afford to. This sounds like responsible thinking, and it is, but unfortunately too often it's also impractical and self-defeating. More often than not you can't afford *not* to expand if you want your business to soar. And, if it takes capital to expand, you must be willing to incur some debt. Don't look upon this debt as something unpleasant. Regard it simply as a leverage tool—as a means of moving your business off the ground. There is a saying, "Nowadays anyone who isn't in debt is probably underprivileged." This saying is particularly applicable to fledgling home-basers.

Legislation and insurance ignorance. Knowledge of legislation or insurance is not particularly exciting. And most home-basers are too busy to bother. That's the kind of stuff you delegate, right? Not totally. Don't rely exclusively on the professionals for what your options are or what's going on. Keep yourself informed of facts, laws, and changes that can influence your income or well-being. Are you aware, for example, that you gain depreciation deductions by speeding up planned equipment purchases? The IRS regards equipment and machinery purchased in December the same as if it were purchased at any other time of the year. This means don't wait until January to get the printing machine your business needs if you want to snare depreciation deductions for this year. Buy in December. (Of course, if you want your depreciation deductions for next year, then you should wait until January to purchase.)

Similarly, you should be aware of insurance events that can be beneficial to you. For example, there is now an insurance offered called product protection insurance. Remember the Tylenol scare of 1982? As a result of this scare protection is now available that will insure small business owners against product tampering. If you're producing the kind of product that might involve you in a whopping lawsuit and certain bankruptcy as a result of product tampering, you should know all there is to know about this new offering and consider purchasing it immediately. Don't focus so closely on the day-to-day details of your operation that you fail to realize that these details and your whole operation could be seriously affected by ignorance of seemingly remote legislation or insurance regulations.

Letting bankruptcy end your business. Suppose that dreaded event cccurs. You go bankrupt. Does this mean it's all over? the end of the road? your dreams are dead? For too many home-basers the answer is yes. It's a mistake to think this way and a mistake to give in to bankruptcy.

Your business may go bankrupt because of a big lawsuit, bad economic events, or unexpected competition. Things within or beyond your control can do you in. But you don't have to be permanently undone. A lawyer experienced in bankruptcy laws can help your business get a second chance, correct wrongdoings, or both.

Perhaps you've heard the terms "chapter ten" or "chapter eleven." These are legal reorganization procedures which enable a bankrupt company to get back on its feet by paying its creditors in a planned or negotiated manner. Often it's not only to your benefit, but to your creditor's benefit to agree to these procedures. (They are paid money they might otherwise never see.) In addition to these procedures there are other technical ways that a company can be bailed out of bankruptcy. Keep in mind that federal laws are devised to resurrect dying small businesses, not to force them into extinction. Also remember that the problem which led you into bankruptcy may be something that you can easily take steps, or make plans, to prevent in the future.

11

CURING FIGUREPHOBIA

Figurephobia is fear of figures and figuring—a fear of working with numbers, calculations, graphs, charts, computers, business machines, or anything remotely related to mathematics. If you have a strong, or even mild, case of figurephobia, it can doom your business. You must recognize it and treat it. *Failure to treat figurephobia is the biggest mistake a home-baser can make.*

Many home-basers are figurephobics. For one reason or another they don't treat the condition and never realize how closely related it is to the fact that their businesses aren't expanding. Because of figurephobia's deadly impact, rather than including it with the other common home-based business mistakes covered in the previous chapter, this chapter is devoted to its symptoms, effects, causes, and cures.

SYMPTOMS

Figurephobia can be successfully treated, and doing so can make your business grow. However, you can't treat something that you're not recognizing as a problem. What are the clues?

Knowing and not knowing. The symptoms of figurephobia are not so acute that you look at a number and pass out immediately. However, they are fairly evident. Chances are that you've developed the habit of ignoring these symptoms. For example, someone asks you how many miles per gallon your delivery truck is getting. Instead of figuring it out from facts on hand, you shrug or guess. Or your accountant uses words like "average" or "ratio" or "percentage" and you feel a blankness. Or a customer hands you a graph or table that he regards as a good pictorial summary and your heart begins to pound. Or a salesman shows you a computer printout and you don't even want to take it in your hands.

These danger signs have been around for a long time and you know it. But you keep pushing them aside. You've never liked to triple a recipe, figure a tip, or do your bank reconciliation. Formulas make you freeze. Figures fatigue you. And the metric system? Forget it! Thank goodness you're out of school and don't have to learn it. Get the picture? The symptoms aren't deeply buried or inscrutable. They're there; but you're not letting them bother you. Maybe if they all ganged up on you in one afternoon, you'd recognize the magnitude of the problem. But since you're not constantly plagued, why think about it? It's too disconcerting.

One home-based figurephobic became so good at not thinking about it that when she finally treated herself to the adding machine she had been wanting for months, she didn't use it for half a year. She admired it. She bought accessories for it. She showed it proudly to her friends. But she never read the instruction manual because she was certain it would be unclear, and never touched a key for fear of breaking the machine. It wasn't until her husband flipped through the manual, forced her in front of the machine, and told her what to do, that her hands ever pressed the "on" button. After a week of anguish, she became an expert on the machine. She now loves it and doesn't know how she ever did without it. But so strong was her fear of figuring out how to use it that she would have done without it indefinitely had her husband not realized the degree of her machine avoidance.

Avoidance. The above home-baser knew that she was afraid to figure out how to use her new adding machine. Yet in a way she didn't know. She knew she felt tension at the thought of mastering the machine, yet she didn't label the tension as figurephobia, and say, "Here is a problem which affects several areas of my life—a problem which I must analyze and treat."

Avoidance is a classic symptom of figurephobia. You avoid those chores that in some way or another involve figures and figuring. And when you can't avoid them, you experience definite physical symptoms. Your head aches, your vision blurs, or you have muscle spasms in your shoulders. And even at this point you don't say, "I must do something about this aversion to dealing with technical data." What you tend to do is treat the physical discomfort, not the source of it; and, if possible, develop a technique to avoid the chore in the future.

Delegation. This is the technique that most home-basers develop to avoid figure-related chores that must get done. They delegate them to someone competent and willing. First you avoid billing your late-paying accounts because you don't want to compute the interest they owe, and then when you realize your cash flow is suffering, you ask your bookkeeper or accountant to compute the interest charges for you. Ask yourself how many of the tasks that you delegate are figure-related.

Delegation is a necessity. As a business owner you can't be in all places or doing all things. But delegation out of fear is not a necessity. It is a habit—an indulgence developed to handle a fear that should be treated. And if most of the tasks you delegate are number-related, it is quite possible that this delegation is a symptom of figurephobia.

Computer rejection. The fact that you're not aching to install a terminal in your home is not an indication that you're a figurephobic. Nor is the fact that you're sick of the computermania that has embraced the nation. Or that you're bored by the "chipheads" who, when they speak of bits or bugs or characters, aren't talking about anything you know. However, if you find yourself strongly shunning everything computer-related, this may be a clue that you are a figurephobic.

One home-based importer got very upset when her accountant said she needed a computer for inventory control. She knew her manual procedure was taking an inordinately long time and that the results were often incorrect. Yet the thought of transferring to a computer system made her irritable. She came up with several flimsy reasons why it was a bad idea. Her accountant insisted that once she learned how to work the program, she'd love it. She'd find herself able to concentrate on aspects of her business that she was neglecting. She'd eventually be able to use it in other ways that would further help her business. He got nowhere until he brought in a demonstration model, sat her down, and said, "Look, all you have to do is this." He was patient, but persistent. She couldn't help but agree she had been unreasonable, that the computer could save her hours of effort and many mistakes. She even admitted ultimately that she had never liked working with numbers, and working with them on a screen had terrified her. It took time and some self-analysis for her to become a computer convert, but when she did she was a happy and successful one.

If you have philosophical or sociological reasons for disliking computers, that's one thing. But if you are rejecting even the thought of using them when you know that it is in your business's best interest that you consider doing so, take heed. This sort of computer rejection, particularly if combined with the other symptoms, can signal a definite need for immediate attention.

EFFECTS

Figurephobia is the unyielding albatross of home-basers who have never learned to become comfortable or confident with numbers. It prevents their businesses from ever soaring. The effects, or by-products, of this fear are so damaging that they can not be canceled by having a fine product or by providing excellent service. Generally the effects can be classified in these four ways—all of them business-dooming:

You have no overall understanding of your company's financial status. You may be an expert at production, sales, or both. You can envision new product designs and new markets. But you cannot envision a clear, detailed financial portrait of your overall operation. This means you can be creating beautiful merchandise or coming up with eager buyers daily, and still be just two steps away from bankruptcy.

A home-based apparel distributor was shocked when her

accountant told her she was in serious financial trouble. How could she be? She wasn't in difficulty the previous year and sales then were far less. This woman hadn't taken the combined impact of four major developments into account: her sales were now greater but her overhead expenses, particularly her travel-related ones, had become disproportionately high; there were a large number of returns, and she hadn't calculated exactly how large; some key customers were late in paying, which had resulted in her taking out a high-interest loan; and, as her sales were for a multilevel company, she was currently selling on a different "level," with a different commission structure than she had been in the previous year—a structure that was smaller. This woman was so taken with the immediate situation—a seemingly endless flood of orders and reorders—that she put off monitoring her overall situation. Even when her accountant gave her advice and alternatives that might have saved her business, she was unwilling to become financially cognizant and ultimately went out of business.

You relinquish crucial control. This has been the undoing of several otherwise conscientious home-basers. Because of their fear of dealing with figures and calculations, they delegate the entire task to others and in doing so lose control of their businesses. You can delegate financial control to the most honorable and capable professionals, and you should; but you should never delegate so much that you lose the capacity to govern your company's financial destiny. You can completely delegate your domestic chores, or your company's routine tasks, without losing control of your business. But if you delegate all financial matters, then your business is endangered. You must retain major control; and, if you have figurephobia, chances are you may not.

You make poor operational decisions. As discussed above, you may not purchase a computer that can save you time and labor for fear of having to figure out how to use it. Or, just as defeating, you may price foolishly (too high or too low) because you dread the thought of sitting down, calculating all your costs to the penny, and coming up with an appropriate price per product. A major portion of the decisions you must make in regard to your business are figure-related. Yet, if you are figurephobic, you can easily make the wrong decisions, or procrastinate and by doing so delay or deter new business.

You overlook opportunities. One home-baser who was fortunate enough to have a healthy cash flow was told about a bank service whereby her cash reserves could be maximized. They could be electronically transferred from her noninterest-bearing company checking account to an interest-bearing no-load mutual fund where they would safely earn daily dividends; then, when bills had to be paid, the money would be moved quickly and easily back to her checking account. The moment she heard the plan, she discounted it—not because she believed it was a bogus opportunity, but because it unnerved her to think about cash flow, interest, and electronic transfers.

Banks and other institutions will occasionally present small business owners with profit-making opportunities. So will suppliers, ad agencies, customers, and other business contacts. Many of these opportunities will involve figuring interest rates, percentages, commissions. If you have figurephobic tendencies, you will be inclined to overlook these opportunities or dismiss them without evaluating them at all.

CAUSES

Just as you should be aware of the symptoms and effects of figurephobia, you should also be aware of its causes; you will feel less uncomfortable with it and be more willing to face it and take steps to cure it. Also, if you are a parent, you will be alerted to what not to do or say to your children. Figurephobia is caused by one or more of the following:

You had negative experiences with mathematics as a child. Figurephobia is most frequently traced back to school days. You didn't understand the "whys" of carrying numbers, or of division, or of geometry or algebra. Instead of slowly and patiently explaining them, your teacher ignored your needs, rushed to the next lesson, perhaps embarrassed you at the blackboard, or discouraged you by saying, "If you think this is hard, wait until you get to intermediate algebra." This is how figurephobia often starts and grows. You turn to a teacher for help and get none. You turn to a parent and find he doesn't understand the stuff himself. You turn to a sibling who tells you you're stupid. And finally you turn to your text and it's worse than all the others put together. Then you stop turning and start fearing—certainly not the foundation for loving number-related tasks or ever excelling at them. Add to all this possible test anxiety, the sequential aspects of math—the fact that you're being rushed to part two without fully understanding part one; the fact that the need for speed, accuracy, and drill are unrelentingly stressed; and that rigid memorization is constantly demanded—and what do you have? A lot of excellent reasons to hate mathematics and anything related to it.

You were influenced by parental prejudices. Many parents used to tell their daughters that math is for men, that it's unfeminine or unnecessary for girls or women to be concerned with it. Or they'd say, "Some people have a head for math and others don't," implying that you'd probably never be able to develop even basic math skills no matter what you did. Today both these beliefs have been debunked, but the conditioning of early years dies hard.

You were led to believe that math is strictly logical. It is logical, but it is intuitive first. Yet the intuitive aspects of math are seldom acknowledged by the authorities in your life. You are not encouraged to follow your instincts if in doubt, but to follow rules. The world's greatest mathematicians will tell you this is bunk. But you weren't taught or guided by the world's greatest mathematicians.

You were led to believe that math "naturals" do things differently than you. More bunk. They count on their fingers. They approximate when they can't come up with exact answers (which aren't always necessary). They figure slowly if they're tackling something new. They often have lousy memories (math requires understanding concepts, not having a great memory). They don't necessarily persevere intensely (they get many of their flashes of illumination during periods of rest). They work much as you do. But for some reason a mystique surrounds math whizzes, and you bought that mystique and believed maybe you just weren't cut out for math.

CURES

You are now motivated, mature, and a businessperson. As a student, computing interest rates and figuring averages seemed like academic stuff—not the stuff of the real world. Now you know, like it or not, that they are the stuff of the real world, particularly the world of business. Figures and figuring are the language of commerce. "Mathese" is as much an international language as English. You may have closed your eyes to your figurephobia for a long time, but you can't anymore if you want your business to really grow. You see the problem of not being able to speak in terms of percents, discounts, equity, and interest rates. Let's go now from seeing the problem to doing something about it:

Determine in advance where you want to begin and end. You don't need to know all about math or to become a number whiz. What you need is to become number-comfortable with the kinds of numbers, problems, and procedures that are a part of your business life. Set realistic goals for yourself. Everything covered in the first eight years of school can be comfortably covered in a matter of months by reading a single review book. However, you don't have to learn everything and you shouldn't start with a review book. One home-baser realized she just wanted to learn some basic arithmetic and business math, "nothing heavy, just enough so that I don't panic at the thought of figuring out how much cheaper it is to buy by the gross than by the dozen." Don't make grandiose blueprints and set yourself up for possible failure—just simple, immediate, and realistic plans. Write down on a slip of paper exactly what you'd like to start learning, what you feel you need to know for your business, and at what point you'll feel you've learned as much as you want and need to for now. (You can always expand to grand heights later should you so desire.)

Get "human" help. Starting with a book, even a good one, is not a figurephobic's best first move. What you need is trained, sympathetic, nonjudgmental, therapy-oriented professional assistance. And today it is available. Math-anxiety workshops or clinics are being offered through local colleges, continuing education centers, community organizations, and corporations. Generally these courses are short, inexpensive, provide "hands-on" experience (be it hands on a pencil or hands on a computer), and require no tests or homework. Supplemental manuals may or may not be used; and no grades are given. Initially the focus is on approaching your fear of figures and figuring, rather than on problem solving. You are made to realize that your anxiety is commonplace. You learn how it works to block you, and how you can decrease it. The environment is supportive, informal, nonpunitive. Nothing like school. Often the setup looks like a living room, with coffee and a snack provided. Rather than feeling it is something you must "bear with," you begin to look forward to each weekly session. In this slow-paced, friendly, "math without wrath" atmosphere a sense of restoration occurs. You begin to remember or analyze when and why your phobia began. One home-baser realized that her phobia, though accentuated by poor teachers and teaching, actually began because her father was frequently unemployed. The subject of figures and money was associated with problem periods in her life. Her parents frequently fought about money and their fights had frightened her. Once this woman understood and dealt with the emotional baggage she was carrying, she felt free to "leave the psychology behind and plunge into the arithmetic."

Plunge ahead. In the workshop, and once you leave it, go full steam ahead. Make mistakes; expect to feel frustrated (a little frustration, and even a *little* anxiety, is good for you). Don't spend time figuring out how to avoid mistakes, paralyzing yourself into inaction. Do a moderate amount of preliminary studying, but make sure you experiment all along the way. Trial-and-error learning is great. Also learn to trust your intuition. Don't be sure you're wrong because you've arrived at an answer or conclusion through intuition more than logic. Take the time to examine the logic behind your intuition, but don't dismiss your intuition. There is no clear division between intuitive and logical thinking—they're both products of your life experience. If an exporter tells you he wants a 20% discount on your wholesale price, and your markup is 25%, is it intuitive thinking, or logical thinking, that first brings you to the conclusion that a 5% profit is not worth bothering with? And does it really matter, as long as you ultimately examine your decision rationally and act in your best interest?

The safest way to plunge ahead is by starting with easy and enjoyable problems. By doing this you can set the stage for your success, build on it, and put yourself in the frame of mind to expect (and feel capable of achieving) more success. A home-based artist who conquered her figurephobia started her plunge with toys. She bought simple, nonthreatening math games and tech toys designed for children in elementary school and quickly found herself having an enormous amount of fun. Her nieces, nephews, and friends' children became her eager playmates and sources of inspiration. By playing with these youngsters she started to adopt their carefree attitude of glancing at the instructions and plunging right in. If one button or card didn't produce the right results, she'd try another and another, and then check again with the instructions—plain, uncomplicated, nonstudentlike fun. Eventually she worked up to advanced games and toys, and started transferring her newly acquired know-how to her business activities with excellent results and with little fear attached.

Be a note taker. There is no one right way to plunge ahead. For the above artist, children's games turned out to be an excellent method. For someone else, hypnosis or some other technique might work well. But whatever technique you use to get yourself plunging, always take notes along the way. Put to paper your feelings, ideas, any important information or facts you come up with, and, most important, any questions you have (and get them answered).

Your notes become a record of your progress. As you read through them and return to them, you will see how far you've come, how your fears are shrinking and your confidence is growing. Reading these notes will reinforce your determination to forge ahead. Also you will realize that you are no longer a child—you can find answers to your questions, help in understanding what you can't figure out, and aid with the little how-to's that are escaping you.

In addition to taking notes, write down any lingo that hits your ears or eyes. You become more comfortable and confident with numbers by learning the lingo of business, math, and computers. When you come upon terms such as "cost effective," "median," "variable," and "interfacing," don't lose them and don't let them make you feel lost. Write them down; get definitions for them; and practice using them. (Of course, don't become the kind of jargon bore who walks around telling yawning friends about his "cost-effective machine that interfaces with . . . .")

Learn to ask and request. Again write down and get answers to your questions. Don't be afraid to ask questions, even if you think they're stupid. Only the worst and most insecure snob will look at you and say, "But it's so obvious." None of this stuff is obvious until you've grasped it, practiced it, and know it well. Ask for explanations of any procedures that you don't understand. Rare is the person who won't gladly show you how to convert a decimal to a percentage (unless, of course, he doesn't know how himself). However, don't let yourself in for pain by asking questions of people you don't feel comfortable with. Seek help from capable, nonjudgmental, pedagogically gifted people whom you like and feel will be pleased to help you.

In addition to asking questions, get in the habit of requesting private "think time." You need time alone to analyze figures and make correct decisions. Don't permit yourself to be rushed into a cursory scan when a close inspection is necessary. If handed a sheet of figures by someone standing over your shoulder waiting for an immediate response, say, "I want to examine these figures closely; I'll be back to you tomorrow." Never let yourself be pressured into an on-the-spot performance. Being rushed, or forced to make calculations with all eyes on you, may have contributed largely to you becoming figurephobic in the first place. Don't tolerate it now; request all the time you need to feel comfortable and competent.

Practice and review. Mathematics prose, like poetry, requires reading and rereading. Facility with figures takes time, concentration, practice, and review. It requires mental exercise; and, just like physical exercise, it's difficult at first, but the more you do it, the easier it gets. And ultimately, just as regular physical workouts put your body in good shape, regular mental exercises put your mind in good condition.

Practice and review during your peak mental periods—when your mind is at its strongest. A half-hour daily is adequate. If you find yourself working longer, take breaks, walk around a bit. Give yourself digestion time; give your unconscious a chance to work. Don't push yourself. Understanding and speed come from frequent repetition, not from irregular endurance drills. Certainly some math is hard, but not what you need to know to gain and maintain total financial control of your business. The math and calculation skills you need to master require a commitment to some mental perspiration, but not any great, creative inspiration.

Just as you probably always have a dictionary on hand, you should also have one or two good mathematics review books on hand—books that cover the basics relevant to you (tasks such as computing interest, figuring probability, working with fractions, reading a balance sheet). Take the time to choose a couple of well-written, step-by-step guides that you'll enjoy turning to. There are many good review books available. Generally, if you find the first five to ten pages easy, you've found a book that is right for you.

Reword and estimate. A great deal of the difficulty people have with math has to do with translating a verbal problem into a mathematical expression. How, for example, do you reword into simple and workable mathematical terms, "If it takes two truck trips to deliver eight custom-made chests, how many truck trips will it take to deliver forty of these chests?" If you know a bit about algebraic proportions (this isn't the only way to solve the problem), and write:

$$2/8 = X/40$$
$$8X = 80$$
$$X = 10$$

you'll get your answer in seconds. But, if you don't reword the problem into a mathematical equation, you can find yourself twitching. You know the problem is not hard, but you just can't think of a quick answer. This is why it's important that you reword. A large part of being figure-comfortable is being conversion-capable. In addition to learning how to convert a verbal question into a numerical equation, make sure you learn when and how to use these equations. Knowing mathematics without knowing when or how to apply it is nonproductive. Again, it's not hard to learn how to become a "translator," but it takes some practice.

Besides translating verbal problems into solvable equations, also get into the habit of translating single terms so you can work with them. For example, if someone asks you to compute 8% of $50, translate the "of" $50 to "times" $50. Or if told that the "difference" between the monthly sales figures of two suppliers is negligible, check how negligible it is by letting the word "difference" be your clue to "subtract" the smaller sales figure from the larger one. Words like "of," "difference," "square," "cube," "quotient" are procedural clues. "Square 5" will only create anxiety until you translate "square" to "multiply by itself the number———." (Thus "square 5" means 5×5, or 25.)

Translating involves sorting out relevant information and putting it into terms that will give you answers you need. Rewording is one major part of translating. The other part is estimating. Frequently it's unimportant that you get an exact answer. If you're considering purchasing a dozen crates that sell for $1.89 apiece, and you want an idea of how much you'll have to spend, multiply $2 times twelve. It's time-wasting to be wedded to precision with a calculation such as this.

Even with harder things, get into the habit of estimating, if you're not in need of an exact answer. The more you estimate, the more skillful you become. If you want a rough idea of how much it will cost you to exhibit at a certain trade show, you don't need to add in the cost of every possible cup of coffee you might drink.

Focus on what you *can* do and have done. One of the reasons a lot of schoolchildren do poorly on math tests is that they spend too much time on the problems they can't solve. They fail to move on to what they can do, and then, if time permits, go back to the trouble spots. They become knotted up over their inadequacies. Don't fall into this trap while you're learning basic mathematics. Focus on what you've achieved and are achieving. Build slowly and sequentially to overall competence. Don't get tense if you find probability harder than proportions. Some procedures will come to you more easily than will others. But eventually you'll get them all. You'll learn whatever you need to know.

While you're learning, don't be magnetized by the biggies. Don't worry about computing compound interest until you've mastered figuring straight interest. Reward yourself for what you've already learned. Periodically get yourself concrete symbols of your success. One home-based importer bought a globe she had always wanted for her office. Every time she looks at it, she feels self-congratulatory and inspired to perform a few necessary calculations and continue in her efforts to conquer her figurephobia. She is currently learning to type in preparation for working a computer keyboard and ultimately rewarding herself with a word processor.

Plan on remissions. There will be times you'll panic, even once you've gone the distance. But you'll panic a lot less and recover a lot quicker than you used to. Progress is not steady and even. Don't get upset if you feel a blankness when faced with figuring something you know you've learned how to do or that you've yet to learn how to do. And don't chastise yourself! Many great mathematicians periodically make mistakes with the simplest calculations. There will be remissions; but there will also be spurts when you feel you can figure out answers to questions that have baffled generations of economists.

You may completely cure your figurephobia, or you may treat it to the point where it is manageable and you can function well even though you'll never be a mathophile. What matters is that you reach a plateau where you are comfortable, competent, and confident with figures. At this point you'll feel a powerful sense of accomplishment and freedom. Your business will benefit substantially, as you will personally.

Conclusion

While you're doing everything mentioned in this book to make your home-based business soar, do one more thing—have a little "chutzpah." Sometimes it works wonders when everything seems to be moving too slowly.

A home-based stationer was eager to gain entry to the office of an important department-store buyer. It would be the highlight of her career to establish business relations with this particular buyer. But the buyer was impossible to see. Entering the outer office, the stationer handed her business card to the buyer's receptionist, who took it to the buyer. As the stationer peeked through the office door which was slightly ajar, she saw the buyer rip it to pieces and discard it. The receptionist came back to the stationer and said apologetically that the buyer could not see her. "May I have my business card back please?" requested the stationer. The receptionist, a bit embarrassed, returned to the buyer. She was quickly sent back out again, this time with a dime and the message that the buyer was sorry, but the card had been destroyed. The stationer stood tall, drew another business card from her wallet, and gave it to the receptionist. "Please take this back inside and tell your boss I sell two cards for a dime," she said.

The stationer got to meet the important buyer. She got a substantial order. And for many years the two women enjoyed a profitable business relationship.

Appendix

Representative Mailing-List Brokers

There are dozens of companies throughout the United States that compile, own, and rent mailing lists. Here is a representative list that you can consult if you are considering direct-mail marketing.

Accredited Mailing Lists, Inc.
3 Park Ave.
New York, NY 10016

Addresses Unlimited
14621 Titus St.
Van Nuys, CA 91402

AZ Lists, Inc.
270 Mason St.
Greenwich, CT 06830

Beauty Mail Co.
5414 West Division St.
Chicago, IL 60651

Bird Corp. Kids List
9110 West Dodge Rd.
Omaha, NE 68114

Ceil Levine Screened Mailing Lists, Inc.
250 W. 57th St.
New York, NY 10019

Concepts for Children, Inc.
607 Palisades Ave.
Englewood Cliffs, NJ 07632

Fred E. Allen, Inc.
Allencrest Bldg.
Mt. Pleasant, TX 75455

Heart Of America List Co., Inc.
PO Box 1090
Blue Springs, MO 64015

List America, Inc.
1766 Church St. NW
Washington, D.C. 20036

List Company
1200 Summer St.
Stamford, CT 06905

Missouri-National Mailing Lists Co.
2200 East Sunshine, Ste. 309
Springfield, MO 65804

National Business Lists, Inc.
162 North Franklin St.
Chicago, IL 60606

Omega List Co.
8330 Old Courthouse Rd., Ste. 700
Vienna, VA 22180

PCS Mailing List Co.
30 Central St.
Peabody, MA 01960

Steve Millard, Inc.
Spring Hill Rd.
Peterborough, NH 03458

Regency Group
80 South Lake Ave.
Pasadena, CA 91101

Total Media Concepts, Inc.
362 Cedar La.
Teaneck, NJ 07666

Religious Lists, Inc.
43 Maple Ave.
New City, NY 10956

Walter Karl, Inc.
135 Bedford Rd.
Armonk, NY 10504

Representative Multilevel Marketing Companies

The following is a small guide to the many multilevel opportunities that exist for home-basers. In addition to handling your own product line you may find it very profitable to tie in your product with the offerings of one of these companies. The multilevel field changes quickly. Firms frequently go out of business and new ones are constantly appearing on the scene. For more information about specific types of opportunities available, you can consult:

The National Association for Multilevel Marketing
PO Box 457
Citrus Heights, CA 95611

Food Products

Dyna Life, Inc.
2160 Bradford St.
Clearwater, FL 33520

Meadow Fresh Farms, Inc.
PO Box 31105
Salt Lake City, UT 84130

Southeast Marketing
12374 Aladdin Rd.
Jacksonville, FL 32223

Health, Beauty, and Skin-Care Products

Afton Jojoba, Inc.
PO Box 156
Gilbert, AZ 85234

Aloe Vera Products, Inc.
PO Box 28211
Tempe, AZ 85282

Burgess Health Products
7240 SE 71st Ave.
Portland, OR 97206

Chrissie Cosmetics, Inc.
6124 Harne Ave.
Shreveport, LA 71108

Lightforce Co.
1115 Thompson Ave.
Santa Cruz, CA 95062

Mary Kay Cosmetics
8787 Stemmons Freeway
Dallas, TX 75247

Sanasu International Inc.
PO Box 82144
San Diego, CA 92138

Vital Corp.
4355 West Tropicana
Las Vegas, NV 89103

Wholesale Nutrition Club
PO Box 3345
Saratoga, CA 95070

*Home, Car, and
Personal-Care Products*

American Free Enterprise
PO Box 1013
Sedalia, MO 65301

Amway Corp.
7575 East Fulton Rd.
Ada, MI 49355

Better Living Products, Inc.
495-A Busse Rd.
Elk Grove Village, IL 60007

Executive Marketing Group Ltd.
PO Box 65
Clayton, NJ 08312

Gameworld
1314 La Loma
Berkeley, CA 94708

W. T. Rawleigh Co.
223 East Main St.
Freeport, IL 61032

Shaklee Corp.
444 Market St.
San Francisco, CA 94111

Jewelry and Clothing

Act II Jewelry, Inc.
Leyland Ct.
Bensenville, IL 60106

Beeline Fashions
100 Beeline Dr.
Bensenville, IL 60106

Helen Marie, Inc.
PO Box 1000
Derry, NH 03038

National Diamond Exchange
400 Tidd Dr.
Galion, OH 44833

Sarah Coventry, Inc.
Sarah Coventry Pkwy.
Newark, NY 14593

Stationery Products

Jay Clark Co., Inc.
5328 Central Ave.
St. Petersburg, FL 33707

V.I.P. Print Shop, Inc.
1915 Southeastern Ave.
Indianapolis, IN 46201

Representative List of Trade Shows for Home-Basers

The following is a small list of the many trade shows where home-basers can sell their products to industry buyers or purchase wholesale from industry sellers. For information on other kinds of trade shows held, dates, and places, in addition to consulting your trade publications and trade association, you can also consult:

230   How to Make Your Home-Based Business Grow

The Generic Directory of Trade Shows,
Meetings & Conventions
available in many libraries and published by:
Hendrickson Publishing Co.,
79 Washington St.
Hempstead, NY 11550
(516) 483-6881

This directory has events classified in over 130 industry fields; over 19,000 events are listed through the year 2000. Or see:

The International Association of Fairs & Expositions
MPO Box 985
Springfield, MO 65801
(417) 862-5771

American Home Sewing
  Association Trade Show
American Home Sewing
  Association
1270 Broadway, Ste. 1007
New York, NY 10001
(212) 836-8820

Atlanta Gift Show
Atlanta Merchandise Mart
240 Peachtree St., Ste 2200
Atlanta, GA 30043
(404) 658-5678

Decorative Accessories Show
National Fairs, Inc.
45 Franklin St., Ste. 301
San Francisco, CA 94102
(415) 558-8011

Frame O Rama
408 Olive St.
St. Louis, MO 63102
(314) 421-5445

Furniture & Accessories Show
Karel Exposition Management
2301 Collins Ave.
Miami Beach, FL 33119
(305) 534-8321

International Toy Fair
International Trade Shows
545 Fifth Ave.
New York, NY 10017
(212) 687-1185

Kitchen & Bath Show
National Exposition Co., Inc.
14 W. 40th St.
New York, NY 10018
(212)391-9111

National Fashion & Boutique
  Show
Larkin-Pluznick-Larkin, Inc.
210 Boylston St.
Chestnut Hill, MA 02167
(617) 964-5100

National Kids Fashion Show:
see National Fashion & Boutique Show

National Merchandise Show
Thalheim Expositions, Inc.
98 Cutter Mill Rd.
Great Neck, NY 11021
(212)357-3555

National Shoe Fair
230 W. 55th St., Ste. 22D
New York, NY 10019
(212) 246-3410

National Stationery Show:
see New York (etc.) Gift Show

National T-Shirt Show
Conference Management Corp.
17 Washington St.
Norwalk, CT 06854
(203) 852-0500

Needlework Industry Showcase
Needlework Markets, Inc.
PO Box 533
Pine Mountain, GA 31822
(404) 663-2495

New York (also Washington,
 Boston, Atlantic City,
 & Chicago) Gift Show

Little Brothers Shows, Inc.
261 Madison Ave.
New York, NY 10016
(212) 986-8000

Pacific Jewelry Show
605 South Olive St., Ste. 714
Los Angeles, CA 90014
(213) 628-3171

Premium & Incentive Show:
see National Merchandise Show

San Francisco (also Seattle,
 Portland, & Las Vegas) Gift
 Show
Western Exhibitors, Inc.
San Francisco, CA 94123
(415) 346-6666

West Coast Stationery &
 Graphics:
see San Francisco (etc.)
 Gift Show

Western Shoe Association
 Convention
Western Shoe Association
110 E. 9th St., No. A 772
Los Angeles, CA 90079
(213) 629-2627

Woodworking, Machinery, &
 Furniture Supply Fair
Marketing Association Services
1516 S. Pontius Ave.
Los Angeles, CA 90025
(213) 478-0215

**SAMPLE OF A THREE-PART FORM SIGNED BY
"BUYER" AND "SELLER" IN A BARTER
TRANSACTION SET UP BY A TRADE EXCHANGE.**

SAMPLE FORM FILLED OUT
BY BARTER CLUB APPLICANT

Barter Advantage Inc.
1751 2nd Avenue
New York, N.Y. 10028
(212) 534-7500

MEMBERSHIP APPLICATION
Print Clearly

I.D.# ☐☐ ☐☐☐☐

APPLICANT'S LEGAL NAME _____
FIRM'S NAME _____
BUSINESS MAILING ADDRESS _____
 CITY _____ STATE _____ ZIP _____
 BUSINESS TELEPHONE NUMBER (AREA CODE) _____
HOME ADDRESS _____
 CITY _____ STATE _____ ZIP _____
 HOME TELEPHONE NUMBER (AREA CODE) _____

If applicant's principal location is different than mailing address or if there are other operating locations, list on reverse.

APPLICANT IS: ☐ CORPORATION ☐ PARTNERSHIP
 ☐ A PROPRIETORSHIP ☐ INDIVIDUAL
 MULTIPLE LOCATIONS ☐ NO ☐ YES (list on reverse side)

APPLICANT PRINCIPAL(S) OR OFFICERS: (Title)

_____ TYPE OF ACCOUNT
_____ ☐ OPEN ☐ CLOSED ____ PER ____
_____ ☐ NF ☐ PF ____

CATEGORIES OF GOODS AND/OR SERVICES: _____

REFERENCES: BANK _____ BRANCH _____
 TRADE _____ TEL. _____
 CUSTOMER _____ TEL. _____
 ADD'L. _____ TEL. _____

CARDS DESIRED FOR:

1) _____ 3) _____
2) _____ 4) _____

TAX PAYERS I.D. NUMBER _____ MEMBERSHIP FEE $ _____
EMPLOYER I.D. NUMBER _____ FIRST YEAR DUES T$ _____
SOCIAL SECURITY NUMBER _____ (In Trade)

All information I've given on this application is true and correct. I understand that you will confirm the information and retain the application whether or not my application is approved.

You are also authorized to receive information on my credit. You can answer questions and requests from others like stores or credit, etc...

FOR OFFICE USE ONLY:

Application Approved: _____ BA1 Representative
Credit Line Approved: (Amt.) _____ Initials _____

_____
SIGNATURE

TITLE _____ DATE _____ ACCOUNT EXECUTIVE _____

WHITE-BROKERAGE COPY YELLOW-MEMBERSHIP KIT COPY PINK-DIVISION OFFICE COPY

Appendix 233

SAMPLE OF AN AGREEMENT
SIGNED BY A BARTER CLUB MEMBER

Barter Advantage Inc.
1751 2nd Avenue
New York, N.Y. 10028
(212) 534-7500

MEMBERSHIP AGREEMENT

This agreement made and entered into on the date shown herein, by and between BARTER ADVANTAGE INC. hereinafter known as BAI, and the Individual, Corporation, and/or Partnership, hereinafter known as MEMBER, do hereby mutually agree to the following:

1. MEMBER agrees that BAI is a service organization whose purpose is to direct members to each other for reciprocal trading, accordingly MEMBER shall not hold BAI responsible for disputes arising from transactions among the membership and MEMBER agrees to indemnify and hold BAI harmless against any and all such disputes. However, MEMBER agrees to voluntarily place such disputes before an arbitration board, sponsored by BAI, whose decision is binding upon all members.

2. MEMBER agrees to sell products and/or services for Trade Credit at their prevailing price, to other members.

3. A Line of Credit of $ _____ has been issued to MEMBER upon execution of this Agreement by an authorized Officer of BAI.

4. MEMBER has the right to cancel Membership at any time by balancing the account in accordance with the existing rules and regulations of BAI, as supplied to MEMBER upon signing membership agreement.

5. BAI has the right to cancel a Membership upon breach of Agreement or failure to comply with the existing rules and regulations of BAI.

6. MEMBER agrees to pay BAI a CASH service and Accounting Fee of 8% on trade purchases made from BAI Members. Service fees are due and payable 10 days after invoice and is considered in breach of this agreement 30 days from invoice date.

7. The initial membership fee of $600 ($400 Cash and $200 Trade) will be charged upon execution of this agreement. Subsequent annual dues will be $200 cash and $100 trade dollars.

8. In the event of a breach of this Agreement by MEMBER, MEMBER agrees to pay all reasonable costs, such as litigation expenses, attorney fees, court costs, collection costs and/or interest.

9. This agreement cannot be assigned, transferred or sold without prior written consent of BAI and is binding upon MEMBER's heirs, successors, assignees, and/or administrators of MEMBER's estate. This agreement cannot be amended verbally and any exceptions shall be in writing from an authorized Officer of BAI.

10. MEMBER acknowledges BAI Rules and Regulations, attached hereto and are binding upon MEMBER as are the conditions and provisions of this Agreement.

11. Each MEMBER shall be personally and individually liable for observance of all the rules, regulations and payments made hereunder.

APPROVED BY BARTER ADVANTAGE INC.   ACKNOWLEDGED AND APPROVED BY

_____   _____
ACCOUNT EXECUTIVE   AUTHORIZED SIGNATURE MEMBER

_____   _____
OFFICER BAI   TITLE

_____   _____
TITLE   COMPANY NAME
DATE OF ACCEPTANCE   DATE OF APPLICATION

Self-Assessment Questionnaire

Anybody can learn to be a good entrepreneur. However, there are certain traits usually found in supersuccessful entrepreneurs, small business builders and home-basers alike, which give them a head start. If you possess these traits, you are fortunate since you'll find it easier than many others to make your business soar. If you don't possess them, you can work on developing them.

The more "yes" answers you give to the following questions, the more naturally suited you are for entrepreneurship and home-based business supersuccess.

Are you:
1. highly energetic?
2. gregarious?
3. competitive?
4. happy working alone?
5. ambitious?
6. highly motivated to become wealthy?
7. aggressive?
8. adventuresome?
9. decisive?
10. informed about overall happenings?
11. well informed about economic and business trends?
12. a divergent and convergent thinker (do you focus on the big and little picture)?
13. innovative or imaginative?
14. a born leader?
15. self-critical, yet also self-confident?

Supplementary Reading List

1. Behr, Marion and Lazar, Wendy. *Women Working Home*. Edison, N.J.: WWH Press, 1981.
2. Blake, Gary and Bly, Robert W. *How to Promote Your Own Business*. New York, N.Y.: New American Library, 1983.
3. Bohigian, Valerie. *Successful Flea Market Selling*. Blue Ridge Summit, Pa.: Tab Books, 1981.

4. Bohigian, Valerie. *Real Money from Home: How to Start, Manage, and Profit From a Home-Based Service Business*. New York, N.Y.: New American Library, 1985.
5. Curtin, Richard T. *Running Your Own Show*. New York, N.Y.: New American Library, 1983.
6. Friedlander, Mark P. *Handbook of Successful Franchising*. New York, N.Y.: Van Nostrand, 1981.
7. Greene, Gardiner G. *How to Start and Manage Your Own Business*. New York, N. Y.: New American Library, 1983.
8. Joffe, Gerardo. *How You Too Can Make at Least $1 Million (but Probably Much More) in the Mail-order Business*. New York, N.Y.: Harper & Row, 1979.
9. Kogelman, Dr. Stanley and Warren, Dr. Joseph. *Mind over Math*. New York, N.Y.: McGraw-Hill, 1978.
10. Lewis, Mack O. *How to Franchise Your Business*. New York, N.Y.: Pilot Books, 1980.
11. McVicar, Marjorie and Craig, Julia F. *Minding My Own Business*. New York, N.Y.: Richard Marek Publishers, 1981.
12. Stevens, Mark. *36 Small Business Mistakes—and How to Avoid Them*. New York, N. Y.: Parker Publishing Co., 1981.
13. U.S. Department of the Treasury. *Importing into the United States*. Write to: The Department of the Treasury, Customs Service, Washington, D.C. 20229. The cost is $5.50.
14. U.S. Government Printing Office. *Export Marketing for Smaller Firms*. Write to: U.S. Government Printing Office, Superintendent of Documents, Washington, D.C. 20402. The cost is $4.75.

Index

Accountant, 159, 164–66, 214
   presence when applying for bank loan, 156–57
   see also Figurephobia
Advertising, 95–103, 116, 138–39, 202–203
   deciding where to advertise, 96–98, 138, 144–45
   defined, 95
   how to advertise, 100–103, 138–39
   for mail-order business, 137–39, 141–42, 142–45
   run-of-the-mill, 202–203
   timing of, 98–100
   using publicity in ad copy, 113–14
   see also Publicity; Public relations; Samples
Advertising agencies, 102–103
Africa, 178, 183, 186
Agents, 72–73, 118, 125–26, 146, 149
Air conditioning, 16
Algebra, 233
   see also Figurephobia
American Register of Exporters and Importers, 188
American Woman's Economic Development Corporation, 175
Amway, 131
Answering services, 17–18

Antitrust laws, 180
Appearance, 45, 105
Attitudes toward home-based business, 3–4
   avoiding thinking poor, 6–7, 193
   degree of success related to your, 10–13, 194–95
   interest in making your business soar, 47, 61
   sideline thinking, 193–95
Attorney General, 137
Auctions:
   testing your product at, 43, 49–50
   types of, 49
Audio accessories, 176
Automotive equipment, 176
Avoiding dealing with figures, *see* Figurephobia
Ayer Directory of Newspapers, Magazines and Trade Publications, 114

Bad debt insurance, 171
Bankers, 153–59
Bank loans, 153–58, 160
   putting the odds in your favor, 156–58
   what banks want, 153–56
   see also Debt
Bankruptcy, 211
Banks, 153–56, 180

Index

Barter, 5, 81–94, 163
  advice for making best trades, 92–93
  bewares, 92
  explanation of, 81–82
  how to, 88–89
  reasons it isn't used more often, 82–83
  taxation and, 90–91, 93
  types of, 83–86
  what to barter/what to ask for, 90
  when to, 87
  see also Barter clubs and exchanges
Barter broker, 84
Barter clubs and exchanges, 3, 85, 86, 90, 93, 94, 127
  sample forms of, 231–33
  see also Barter
Barter scrip, 93
Better Business Bureau, 137
Bohigian, Valerie, 1–5, 131
Bookkeepers, 166, 214
  see also Figurephobia
Books:
  exporting of, 176
  how-to, 139, 190
  mathematics reference, 223
  supplemental reading list, 234–35
Borrowing, *see* Bank loans
Budgeting your time, 7–10
Bulletin boards, advertising on, 98
Business consultants, 172–75
Business Interruption Insurance, 171
Business plan, 158–59
Buyers and buying offices, 67–72, 149, 226
  agents to visit, 72–73
  corporate, 73–77
  indirect selling to, 149

Cable-television:
  advertising on, 97
  talk show publicity, 112, 113
Call-forwarding service, 18
Capital gains, 90
Cash flow, barter to preserve, *see* Barter
Casualty insurance, 170
Catalogs, mail-order, 139
Chemical products, 176
Children's market, 147–48
  naming a product for, 24–25
Classified-ad barter, 84
CLCU (Certified Liability and Casualty Underwriter), 169
Cleansing products, 176
Clothing:
  exporting, 176
  samples of, 120
CLU (Certified Life Underwriter), 169
Clubs:
  barter, 3, 85, 86, 90, 93, 94, 127
  distributing samples through, 127
Collateral for bank loan, 154, 155
Collectible appeal of product, 37
Color of work area, 14
Commerce Department, 184, 189
  District Office, 184
Commercial barter, 86, 91, 92, 93
  see also Barter clubs and exchanges
Commissions, 12, 126, 131, 134
Community barter, 84–85

Community groups, marketing to, 53–54
Community mixers, distributing samples through, 126
Community programs:
 participating in, 42, 44, 50–51, 115
 sponsoring, 115–16
Competition, 181
 avoiding pettiness, 207–208
 in import business, 190
 pricing policy and, 205–206
 at trade shows, 65
 watching the, 35, 130, 148
Component parts, 176
Computers:
 for mail-order business, 140
 for record keeping, 167
 rejecting, and figurephobia, 214–15
Consignment, selling on, 5, 31, 54, 70–71
Constructive criticism, 46–47, 51
Consultants, business, 172–75
Consumer columnists, 108–109
Consumer confidence, 25–26
Consumer debt, 15, 209
Consumer Product Safety Act, 162
Cooperating with the competition, 209
Cooperative advertising, 73, 102
Corporate market, 73–77, 150–51
 contacts in, 75
 defining the, 75
 presentation to, 75–76
Corporations:
 barter by, 82
 selling to, *see* Corporate market

Cosmetics:
 exporting, 176
 samples of, 119
Cottage-industry trend, 2–3
 statistics on, 4
Craft fairs, *see* Fairs
Credibility of your home as business center, 13
Credit-card buying privileges, 139, 167
Credit investigation and references, 157, 158, 187–88
Credit reporting bureaus, 158
Criticism, constructive, 46–47, 51
Customer recognition of product, 25, 26, 98
Customer testing, 51–52
Customs regulations, 190

Debt:
 business-investment, 15, 209–10
 consumer, 15, 209
 see also Bank loans
Decorating magazines, 14
Delegation of responsibility, 7, 195–96
 figurephobia and, 214
 for production of product, 55, 56, 57
Department-store buyers, 67–72
Dialing for Answers service, 175
Direct mail advertising, 143, 145
Direct Mail Marketing Association, 141, 144
Directory of Magazines with Classified Ads, 139
Direct selling, 128–146
 advantages of, 145–46

Direct selling (*cont.*)
  flea markets, *see* Flea market
  home shop, 129–30, 149
  mail order, *see* Mail order
  multilevel sales, 5, 10, 53, 131–37, 151
  see also Indirect selling
Displaying your product, 28–30
  at trade shows, 65
Distribution of samples, 118, 125–27
Distribution of your product overseas, *see* Exporting
Domestic help, 61
Duties, import, 190

Earnings, *see* Income
Electronics equipment, 176
Employee benefits insurance, 171
Enthusiasm about your product, 38
Enterpreneurial spirit, 154–55
Environmental equipment, 176
"Envisioning" success, 194–95
Equipment:
  borrowing to purchase, 15, 209–10
  bringing machinery into your home, 62–63
  depreciation deductions for, 210
  exporting, 176
  insurance, 171
  supplemental, 15–16
  time-sharing arrangements, 16
  tools of your trade, 14–15
Evaluating your home base, 6–22
  arranging part of home specifically for business, 13–14
  attitudes toward financial success, 6–7
  attitudes toward home basing and your success, 10–13
  budgeting your time, 7–10
  equipment, importance of, 14–16
  flow charts, use of, 8–10, 11
  imitating and learning from successful homebasers, 19–21
  mobility of "home-based" business, 21–22
  telephone services, 16–19
Exclusives, 69
Exercise, 198
Expanding your business, 60–80, 209–10
  corporate market, 73–77
  mass production, 60–63
  plateau periods and continued planning, 77–80
  using agents, 72–73
  trade shows, 63–67
  visiting buyers and buying offices, 67–72
Experts, getting help from, 152–75
  accountants and bookkeepers, 164–67
  bankers, 153–59
  business consultants, 172–75
  insurance agents, 167–72
  laywers and legal experts, 161–64
  Small Business Administration, 160–61
Export Company Trading Act, 180

Exporting, 3, 176–92
  combining importing and, 186–88
  direct, 176–77
  exploring all domestic options before, 185
  export management companies, 177–83
  indirect, 177
  "one-world" concept, 191–92
  piggybacking, 183–84
  products suitable for, 176
Export management companies, 177–83
  finding, 179–80
  getting the best results from, 182–83
  selecting, 180–81
  services provided by, 177–79

Fair Labor Standards Act, 161
Fair market value and barter, 91
Fairs, 43, 127
Family, 21, 201–202
Features, 107–108, 113, 200
Federal Drug Administration, 137
Federal Trade Commission, 143
Federation of Export Management Companies, 179–8, 181
Feedback:
  constructive criticism, 46–47
  from direct selling, 145
  product-testing to receive, 41–42
Figurephobia, 212–25
  causes of, 217–18
  cures for, 219–25
  effects of, 215–17
  symptoms of, 212–15
Financial planning and control, figurephobia and, 216
Financial statements:
  projected, 159, 166
  record keeping, 164–67
Financing, *see* Bank loans; Debt
Flea market, 4–5
  direct selling at, 130–31, 147–48
  distributing samples at, 127
  testing your product at, 43, 48, 130
Fliers, 98, 139
Flow charts, 8–10, 11
Food products:
  exporting, 176
  samples of, 119
Franchising, 78–79
Fraud, 137
Free editorial, 108–109
Friends distributing samples through, 126
Fundraisers, 41, 43
  distributing samples at, 127
  as a profit-sharing vendor, 43
Furniture arrangement, 14

Gift-giving potential of product, 37
Government contracts, 77

Handicrafts, samples of, 121
Health-care products, 176
Heating, 16
High-tech consumer products, 176
Hiring help, 7, 62, 195
Hobby, 165
Home shop, 129–30, 149
  leaving the, 206–207

How-to-books on mail order, 139

"Image making," 44
Imitating successful
  home-basers, 19–22
  in advertising, 142–43
Importing, 186–91
  becoming an importer, 189–91
  combining exporting with, 186–88
Impulse items, mail-order, 141
Income, 4, 7, 129, 159, 193–94
Indirect selling, 128, 146–51
  with agents, 72–73, 118, 125–26, 145–46, 150
  to buyers and buying offices, *see* Buying and buying offices
  to corporate market, 73–77, 150–51
  at trade shows, *see* Trade shows
  see also Direct selling
Institutional market, *see* Corporate market
Instructional materials, mass-produced, 78–79
Insurance agents and coverage, 167–72, 210–11
Interior designer, 14
Internal Revenue Service, 165, 167, 210
International Association of Trade Exchanges, 94
International trade, *see* Importing; Exporting
Interviews:
  publicity, 106
  of successful home-basers, 20–21
Inventory list, 159
Investment debt, 15, 209–210
Investment for multilevel marketing, 136
Isolation, avoiding, 45–46

Japan, 178, 180

Key Man Insurance, 170
Kits, do-it-yourself:
  exporting, 176
  mail-order, 140, 143

Language:
  of ad copy, 101
  foreign, importing and speaking a, 190
  of mathematics, 221–22, 224
Lawyers and legal experts, 161–64
Layoffs, freedom from worrying about, 12
Legislation, keeping up-to-date on, 210
Letter of credit, 188
Liability insurance, 170, 210
Licenses, 144, 163
Life insurance, 171
Lifestyles feature, 107–108, 112, 113, 200
Lighting, 16
"Like-kind exchanges," 91
Listmaking:
  for bartering, 93
  to budget your time, 7–8
  to prepare for getting publicity, 104
Lloyd George, David, 60
Lofts for office space, 13–14
Logo, 25–26, 99
Long-term appeal of product, 36–37
Low-tech consumer products, 176

Index

Machinery, *see* Equipment
Magazines, advertising in, 97, 138–39
Mail distribution of samples, 126
Mailing lists, 109, 126, 139–40, 141
 brokers of, 227–28
Mail-order business, 5, 99, 109, 137–46
 advertising by, 137–39, 141, 142–45
 disappointing results from, 138
 ideal product for beginning, 140–42
 overall plan for building, 139–40
 telephone answering service for, 17–18
 tips and caveats, 142–45
Make-it-yourself formula, mail-order, 141
Make-your-own-presentation, 32
Mall shows, 43
Malpractice insurance, 170
Managerial skills, 154–55
Manufacture of the product, 54–57
 mass production, 60–63
Market:
 advertising geared to target, 101
 ignoring an existing, 203–204
 international, *see* Exporting; Importing
 multimarketing, 43–48, 128–29
 the "right," for your product, 39, 42, 172–73, 203–204

Market approach to selling, 33–34
 modified, 35
Marketing help, hiring, 61–62
Market research, 34
Mary Kay, 131
Mass production, 60–63
Math-anxiety workshops, 219–20
Mathematics, *see* Figurephobia
Media attention, 44
Media awareness and product perfection, 34–35, 36
Media people, getting to know local, 106
Media mix for advertising, 99
Medical insurance, 171
Medical products or equipment, 176
Messages, telephone, 17
Middlemen marketing, 52–54
Mistakes, avoiding common home-based business, 193–211
 allowing stress damage, 197–98
 counting on volume sales, 204–205
 failing to combine service selling with product selling, 200–201
 failing to delegate, 7, 195–96
 ignoring your prime market, 203–204
 leaving home base, 206–207
 legislation and insurance ignorance, 210
 letting bankruptcy end your business, 211
 measuring time unrealistically, 196–97

Mistakes (*cont.*)
  networking nonchalance, 198–99
  pettiness, 207–209
  run-of-the-mill advertising, 202–203
  shutting out family assistance, 201–202
  sideline thinking, 7, 193–96
  thinking all debt is bad, 15–16, 209–10
  underestimating the power of the press, 200
  unrealistic pricing, 205–206
Mobile home base, 21–22
Modifying and updating your product, 36–37
  for different mediums, 62
Modules, 13
Morley, Christopher, 151
Multilevel marketing ("direct sales"), 5, 10, 53, 131–37
  being right for the product you're selling, 133–34
  for more than one company, 135–36
  physical stamina for, 134
  price and commission structure for, 135
  recruiting, 132–33
  representative list of companies, 228–29
  social skills for, 133
  super product for, 133
  things to beware of, 136–37
Multimarketing, 43–48, 128–29
  avoiding isolation, 45–46
  being personable, 45
  engaging in "image making," 44
  example of, 43–44
  expending energy, 45
  interest in making your business soar, 47
  welcoming constructive criticism, 46–47
Multi-purpose product, 32–33

Naming your product, 24–25, 26
National Association for Multilevel Marketing, 137
National Association of Export Management Companies (NEXCO), 179–80, 181
Negotiating with buyers, 68–69
Networking, 20, 67, 73, 198–99
New product, advertising a, 100
Newspapers:
  advertising in, 96–97
  publicity in, 107–109, 200–201
NEXCO, 179–80, 181
"No-frills" market, 28
Novelty items, samples of, 120

Occupational Safety and Health Act, 162
One-to-one barter, 83
"One-world" concept, 191–92
Order forms, 66, 139
Organizational skills, 154–55
Out-of-country labor, 63
Overseas markets, *see* Exporting; Importing

Package design, 26–28, 186
  for exporting, 183, 186
  for mail-order products, 142

Index

Partnership insurance, 170
Party-plan selling, 41–42, 53, 132, 133, 134
Perfume, 176
Permits for mail-order business, 144
Persistence, 71–72, 76
Personability, 45, 105, 111, 112
Personalized presentation, 32
Pettiness, 207–209
Photographs, 105, 109
Piggybacking, 183–84
Pizzazz piece, 122–23
Plagiarism, 163–64
Planning for the future, 77–80, 158–59, 216
Plateau periods and continued planning, 77–80
Plethora piece, 124–25
Portable office, 14
Portable telephone, 6
Postal Inspector, 137, 144
Post-office box, 110, 111
"Pre" method, 62
Premium items, 74
Presentation of product, 32–33
  to corporate market, 75–77
Press release, 112
Pricing policy, 30–31, 58–59, 61, 204–206
  counting on volume sales, 204–205
  "overpriced" vs. "priced too high," 30–31
  self-defeating, 7, 61
  at trade shows, 66
  unrealistic, 205–206
Printed goods, samples of, 119
Priorities, setting, 8–9
Product, perfecting your, 23–26
  being certain your product is "right," 23–24
  enthusiasm about your product, 38
  logo for product, 25–26
  long-term appeal, 36–37
  naming your product, 24–25, 26
  package design, 26–27
  presentation of product, 31–33
  pricing policy, 30–31
  product approach vs. market approach, 31–35
  product display, 28–30
  the right market or place, 39
Product approach to selling, 34–36
Production procedure, 55–57
  mass production, 60–63
Production Protection Insurance, 170, 210
Professionalism, 195
Publicists, 103
Publicity, 103–14, 200
  defined, 95
  how to get, 103–106
  how to use, 112–14
  kinds of, to go after, 106–12
  see also Advertising; Public relations; Samples
Public relations, 114–16
  charitable events, 115
  defined, 95
  underwriting community projects, 115–16
  see also Advertising; Publicity; Sampler
Public service, 44
Public speaking, 44, 50–51, 111
Pyramid schemes, 136

Quality control, 71
Questionnaire, self-assessment, 234
Quotas, import, 190

Radio:
  advertising on, 97
  talk-show publicity, 112–13
Recording devices, telephone, 18
Record keeping, 93
  accountant or bookkeeper to assist in, 164–67
  computerized, 167
  for mail-order business, 144
References:
  when bartering, 88
  business, 159
Rejection risks, 41
Relatives, 21, 201–202
Reorders, 36–37
Repeat-need product, 36–37
Replica samples, 121, 122
Résumé, personal, 159
Risk-taking, 40–42
  rejection risks, 41–42
Role models, learning from, 19–21, 194

Sales or offers:
  advertising, 100
  publicity, 109–10
Samples, 116–27
  "ample sample," 117, 118
  for buyers, 71, 118
  characteristics of the "simple sample," 117
  with direct mail advertising, 145
  distribution, 118, 125–27
  good simple-sample products, 119–20
  pizzazz piece, 122–23
  plethora piece, 124–25
  for publicity packet, 105, 110
  replica sample, 121, 122
Sarah Coventry, 131
Scientific instruments, 176
SCORE(Service Corps of Retired Executives), 166
Seasonal advertising, 99–100
Self-assessment questionnaire, 234
Selling agents or reps, 72–73, 118, 125–26, 146, 149–50
Seminar publicity, 110–11, 113
Seminars, 43, 127, 190
  finding a business consultant at, 174
Service selling, combining product selling with, 200–201
Shaklee, 131
Shipping of mail-order products, 142, 145
Short-term loans, 155–56
Sideline thinking, 193–95
Small Business Administration, 77–78, 137, 160–61, 162, 166, 180
  loan assistance from, 160–61
Sponsoring community projects, 115–16
Sporting goods, 176
Spot O'Time, 141
Standard Rate and Data, 138
Stolen merchandise, 92
Stores, selling to, *see* Buying and buying offices
Stress damage, 197–98
Students, hiring, 62
Successful Flea Market Selling (Bohigian), 5, 131
Suppliers, 57–59
  at trade shows, 66

Surveys, 101–102
Swap-meet barter, 83–84

Taiwan, 178
Talk-show publicity, 112
Taxes, 165, 166, 210
  barter and, 90–91, 93
Teaching, product-related, 43–44, 129, 200–201
Teaching aids, mass-produced, 78–79
Teleconferencing, 19
Telephone, 16–19
  answering services, 17–18
  business consulting service, 175
  during business hours, 17
  call-interrupt system, 18
  800 number "hotline," 145
  investigating available service options, 18–19
  messages, 17
Television:
  advertising, 97
  talk-show publicity, 112, 113
Testing your product (and yourself):
  finding the right suppliers, 57–58
  multimarketing, 43–48
  outlets and methods for, 42, 48–52, 130
  production procedures, reevaluating, 55–57
  risk-taking, 40–42
  in shallow waters, 40–46
  small-scale wholesaling, 52–54
Thank-you notes, 106
Theft insurance, 171
Time management, 7–10
  measuring time realistically, 196–97

Tools, 176
Trade, *see* Exporting; Importing
Trade associations, 162, 163, 165, 180, 184
Trademark, *see* Logo
Trade offices in foreign countries, 189
Trade publications, 64
  advertising in, 97
Trade shows, 3, 63–67, 147–49
  alerting customers of your participation at, 66
  booth-sharing, 64–65
  buying, learning, and networking at, 66–67
  distributing samples at, 125
  eye-catching displays for, 65
  getting a good location at, 65
  indirect selling at, 147–49
  international, 177, 183, 187
  orders received at, 65–66
  pricing at, 66
  representative list of, 229–31
  selecting, 64

United Parcel Service (UPS), 145
Upgrading your market, 31
"Used goods," barter of, 91

Volume sales and pricing policy, 204–205

Wholesaling, 5, 148
  small-scale, 52–54
  see also Exporting
Workers' compensation insurance, 171
Writing publicity pieces, 104–105

Yellow pages, 96